No Hurry
In
Africa

Brendan Clerkin

ORIGINAL WRITING

ISBN: 978-1-906018-34-4

A CIP catalogue for this book is available from the National
Library.

Published by Original Writing Ltd., Dublin, 2008.

Printed in Ireland by Cahill Printers Limited.

FOREWORD

DELOITTE are delighted to support Brendan in bringing this book on his experiences in Africa to publication. Our firm is committed to supporting a wide range of voluntary groups and projects as part of our community programme. We are immensely proud of the support that our people have given to numerous organisations and charities both at home and abroad.

What makes Brendan's experience unique is the fact that it was his accounting skills which enabled him to help people in Africa – his conviction, spirit and commitment to this work is an example to all of us.

Congratulations to Brendan on this magnificent achievement and on a thoroughly enjoyable memoir of his trip!

Pat Cullen,
Managing Partner, Deloitte

INTRODUCTION

This book is an account of an extraordinary year in East Africa. The author's motives for going there after leaving college were mixed: to seek what might be the last great adventure of his youth; to avoid the responsibilities of the real world as long as possible; and, through voluntary work, perhaps to 'do some good in the world.'

On arrival in Kenya in September 2005, Brendan worked for months on a project to establish a village for AIDS orphans and their carers in the remote Kitui region, working among the genial Akamba tribe. He befriended a gallery of saints, sinners and eccentrics—both African and European.

In Nyumbani, he lived a blistering four-hour cycle ride from the nearest store. As one of the very few white people in an area larger than Ulster, he was often treated like a celebrity; they took him to their hearts, their homes, their weddings and their funerals. He had numerous marriage proposals. As a Project accountant during a period of severe drought and famine, he worked with people who refused to work unless a goat was sacrificed to a large python to which they prayed for rains. One of the village workers had his left buttock eaten by a hyena after he fell into a drunken sleep by the roadside.

He took time out to travel extensively throughout Kenya, Tanzania and Uganda. He suffered frost-bite near the equator, scaling both Mt. Kilimanjaro and Mt. Kenya; he fled the immigration officers over the border into Uganda, where he swam with crocodiles and hippos in the River Nile; he explored exotic Zanzibar and the Serengeti game park. The slums of Nairobi were as depressing as the spirit of the people was life-affirming. He rescued a Kenyan woman who was being swept out to sea on New Year's Eve. He travelled with some of the dwindling band of Irish missionaries through the Rift Valley, and among the primitive Turkana tribe whose warriors often go naked except for their spears and AK-47s . . .

The book becomes an engaging narrative through a full year in Africa, bulging with amusing personal anecdotes, sprinkled with interesting stories of Kenya past and present, and full of personal insights that will challenge any reader's view of Africa and her people.

Part of the price of this book is donated to the education of children in Kitui.

ACKNOWLEDGEMENTS

There are so many people I feel deserve acknowledgement for their help and encouragement, both during my time in Africa and in the making of this book. I began writing this during a few rainy days after I came home, so that I would not forget it all in a few years' time. I intended to spend only a few days at it so I would have something for myself to look back on. Then a few people along the way told me it was a good read, but that I should improve it in various ways.

I would like to thank in particular Pat Close who probably guided me through its progression more than anyone. I must also express my gratitude to the O'Donnells of Ardara—Cian and Fionntán, my brother Aidan, Fr. Liam Kelly, Wambua Singa, and Seamus Murray.

I am very grateful to Pat Cullen for his generous backing; also to Mike Hartwell, Gerry Keating, Marianne Leonard, Claire Quinn, and those in Deloitte for their terrific support for this project.

The writing of this book owes much to my parents Séamus and Pauline for inspiring my love of learning and adventure, as well as for their valued advice while composing it.

I would like to thank my editor Cleo Murphy, and the people of Original Writing for the opportunity to publish this account.

Jean Spindler deserves a special mention for her marvellous animations and the front cover. Bartley Sharkey did me a huge favour by creating the maps of Kenya and Kitui, and Michael Higgins also in creating the website.

I must express my appreciation to Fr. John Gilligan of DCU, as well as Margaret Murtagh and John Murphy of Gaisce.

There are many people whom I knew in Kenya who are not even mentioned in the pages of this book, but who warmly welcomed me wherever I went. I would especially like to express my deepest appreciation to the Irish missionaries throughout Kenya for their unfailing hospitality, and for making my time there so enjoyable, and also to the African people of Kitui for their friendships and the terrific welcome I received from every one of them.

During my time in Africa, there were many people who sent donations for the people of Kitui. I think nearly all of them are far too modest to want to be named, so please know your wonderful generosity is making a difference. Finally, without ever even asking any of them, Bríd and a whole army of friends from college (and even some of their friends) were busy raising a huge amount of funds in Ireland for projects around Kitui. Again, I know many of them are too modest to want to be mentioned, but I have to congratulate them on their superb work.

This book is dedicated to Packie Ward who passed away only days before I left Kenya.

It is also dedicated to 'Nana' Clare McGarrigle who passed away a few months after my return to Ireland, but always encouraged me to write it all down

CONTENTS

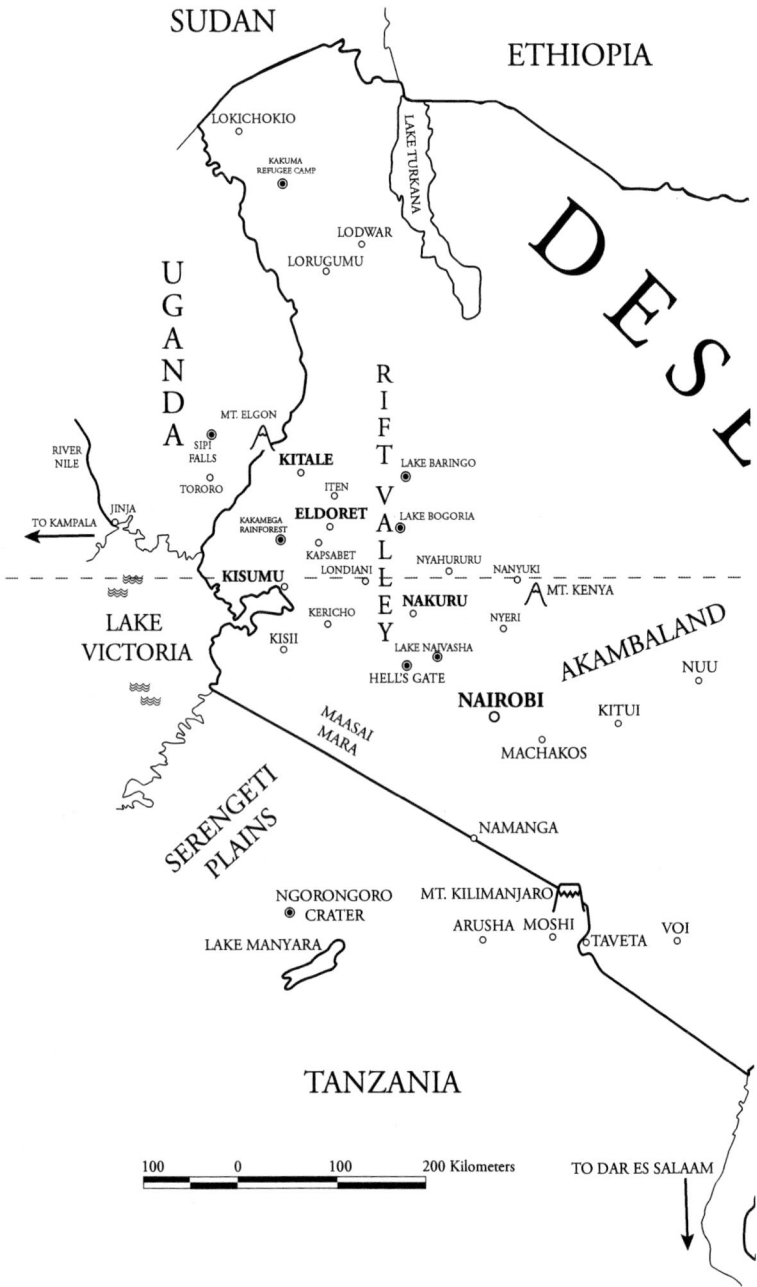

SUDAN

ETHIOPIA

LOKICHOKIO

KAKUMA
REFUGEE CAMP

LAKE TURKANA

LODWAR

LORUGUMU

U
G
A
N
D
A

DESL

RIVER
NILE

MT. ELGON

SIPI
FALLS

KITALE

LAKE BARINGO

RIFT VALLEY

TO KAMPALA

JINJA

TORORO

ITEN

ELDORET

LAKE BOGORIA

KAKAMEGA
RAINFOREST

KAPSABET
LONDIANI

NYAHURURU

NANYUKI

MT. KENYA

KISUMU

NAKURU

NYERI

LAKE
VICTORIA

KERICHO

KISII

LAKE NAIVASHA

AKAMBALAND

NUU

HELL'S GATE

NAIROBI

KITUI

MAASAI
MARA

MACHAKOS

SERENGETI
PLAINS

NAMANGA

NGORONGORO
CRATER

MT. KILIMANJARO

ARUSHA

MOSHI

TAVETA

VOI

LAKE MANYARA

TANZANIA

100   0   100   200 Kilometers

TO DAR ES SALAAM

Larger Area Map

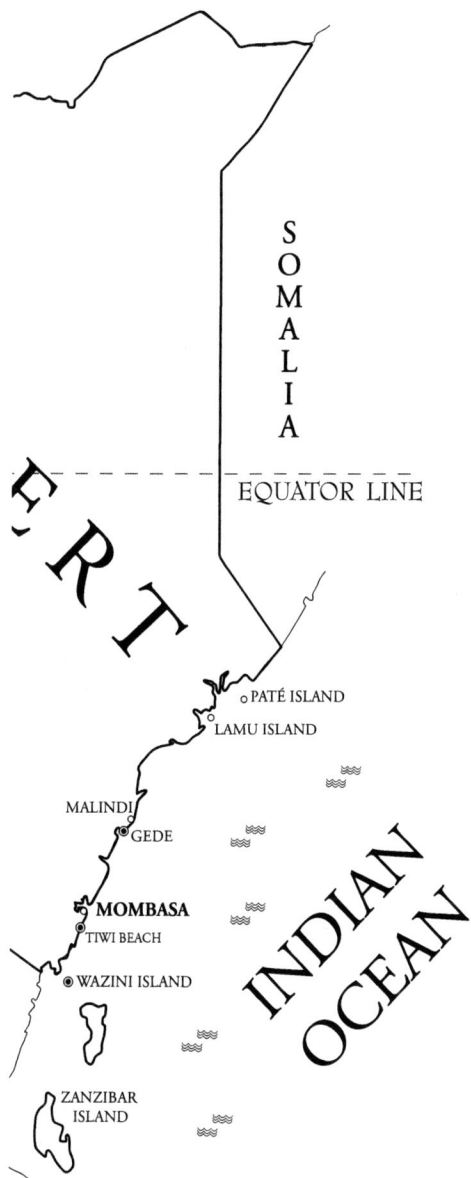

SOMALIA

- - - - - - - - - - - - - EQUATOR LINE

'ERT

o PATÉ ISLAND
° LAMU ISLAND

MALINDI
◉ GEDE

◼ **MOMBASA**
◉ TIWI BEACH

◉ WAZINI ISLAND

INDIAN OCEAN

ZANZIBAR
ISLAND

Local Area Map

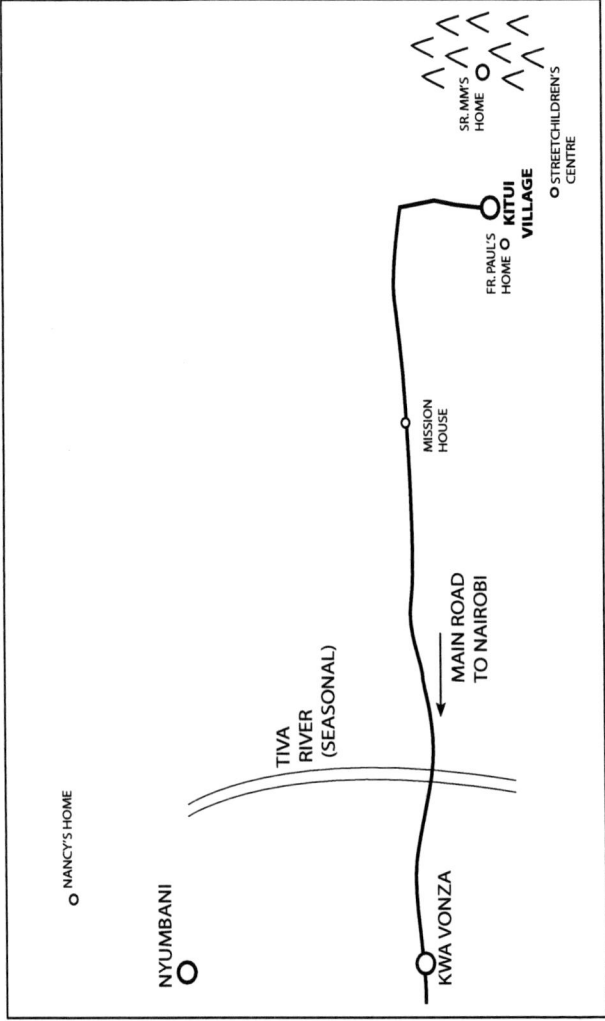

NYUMBANI

o NANCY'S HOME

TIVA
RIVER
(SEASONAL)

MAIN ROAD
TO NAIROBI

MISSION
HOUSE

KWA VONZA

FR. PAUL'S
HOME o **KITUI
VILLAGE**

SR. MM'S
HOME O

O STREET CHILDREN'S
CENTRE

LIST OF ILLUSTRATIONS

PROLOGUE

'Whites have watches, blacks have time'
(Kenyan proverb)

I can remember the moment very clearly. I was sitting at my desk in the PricewaterhouseCoopers offices in Dublin during the college holidays in the summer of 2003. An e-mail arrived from a good friend who was on a J1 summer work visa in New Jersey, USA. His message was not so much, 'Wish you were here'; it was more along the lines of, 'I bet you wish you were here!' It set me thinking.

It was a pleasant sunny day. During lunch-break, I ambled down to the Grand Canal to eat my salad sandwiches on a bench, sitting beside the statue of Patrick Kavanagh. As I sat there, two thoughts crossed my mind. The first was—what am I doing here working in an accountancy firm in Dublin? The second was—I am going to Africa.

This second thought, which had come from God knows where, was quickly forgotten. Later that summer, some friends and I went inter-railing around Eastern Europe, from the Baltic to the Black Sea, for over a month. Halcyon days of innocent mishaps and harmless mischief, hours spent trying to chat up the stunning blondes of those countries, hardly being able to spend our money because everything was so cheap, and taking a last glimpse before the EU would transform the eastern bloc once they all joined the following year.

I did the J1 visa gig myself the following summer. I worked as a lifeguard at a summer activity camp in Maine, with a month at the end for the classic American road trip. It was only after that summer that Africa came back into my head. Of all the places in Western Europe, Eastern Europe and the United States that I had visited, the region that most appealed to me was Transylvania in Romania. The scenes I had witnessed there remained fixed in the album of memory: horses pulling wooden carts stacked with hay, everybody going about their business on foot or on bicycle, forty or more workers cutting corn in a field . . . It was the sedate way of life which appealed; it seemed that things had not really changed a great deal since the days of Vlad the Impaler. I did not know it then, but that step back in time was in some ways a preparation for Africa.

Any seasoned traveller will tell you that the real characters and the friendlier locals tend to be found in poorer regions not yet in the viewfinders of coach loads of Japanese tourists. There is an appealing innocence and spontaneity amongst people unused to tourists. I like that, though it is not to everyone's taste. Most of those who travel after leaving college in Ireland spend a year working in bars in Australia and socialising most nights with other Irish, maybe having spent a while in Thailand or South America beforehand. They all have a fantastic time on Bondi Beach or in Byron Bay.

But Australia just did not appeal to me. Everyone comes back with much the same stories. I wanted more of an adventure, to go somewhere that entailed some risk, to experience places that did not have McDonalds and Irish bars, places where few of my generation had ventured before. It would have to be somewhere in the Developing World. The idea of voluntary work was taking shape in my head. I really wanted to live the life of the place, not just observe it. That might prove to be adventure enough. A bit of sun would be a bonus!

However, I was contracted to train as a tax advisor with Deloitte & Touche for three years immediately after college; they were sponsoring the Masters in Accounting that I was studying at Dublin City University. So, with some trepidation, I rang them up in late 2004 and told them of my desire to volunteer for a year in Africa. They got back to me a few days later.

'No problem,' they said, to my great delight and gratitude.

The next decision was what exactly I would do for the year. One by one, those friends who had expressed an interest in joining me pulled out. One spent all his 'Africa' savings during rag week in Galway! It became clear I would be going on my own. Then there was the problem of expense. Some voluntary organisations were asking for thousands of euro for me to volunteer with them for a couple of months. I drew up a tentative plan to volunteer in Ghana, travel on to East Africa, then the Middle East, and catch the Trans-Siberian railway from Moscow to Beijing. Well, things fall apart.

One particular day in college, still pondering what to do, I remembered being at a Mass in DCU a few months previously, where the chaplain gave a sermon about a recent visit of his to a friend who was a Kiltegan missionary in Kenya. It had struck a chord with me at the time because some of my relatives had worked in Africa. I went to talk to the chaplain about it. Through him, I contacted a missionary in Kenya called Fr. Paul. He suggested that I work at a project in his Diocese, in a region called Kitui. They could use someone with accountancy skills. And that was it; Kenya it would be . . .

. . . Which is how I found myself on a plane bound for Nairobi in September 2005. I was leaving behind a family deeply concerned about my safety. I was leaving behind the hustle and bustle of city life in Dublin; leaving behind life in Celtic Tiger Ireland and one of its ideological bastions, DCU. I was taking time out from all that. Time for possibly the last great adventure of my youth. Time, perhaps, to 'give something back' and, however briefly, to 'do some good in the world,' as the volunteer literature puts it. Time would tell.

And there was a further complication. Some time before the end of college, but after I had made my plans, I had fallen in love with a girl on my course. It tore me to leave Bríd behind for a whole year. Looking ahead, it seemed like a very long time. But maybe I could learn patience, like the Africans in the Kenyan proverb: 'Whites have watches, blacks have time.'

CHAPTER 1
NOT LIONS, LADYBIRDS!

PEOPLE WORRY ABOUT YOU WHEN you tell them you are going to Africa. For a start, they worry about all those nasty tropical diseases. They have seen films and documentaries on television in which the intrepid travellers and explorers were laid low by something viral, horrible and occasionally fatal. Mothers, understandably, worry more than most.

'Look, Mammy,' I explained again, 'I've had all the injections: yellow fever, tetanus, diphtheria, rabies, cholera, typhoid, hepatitis A, B, C, and probably X, Y, and Z as well. I have arms like a junkie!'

'They say malaria is the worst,' she observed nervously.

'I promise to keep taking the tablets.'

'And there are all those wild animals. I read somewhere that buffalo are the most dangerous, worse than the lions, the hippos, the crocodiles . . . '

'I'm told hyenas are fairly treacherous!' my father interjected.

Yes, they were all rather worried. Nobody, including me, was worried about ladybirds, though. I should have been.

I spent my first night off the plane as a guest of the Kiltegan Fathers in Nairobi. I had been met at the airport by a member of Fr. Paul's lay staff named Stephen, who explained that Fr. Paul had recently left on a fund-raising trip to Ireland. Fr. Paul was the administrator of the Kitui Diocese, in effect the acting Bishop. It was through him that I had been assigned to a role as an accountant on the Nyumbani Village Project. Before I retired for the night, Stephen, a middle-aged man from the Akamba tribe, told me to get a good sleep because we would be up early to travel to 'base camp' in Kitui village the next day. Kitui District is in the Akamba heartlands, about three or four hours from Nairobi.

There is nothing quite like a nine hours plane journey to ensure a sound night's sleep. I regained consciousness around 8am, quite late by African standards, and within half an hour, we were on the road. It was to be my first sight of Kenya in daylight. I remember being overwhelmed by the scenes that morning as we made our way to Kitui. From the front seat of the battered old jeep, I tried to take in the endless straggle of the Nairobi suburbs, the crazy kamikaze drivers, the corrugated iron shacks, and the deteriorating roads, rutted and pot-holed. Beyond the city, the road traverses the Nairobi National Park, and I had my first excited sightings in the wild of ostriches, gazelles and warthogs.

The Park eventually surrenders to a parched barren landscape, sparsely populated, studded here and there with isolated round, thatched mud-huts. After Machakos, a disorderly tangle of a town, the road twists and clambers up a terraced mountain. The countryside is more fertile now, with lots of tiny villages and scores of pedestrians strolling or striding along under a sweltering sun. Across the mountain, the brown barren bush returns, with an occasional acacia tree or tiny roadside hamlet. Classic African landscape. Near the village of Kwa Vonza, the soil becomes noticeably redder in colour and tiny fields show traces of valiant attempts at cultivation.

Several more kilometres further on lies the decent-sized village of Kitui—my destination and my base for the foreseeable future. The capital of Kitui District, it consists of three or four interwoven streets and is home to a few thousand people. The village appears a bit anarchic, and at first glance has very little of note to distinguish it. In the months ahead, I would get to know it well, and to appreciate its intriguing people.

Apart from the sensory overload along the way and a slight headache (which I attributed to jet lag and to altitude), I had enjoyed the dusty, bumpy, shake-rattle-and-roll of the journey to Kitui with Stephen. He had answered patiently my endless questions. My first impression of Kenya was that it was a bit like the down-at-heel Ireland of the 1920's newsreels—though obviously a lot hotter. I knew it would take me some time to process all of these new sensations.

'The Akamba are the fifth largest tribe in Kenya,' Stephen told me with discernible pride.

However, they inhabit a very arid region; Kenyans take pity on you, as I discovered later, when you tell them you live there. It is an undeveloped backward area even for Kenya, and populated by a very traditional community. The people of Kitui are cut off by the mountains on the western side, and wedged in by the desert to the east.

Seven kilometres further up a dirt track into the hills above the village, our jeep pulled up outside a modest cream-coloured bungalow opposite what was obviously a school. A woman of about sixty years of age dressed in a bright blouse and long skirt emerged to meet us.

NO HURRY IN AFRICA

'Karibu sana,' she said in very proper tones as she grabbed my hand.

'Huh?' I replied, confused.

'Oh . . . yes . . . welcome, come in. I'm here since the 1970s. Swahili becomes a habit. You must be starving, will you eat?'

This was Sr. Margaret Mary, an impressive-looking Irish Ursuline nun. She had rosy cheeks set in a face that suggested a jolly disposition; it was lightly tanned by decades spent in the African sun. She came from Thurles in Tipperary originally, and still retained something of the accent. I would discover later that she also retained the selfless generosity of spirit that had brought her to Africa as a teacher all those years ago. During my time in Kenya, she would become like an aunt to me.

She summoned her cook in Swahili, an Akamba man of indeterminate vintage, who brought in some rice and a small bit of chicken on a bone. I was famished and I tucked in with relish after the long journey. As I gnawed on the bone, I resolved that I must make learning Swahili a priority. Sr. MM (Margaret Mary), with the curiosity of the exile, proceeded to quiz me for ages about recent events in Ireland.

'I go home as often as I can, Brendan, but I hardly recognise the place anymore. I suppose this is home now.'

That evening, Sr. MM told me about the Akamba people to whose welfare she had devoted her life. As she did so, the cook listened and nodded regularly as if to confirm her story.

'It used to be the Maasai people who held sway here in this part of eastern Kenya,' she began. 'The Maasai were pastoralists. Their neighbours to the south, living around Mount Kilimanjaro and the Taita Hills, were the Akamba tribe. They are one of the many Bantu tribes in this part of Africa. Kitui was endowed with an abundance of wild animals such as lions and elephants, far more than there are now. The Akamba were hunters, experts at using bows and arrows. Later they became successful traders, selling ivory to the Arabs who sailed along the coast.

Anyway, when the elephants around Mount Kilimanjaro were becoming scarcer, the Akamba coveted the land around Kitui where the Maasai lived. As the Akamba hunted the dwindling elephants stocks, they edged ever closer to Maasai territory. Eventually the two tribes clashed in a ferocious battle. The Maasai warriors relied on the spear to defend their lands; the Akamba easily overwhelmed them with their bows and arrows. The Maasai migrated south to where they live today along the Kenyan/Tanzanian border. The Akamba moved north.'

I was getting my first lesson in the complex patterns of tribal conquest, settlement and rivalry that bedevil African affairs to this day.

'There's another darker side to the Akamba story,' Sr. MM continued. 'They sold ivory to the Arabs and grew prosperous while elephants were in plentiful supply. However, when the elephants in Kitui became scarcer as well, a number of the Akamba collaborated with the Swahili traders and found something else to sell to the Arabs apparently—slaves. Most of the Akamba tribe fiercely resisted those people. But that was a long time ago. Anyway, you must be tired after your travels, Brendan. You could do with a good sleep and a bit of rest before you start work at Nyumbani.'

I slept late the next morning and woke up with a slight head-ache. To shake it off, I went for a long exploratory stroll in the afternoon. It had rained for the first time in months in Kitui during the night. The rich earthy smell of parched soil disturbed by rain after prolonged drought is powerful and unforgettable. I breathed it in deeply as I strode along. I met people walking in groups—or was it gangs?—with axes and machetes, and I wondered were they about to murder me. I had been listening to the horror stories people told me in Ireland before I came out to Africa. I need not have worried; the axes and *pangas* were for nothing more sinister than clearing scrub. I greeted them, and told those who understood English that I had come to Kenya to volunteer on the Nyumbani project. I told them I came from a place where it rains all the time. They could not have been more welcoming.

They told me joyfully I must have brought the rain from Ireland, and loved me for it. A woman beamed widely and boasted how she had set out all her seven buckets to catch the rain. It would save many a trip to the dry riverbed several kilometres away, where they dig a hole in the sand to extract groundwater. Sadly, every day after that brought cloudless skies and scorching temperatures. The longed-for late year rains in Kitui never came. In fact, no prolonged rains had occurred since the worldwide *El-Niño* rains of 1998—and those were so strong they washed away the soil.

That first day, the children mobbed me and made such a hullabaloo that the local chief got one of his three wives to call me over to be introduced. He, in turn, introduced me to his 'royal' family who shyly shook my hand. It was not everyday that they had a visit from a tall *mzungu* (Swahili for white person, with some of the connotations of a derogatory term like 'nigger' but not really meant in a hostile way). We then had an impromptu thirty-a-side game of football with a ball made from plastic bags and string on the 'highway,' as they called it. In reality, it was a narrow dirt track. The children were shouting 'how are you, one, two, three, I love you,' over and over and over. Their parents must have taught them to say that whenever they saw a *mzungu*. Clearly most had no idea what they were chanting.

I spent that day and the next in Sr. MM's home. The day after that, she insisted on escorting me the fifty kilometres over the dusty pot-holed dirt track to Nyumbani. My headache returned. Now I blamed it on the jolting brought on by the rutted track. It was not quite the Sahara, but we were driving further and further into the desert—an arid bush landscape, inches deep with fine red dust. There were a few seashells on the ground as well, which gives one a sense of its geological antiquity. This was the time-forsaken place where I planned to be volunteering for the rest of the year. *Nyumbani* means 'home' in Swahili. It had little in common with the homes of my native Donegal, I thought as we arrived.

In the middle of this desert was a vast thousand-acre building site. This was the Village project. I could see about a dozen houses (later to be referred to as Phase I), and a number of silver corrugated iron shacks that served as offices. But what pulled me up short was the sight of maybe five hundred people in this remote place, all busy digging trenches, clearing scrub or hauling clay blocks on ox-carts. It was like a rural African version of a Lowry painting. There was not a white face to be seen. I was feeling nervous, probably for the first time. Where and how could I possibly fit in?

NO HURRY IN AFRICA

A local Akamba woman named Nancy was the first to introduce herself to me in Nyumbani. She was a small but fine-looking woman in her late twenties. She also had more English than nearly any other African I had met so far. More or less the first thing she said to me was,

'Bradan (as she pronounced my name forever more), there are baboons between here and my home, big big baboons, and yesterday they took my sister's baby when I was here, and started throwing the baby among them. Oh, my sister cried and cried.'

Nancy illustrated her cautionary tale with appropriate gestures and arm actions to go along with every sentence.

'Then they left her baby down beside her. But they are dangerous. Be careful of the baboons, Bradan.'

It sounded like good advice! I would recall her cautionary words later.

Nancy showed me to the spartan accommodation which I would share with around ten other workers. I would be working very closely with her, as she was one of the half dozen clerks in the corrugated iron office where I was based. She was quite tiny, much smaller than the other Akamba, who themselves are closer to the height of Pygmies rather than the taller Maasai. She could be very bashful, yet she appeared every Monday morning with a brand new hairstyle. At 6"2,' I probably resembled the BFG, loftily winking down at her to make her blush when she pretended her hairstyle was the same as the previous week's. I found her permanently in a good mood and joking, but she took no prisoners; if a worker tried a fast one, she would go through him or her for a shortcut. She was straighter than a die, not just by African standards, mind, but by those of an older generation in Ireland.

CHAPTER 1 NOT LIONS, LADYBIRDS!

She was incorruptible, and tireless in her work.

The next day, Thursday, my headache returned with a vengeance. I could no longer blame jet lag, altitude or jolting jeeps. I doubted if it was a side effect of the malaria tablets. It was no longer a sort of tingling sensation in the back of my head; it had morphed into a stinging pain that pulsed through my brain every time I moved. I was comparing it to something like electroconvulsive therapy without the benefit of anaesthetic.

Whatever it was, it was sapping my body of energy, levels of which were already depleted by the African sun. I was embarrassed that I was ill so soon. I knew it was my mother's worst fear. Sr. MM picked me up the next day, Friday, to spend the weekend at her house, and I confessed my condition to her. One or two lesions had appeared on my face, and were soon proliferating. She drove me to a doctor of Indian descent in Kitui village. He seemed baffled. After boasting that he studied in London—in an attempt to impress us, I think—he prescribed three different kinds of antibiotics that I had to take over the weekend. To be sure, to be sure, to be sure, I felt like saying. They did nothing for me. At least, I was not getting any worse.

On Monday morning, I insisted on returning to Nyumbani. Nancy called in the local herbal doctor, a grey-haired *mzee* called Mutinda. It was not very encouraging to be told he had a good reputation for healing sick animals. Hocus pocus, I was thinking. He appeared as I was sitting disconsolately on the step at the house. He muttered things in English that I did not take in, because I was wondering how he had acquired his shiny gold tooth. He had a gentle face, though, and a confident manner. He was a respected elder and community leader. Just as another electric

27

shock buzzed through me, he promptly disappeared.

'Am I cured now, Nancy?' I asked, straining to be funny, and trying to disguise my fears.

She was throwing the bones left over from our lunch to the hungry pups.

'Ah, no Bradan, wait, wait.'

She chuckled at the silly *mzungu* thinking himself cured.

Soon Mutinda returned with an off-white liquid mix in a wooden container and spread it on my cheeks and around my face.

'It is a mixture of aloe vera, water, sugar, and garlic. Good, good, good,' Mutinda enlightened me in a soft gravelly voice as he proceeded to smear it over my upper torso. By now, there were half a dozen spectators. My pale Irish body was a terrific source of interest, even amusement, to them all.

'Were you in Nairobi?' Mutinda asked.

I told him I had stayed with the Kiltegan Fathers in Nairobi the night I arrived off the plane.

'It's a Nairobi fly, yes; what's it known as in English . . . a . . . a ladybird, yes. It walked along your face as you slept and urinated here and here and here.'

He touched the lesions on my face. Of all the African beasts that exist or that had starred in my parents' imaginations, the creature that felled me turned out to be a ladybird!

Whether it was the delayed effect of the antibiotics, or Mutinda's magic mix, I will never know, but within a few hours I started to feel slightly better. Later I discovered that every tribe has their own tried and tested herbal remedies made from roots and plant-leaves. There are cures for more or less every ailment (except the big one, of course—AIDS, which one dubious theory claims began when a man in the Congo had sex with a monkey). And here is the crux of one of Africa's problems. They are beginning to lose these effective herbal remedies, but have only limited access to Western medicine. In essence, many African tribes are losing the best of their indigenous ways, but have yet to gain the benefits of Western ways in areas like medicine.

You always feel a lot better when you realise you are not going to die, at least not yet! Thanks to Mutinda's remedy, I was feeling well enough the next night for some serious socialising. An affable twenty-one year old mechanic, Kimanze, had offered to take me to a hostelry in Kwa Vonza village. He thought himself quite the cool boy, did Kimanze. He had a wide mischievous smile, and darker skin more akin to the Luo tribe, and not the lighter hue of his own Akamba people. He had borrowed a motorbike, and he carried me and two of his African friends into the night, travelling at ten kilometres an hour—without the benefit of headlights. Later, when I told my Irish friends about four of us on a motorbike, they were incredulous. It can be done, but I would not recommend it!

Under a clear night sky, brilliant with stars, we suddenly came upon a security checkpoint. Two stroppy-looking policemen were pointing Kalashnikovs at us. Kimanze negotiated on our behalf. In this sticky situation, he opted for bribery rather than blarney, and asked me to pay the police the equivalent of five euro so they would let us all go. It is a fair amount for a policeman there. Forget South Armagh, I thought, this place is real Bandit Country.

That night was my first experience of a Kenyan pub, in the tiny village that is Kwa Vonza, about fifteen kilometres from

NO HURRY IN AFRICA

Nyumbani. The pub was a remarkable place, a fifteen-foot square shack, but with the grand name of 'The Paradise Hotel.' It was lit by a single glowing tilly-lamp. There were two dogs scratching themselves in the middle of the concrete floor, and a few old men chewing *miraa* (a foul tasting legal African narcotic) on the shaky, plain wooden benches. There were not any women, and the only choice of beverage was between a warm bottle of Guinness and an equally warm bottle of Tusker beer. Nothing else at all. The 'toilets' consisted of relieving oneself against the outside wall in the dark. Oh, and there were constant requests from the Africans for the rich *mzungu* to buy a round—which cost the equivalent of five euro for the whole house.

That particular night, one drunk had a call of nature and stepped on a snake. He was in screaming agony until a 'black stone' was brought.

'It will suck the poison out,' Kimanze explained.

A 'black stone' is a rare form of sedimentary rock that, when placed over a bite, will absorb the snake poison from the blood. Nearly every home has one in these parts, but it must be thrown out after having been used once.

'Welcome to Kitui!' Kimanze proclaimed, watching me view this process with fascination.

I stayed in his home that night—a round, thatched mud-hut of one, virtually furniture-less, room that was lit by a paraffin hurricane lamp. Boy, these Africans have nothing, I was thinking. I would discover in the year ahead how this was true only in a superficial sense. I had been in Africa for a week and I had a lot to learn.

The four of us squeezed into two single beds, malarial

CHAPTER 1 NOT LIONS, LADYBIRDS!

mosquitoes buzzing incessantly as I drifted off to sleep. My head was teeming with impressions of my first extraordinary week in Africa. If my mother could see me now! My final thought before losing consciousness was of the headline if it ever made the *Donegal News:* 'Letterkenny man laid low in Africa by a ladybird.'

CHAPTER 2
A DAY AT THE OFFICE
(LIKE NO OTHER . . .)

THE DIRECTOR OF THE NYUMBANI Village Project was a commanding figure. An architect from the Kikuyu tribe, Kiragu was a man in his early fifties, quite tall, with a shaven head and mobile features that suggested a quick intelligence, imagination and resourcefulness. He welcomed me to his humble office with a warm smile and, in perfect Queen's English, acquainted me with what the Nyumbani Project was all about.

Speaking with passion, he began by outlining the devastation wrought by AIDS in Kenya and throughout Africa. There was (at that time) something like twelve million children orphaned by the pandemic across the Continent. In some Nairobi slums, the infection rate was close to 40 per cent. Kenya was facing an appalling crisis.

'Nyumbani Village is our response to the pandemic' he explained. 'We want to establish a model settlement for HIV-AIDS orphans in sub-Saharan Africa. If we succeed, others can go down the same road. When we are up and running, we plan to house and nurture 1,000 orphans as well as their elderly guardians—in most cases their destitute grandparents. You see, Brendan, the middle generation of parents has died from AIDS; we refer to them as "the lost generation."'

He became very animated when he got down to the details of the scheme.

'The Village will include about 150 homesteads, a health clinic, a nursery, a primary school, industrial production and training centres, a multi-purpose community hall, a worship centre, a police post, and a guesthouse.'

I could tell that the man was a visionary. As well as the administrative centre and the necessary infrastructure, he was already looking ahead to providing an ecological management centre and recreational spaces. Glancing out the window at the primitive building site, I could not help but feel that Kiragu was a bit of a dreamer, maybe; but this proud Kikuyu was also one of the most thoroughly inspiring people I met in Africa.

'The whole project,' he continued, 'will have to respect our African culture and traditions. We would hope to create a strong social fabric among the villagers themselves, and between the village and the existing population of the area. Nyumbani is labour intensive, and there will be a lot of employment. We hope to train people in useful and traditional skills such as woodwork and woodcarving. There's a market out there. We already employ around 500 local men and women in a place with no other employment opportunities at all. We will be progressive too. Women will hold many leadership positions, just as they already do in the development of it right now, which—as you probably know—is unusual for Africa.'

Kiragu was wearing a sleeveless jacket and waved his arms a lot as he spoke, as if expending some of his boundless energy. He pushed a folder of documents and plans across the table. With this visionary at the helm, I felt, this dream might just come true.

CHAPTER 2 A DAY AT THE OFFICE (LIKE NO OTHER . . .)

Having drawn breath momentarily, he was off again.

'One of the major principles in the Nyumbani village concept is self-sustainability. This can be achieved on our 1,000-acre commercially viable organic farm. We will grow subsistence food, cash crops, and medicinal plants. Much can be done through using solar energy. Water for irrigating the farm will be sourced from the construction of dams, boreholes and wells. You'll have noticed that the work has already begun.'

Through the office window, I could see hundreds and hundreds of busy people scurrying around like ants, heavy loads being moved by ox-carts, and lines and lines of workers digging foundations and irrigation trenches. I was looking at the biggest building site I had ever seen. Kiragu attracted my attention again and said, almost pleadingly,

'We are desperate for an accountant here, Brendan. Can you start right away?'

He told me that anyone from Kitui District who qualifies as an accountant moves straight to Nairobi, and never returns. It would be impossible to persuade any educated Kenyan to live at Nyumbani unless they were paid extortionate amounts of money. And that, in short, is how I became the management accountant of the whole Village project.

On later occasions, my initially favourable impressions of Kiragu were confirmed. In conversation with him, the simplest thing would spark him into a mesmerising monologue. A vague idea would turn into a detailed plan as his thoughts poured from him, perfectly articulated. He was a good listener too. I told him about self-help projects in Ireland and he listened intently. He was fascinated when I described how the setting up of Credit

NO HURRY IN AFRICA

Unions in rural Ireland helped so many ordinary families to take advantage of developments in the country during the 1960s.

Kiragu's vision and effortless inspiration added fuel to my innate enthusiasm for volunteering.

Over the next few days, I acquainted myself with the systems in place. My immediate challenge was simple: the faster I could make the project run, the more costs I would manage to save, the more homesteads would be built, and the more people would live there. Who would have imagined that all that auditing and management accounting I had studied at college would actually be so useful so soon? From the start I was immediately stimulated, and threw myself at it, becoming a real part of the management of the project.

Everything was being constructed by hand. There was practically no machinery because there would be nothing to run it on. Most wells were developed by men lowering themselves fifty feet or more down into a dark hole using an ordinary rope tied onto something, anything, even a nearby tree. Then it was a matter of chip, chip, chipping away with a hammer and chisel—some wells could be more than one hundred feet deep. None of the labourers ever thought to ask for safety equipment, not even a helmet. At least, we did not have the crazy scaffolding consisting of tree branches of all shapes that are lashed to buildings several stories high that you see around Nairobi. Health and Safety means something different in Africa.

One of my first tasks in September was counting a month's wages in cash for 500 people. I was counting over one million Kenyan shillings in total, one note at a time. One shilling is known as 'a bob,' twenty shillings is termed 'a pound'—a throwback to

British rule—and ninety shillings roughly equalled a euro. The average Nyumbani wage was the equivalent of two-euro per day, an excellent wage for Kitui, or indeed anywhere in Kenya. Even to have steady waged employment is rare enough.

A mêlée very nearly erupted that first week because the wages were very late. Apprehension was increasing, understandably so. Delay meant the workers' children could go hungry, and they could not buy seeds to take advantage of the rains that were due and expected any day soon. However, Nancy and I were finally handing out notes to people as they entered our tiny tin office. Towering over us were two burly men with Kalashnikovs, and another two were standing guard outside the door. I found out later they were special military police with shoot-to-kill orders if anybody caused trouble.

The house where I was staying was only a few hundred yards away. It was one of the spartan village homesteads that had been constructed with clay blocks and roofed with red corrugated iron sheets. I shared it with a fluctuating number of Project workers who lived on-site, three of us to a room. It became congested at times. We were the dozen or so non-locals: the Kikuyus, the Luos, the *mzungu*, the Nairobi professionals. We tended to work in management, or were otherwise required to be permanently on-site.

I was glad to discover that there was at least one other *mzungu* living there, a Rasta from Munich named Leo. He was equally delighted to see me. I think he had been going a bit out of his mind in the previous month in Nyumbani because there had not been another Westerner to see things as he did. Leo had dreadlocks to his shoulders; he had a proper goatee but was generally unshaven. He dressed raggedly, yet was the stereotypical German in so many of his mannerisms. Despite his bedraggled appearance, he was very logical and very methodical. He was a kind of living paradox. The Rasta exterior concealed an orderly German soul.

'The African way of doing things is so unlike the German way,' he complained.

Leo possessed that element of fun that Bavarian people have; he was fond of a beer as well as the occasional joint to relax him when things proved too much. He had been going round the bend of late because his name sounded like the Swahili word for 'today,' and he was forever thinking people were calling him over or talking about him. He was already a good friend of Kimanze, as they worked closely together in trying to build an irrigation system in the sterile land that is Nyumbani. He possessed a restless energy.

Leo told me that, on finishing school, he had arrived in Africa to avoid a year's conscription in the German army.

'I really want to make a difference here,' he told me.

He was innocent, almost naïve, in his idealism in my view. I liked to think I was a lot more pragmatic. Yet, we hit it off right away. The Africans liked him too. With his long hair and German nationality, the Africans christened him 'Jesus Hitler'— apparently without a trace of irony!

Glad that the excitement of payday was over, I wandered down to the tin offices early the next morning. I was whistling a merry tune and waving to people, when I encountered a group of five women. Despite the early hour, they were dancing and singing as they passed by, each wielding a *jemba* (African style spade).

CHAPTER 2 A DAY AT THE OFFICE (LIKE NO OTHER ...)

At the door to one of the offices, I greeted Nzoki, a stout female Akamba clerk with one crossed eye, who was sweeping out the ever-invading red dust with a bunch of dried reeds. She was quite flirtatious.

'How is you, Brendan? . . . How is your family? . . . How is Sr. MM? . . . How is your children?'

This volley of questions was followed by a personal inspection.

'That's a nice shirt, Brendan. You need a wash, your feet are dirty; a *mzungu* should be clean.'

I thought my feet might have been getting tanned, but it turned out she was correct, they could do with a wash.

'I must begin work, Nzoki, I've a lot to do,' I replied, terminating the conversation, but pleased with the natural curiosity and spontaneous friendship of these Akamba people.

No sooner had I reached my own tin office than Nancy subjected me to a similar battery of questions and comments.

I turned on the 1995-model computer, and began tapping away on my calculator and writing up a funding report for Kiragu. I was going hammer and tongs at it for nearly an hour when the computer suddenly conked out. The generator outside had stopped. It often did. I strolled over to see what the problem was. The Akamba will see a problem coming, but invariably decide to do nothing about it until it is too late. Kimanze had seen the generator was low on fuel, but waited until it ran out altogether and, as a result, I lost my work on the computer. Only now did he decide it was time to do something about it—more out of a laid-back attitude than anything else.

While I was outside, I took the opportunity to greet Nzoki

again. She too was outside, organising a group of workers. We shook hands again as one must do every time one says hello to an Akamba, with their elaborate three part handshake. I needed clarification from her.

'Hello, Nzoki, would you be able to help me please? Is this a 1 or a 7?'

I showed her a page from a battered copybook with figures handwritten in pencil.

'How is you, Brendan?'

'Fine still, thanks.'

'How is your family?'

'Well, I still haven't spoken to them since I came to Kenya— but fine, I'm presuming again.'

'How is Sr. MM?'

'Ah, probably an hour older by now, I'd imagine!'

'And what about your children?'

'I still haven't had any children born to me since the last time you were asking.'

'I see you've washed your feet.'

'Em, you wouldn't be able to tell me please if that's a 1 or a 7?'

Nzoki puzzled over the piece of paper for a few moments, 'It's neither, Brendan.'

'So what is it?'

I nearly rolled my eyes.

'A fraction line, it's 8/5?'

'Hmm, that changes all my calculations. Oh well, lucky the generator broke down before I went any further with it. Thanks. See you in a while, my calculator calls.'

CHAPTER 2 A DAY AT THE OFFICE (LIKE NO OTHER...)

I was learning to adjust to the African pace, to accept all their questions, to embrace their ways. Pleasantries always took precedence over productivity.

One of the first things I had to do was to computerise the recording systems. Everything up to then was in copybooks or on sheets of paper. Nobody could easily retrieve any useful or indeed essential information to improve the workings of the project. It frustrated Leo intensely. Everything, from excavating the raw materials for the blocks to cutting and shaping the tin for the roofs, had to be performed on-site.

I quickly realised there would be little point in me putting a whole computerised system in place, only for it to collapse once I left. The other staff, barring Kiragu and his secretary, had never used or even seen a computer before. So I also began to train Nancy and a number of other clerks to type and navigate the computer. In time, they could input the data themselves, and later on again they could begin to use Word and Excel to create and access information they themselves required.

When I finished for the day, I relaxed by dandering down to the dry river and loitering until dusk fell, fascinated by the wildlife. As this was the only place with an abundance of leaves and greenery, all the animals and birds congregated there once the heat seeped out of the day. Whenever I came tramping along, baboons rushed away, monkeys cleared off frightened and chittering, the small deer stared briefly and raced for cover, as did the rock hyraxes, the python, the tiny scampering lizards, the larger monitor-lizard, the pelicans, the birds with shiny white tails two feet long that I did not know the name of, the hyena, the marabou storks, the armadillo type creatures ... amongst others.

41

No Hurry in Africa

One late afternoon, I went exploring alone through the vegetation, further up the course of the dry river than I normally would. For one split second, I froze with fear as I espied in the fading light what looked like two young female lions stretched out on the branches of a tree. They spotted me a second later, staring straight at me for what, at the time, seemed like ages, but could not have been more than a few seconds. Suddenly each of them jumped down from the tree. My heart pounded audibly. Luckily, they turned and ran away in the other direction, and I rushed straight back home. Still breathless, I asked Nancy what they could have been.

'Most likely caracal cats, Bradan, there haven't been lions seen around Nyumbani in two years.'

There is something special about catching sight of all these truly wild animals in their natural environment, not protected by any national park, and living so close to humans. I used to hide under cover for a long time, motionless, seeing nothing, but when I began to leave, I startled everything again. It took me weeks to realise that David Attenborough might have got it wrong—the trick is to keep walking around making as much noise as you can to frighten everything into moving and betraying its presence. On occasions, baboons growled and barked at me like dogs. I recalled Nancy's warnings. They were probably stronger than I was, but they would run away regardless after a few seconds.

The people of the Akamba tribe take an easy-going, rather Jamaican approach to work and timekeeping. This would have suited me grand! It was people of the Kikuyu and Luo tribes I was working with in management, though. There is a phrase still heard in Northern Ireland—to be 'grabbed by the Kikuyus'—

which means to be grabbed by the testicles. It originated from the time of the Kikuyus' ill-fated *Mau Mau* rebellion against the British during the late 1950s. Kikuyus, who are the biggest tribe in Kenya, making up a fifth of the population, are remarkably like the stereotype of the Scottish Presbyterians in their instincts—hardworking and honest, but rather serious and tight with money. The Akambas on the other hand—dare I say it?—can be a bit Irish, with all that that entails.

One day Kimanze, walking beside me with the new boneshaker bicycle he had just bought, put it to me as follows:

'The difference between the two tribes is this. A Kikuyu man will see my new bicycle and work even harder to save the money to buy one for himself. Whereas an Akamba man will see my new bicycle and perform a witchcraft spell so that I lose the bicycle.'

At that point, I decided the 'Irish' analogy went too far!

I remembered hearing Sr. MM explain that the Akamba tribe were, until the late nineteenth century, semi-nomadic hunter-gatherers. I saw traces of this earlier way of life still persisting everywhere. The night watchmen at Nyumbani walked around with bow and arrows. I once saw a watch-man shoot an arrow between the eyes of a snake camouflaged in the ground, just as I was about to step on it. Akambas are all the time knocking birds off a branch with a catapult. One time, I followed Nzoki's husband when he was out poaching wild dik-dik (miniature deer) for food, expertly shooting the elusive animal dead with an arrow. The sad thing is, a dik-dik mates for life with one partner, so its demise leaves a permanent widow—but the hunters usually catch that one too.

After a few weeks in Kenya, I was getting to know some of

the differences between the tribes. If the Kikuyu tended to look down on the Akamba, the Akamba liked to feel superior to the Maasai. As he was clearing up after breakfast one morning, Sr. MM's Akamba cook told me a story about how his own tribe triumphed over the Maasai in their long territorial disputes, before the arrival of the British.

'The elders one day sat down for a peace conference. After some time, arrows rained down from the sky and landed at the feet of the Maasai elders. The Maasai complained that they were being attacked. One Akamba elder stood up and gestured. "Look around, can you see anybody?" The Akamba elder proceeded to explain: "These arrows have been fired by our ancestors." The Maasai were so afraid of the Akambas' deserved reputation for witchcraft that they withdrew straight away.'

He went on to explain, proudly,

'We Akambas had hidden our men behind trees half a mile away. They had been able to aim their bows and arrows with such accuracy that they landed at the feet of the Maasai elders.'

The Akamba people are unused to contact with white people nowadays. When I arrived, there were about a dozen Irish in Akambaland, an area greater than the size of Ulster, and there were no other resident white people at all. Wherever I ventured, the children would silently stare at me, mesmerised, until I spoke. Then the cheering would erupt and I would have throngs of barefoot children swarming around me, screaming and following me for several kilometres. Being the first white person they had ever seen, I was just like a celebrity, a pop star that they wanted to touch and shake by the hand. They would pinch my skin to see if it were real; they would stare, cheer, scream and beg me to take a photograph of them as they mobbed me. When I obliged, even the Akamba adults would run into the frame, and then thank me for taking the photo.

The principal way to get around in Kitui District was by walking, as the vast majority of people regularly did over huge distances. About the only real alternative was a 1950s-style bicycle. These were first imported from China decades ago and, as far as I know, are still being imported from that source. Think of a five-barred gate on wheels, with several middle bars missing! Before I acquired my own bicycle, random people used to offer me theirs to take whenever they saw me walking somewhere in the desert; they were confident that one of their neighbours would bring it back to them that evening. The only other form of transport around Nyumbani was the ox and cart. The second time I was on an ox-cart, I managed to fall off the side. Only my pride was bruised. From one weekend until the next, I might not see a single car. At weekends, I would often go to Sr. MM's. Sr. MM eventually presented me with an old ramshackle boneshaker that had been lying around her girls' secondary school. It needed fixing up. It was actually supposed to be for her caretaker but he was too lazy to cycle and would always send someone else for provisions. After doing my own temporary repair job on it, I had half a dozen parts replaced by one of the many bicycle-repair men plying their trade underneath a tree, and then added a silver bell for good measure.

It is a four hour cycle from Nyumbani into Kitui, the nearest decent village with electricity and foodstuffs. The smaller villages, like nearby Kwa Vonza, have shops—mere shacks—where all the stock is on or behind the counter, often though amounting to no more than a loaf of bread and a hanging goat carcass. Often too, there would be a cat patrolling the counter; whatever about the hygiene, it would keep the rodents and reptiles at bay. There was always an ancient weighing scales sitting on the clay floor. The bigger villages, like Kitui, have colourful noisy outdoor markets, with stalls made from branches lashed together, or wares simply laid out along the ground. Some of the stallholders physically drag you over to their merchandise; some hawkers walk around carrying their bric-a-brac and push it in your face. In the midday heat, many lie asleep on top of their stalls, unconcerned about whether they sell anything or not.

An odd time, I managed to get a lift on the back of one of the very rare motorbikes, usually travelling at white-knuckle speeds over the undulating dirt tracks, weaving in and out among the wandering donkeys and goats along the way. Other vehicles encountered on the road to Nairobi might be buses filled with hens, buses brightly painted with graffiti and emblazoned with names like 'Camilla Parker-Bowles,' 'Princess Di,' or, curiously, 'Fast and Furious—Devil Must Bow.' Passengers rarely wait for the vehicle to stop before dismounting. Visitors to Kenya are always struck by the anarchy that prevails on the roads.

Until people became acquainted with me around Kitui, I was called either '*mzungu*'; or 'Father British'—because the very few white men they meet are priests, and 'British' is the Akamba tribe's generic word for any white person. I heard of one old Irish missionary in Kitui who became so incensed at a small child shouting 'British' to him, that he scrambled out of his rusty jeep, lofted the child up in the air and threatened him,

'Don't you ever call me British again!'

CHAPTER 2 A DAY AT THE OFFICE (LIKE NO OTHER...)

Sure, the child had not a clue (though one day, he too might become aware of post-colonial sensitivities). I was soon being called 'Bwana Kyalo,' an Akamba name meaning 'born after a journey.' If not one of these, then it was 'Mr. Brendan'; or 'Gentleman' (I have never had the privilege of being addressed that way before, or indeed since); or that great title of respect in Kenya, 'Mzee Brendan'—though I suspect an odd time it was conferred in jest!

In those early days in Kitui District, it took me a bit of time to get used to the toilet arrangements. It was a short while before I was able to master the art of correctly aiming while squatting over a small hole in the ground. Sometimes I just did it outside in the bush like everybody else. Such arrangements were not unknown in rural Ireland in the past. It reminded me of Patrick Kavanagh's *The Great Hunger* where he muses: *'And his happiest dream/Was to clean his arse/With perennial grass/On the bank of some summer stream.'*

In the absence of perennial grass in these parts, you can get caught out badly—as I did one day in early October, looking for a suitable harmless leaf to clean myself with after a call of nature. It turned out to be as harmless as a nettle! Every animal and plant in Kitui seemed to be either benign or deadly, with no in-between. Nancy, one time, told me rather quaintly,

'You cannot die from a scorpion sting in Kitui, but you can die from the suffering of the pain it causes.'

Toilet roll is a Western invention that has not yet reached rural Kenya, by and large. It was yet another basic commodity to be acquired after a four-hour bicycle ride from Nyumbani. Cleaning and personal hygiene became a trial all round. When we were lucky enough to have water stored in the house, a shower involved splashing cold water onto myself from a basin. The bike ride from Nyumbani was not undertaken lightly; apart from the effort required in cycling four hours under the African sun, I could not cycle uphill because there were no gears, and I could not cycle downhill because the brakes did not work that well. It made you sort out your priorities, even where hygiene was concerned.

In early October, the day a total eclipse of the sun occurred, when it became strangely darker and cooler for a time during the early afternoon in the middle of the desert, I chanced upon a half dozen naked Akamba washing each other in a small water hole in the dry, sandy, seasonal Tiva River, between Nyumbani and Kitui village. There appeared to be three naked generations of the one family, all enthusiastically waving to me as I cycled by. At the time, I did not even think there was anything strange about this. I was already becoming used to life there.

CHAPTER 3
TO MOMBASA WITH JESUS HITLER

IN MID-OCTOBER, LEO, Kimanze, and I endured a very eventful 600km marathon overnight bus journey southeast to Mombasa on the coast. We were to spend a few days there celebrating Leo's twenty-first birthday. Mombasa is Kenya's second city, the main port for East Africa, and was the first colonial capital during the 1890s. It had been fought over for centuries, chiefly between the Portuguese on their way to Goa in India, and the Omani Arabs who controlled the ivory and human slave trades. The British wrested it from both. Mombasa is a cross between Bombay and Salthill. It is a bustling third-world city, but it is also the country's principal beach resort, attracting large numbers of European sun-seekers.

As much as I loved living so remotely at Nyumbani, I was already impatient to see more of Kenya. At times, I was beginning to find Nyumbani rather claustrophobic, working and living with the same people in a confined area every hour of every day. I had been working hard since I arrived, and was looking forward to going a bit wild. I even dared to hope for a few creature comforts, such as relaxing under a long pleasurable warm shower, and the opportunity to ring home. Yes, I needed this long weekend break.

NO HURRY IN AFRICA

We managed to hit Mombasa right in the middle of Ramadan, the Islamic month of penitential fasting. Hunger and the energy-sapping humidity may have slowed the rest of the population in that overwhelmingly Muslim city, but not Leo's African Rasta friends. Leo had previously lived in Mombasa for over a month when he first arrived in Kenya looking for volunteer work, and had become friendly with some of the many black Rastas there.

We rented out a simple but comfortable chalet near the beach. Kimanze had to answer a call of nature as soon as we arrived. He rushed into the bathroom, saw the Western-style toilet in it, and rushed back out.

'How does this work?' he asked urgently.

Western plumbing was as alien to him as the African 'arrangements' had been to Leo and myself.

Joined by about eight of Leo's friends, we stayed indoors for the afternoon and evening, the roof-fan turning lazily overhead. The Rastas were soon getting high on marijuana all around us. These cosmopolitans were so different to the people of Kitui, that Kimanze felt as much in a different country as I did. It was the British, I suppose, who had brought such diverse peoples together under the common name of Kenyan.

Leo put in an order to one of the Rastas, when the substance was running low.

'Here, can you get me a few hundred shillings worth, whatever you can buy with that,' he requested, as he palmed him the notes (about three euros' worth).

Our eyes popped when, a half hour later, the Rasta returned with a bag full of the stuff for Leo, who nearly had an orgasm looking at it.

Later, we partied well through the night at a giant outdoor session near the beach, where they played reggae versions of songs that were never meant to have the reggae treatment—'Stuck on you' and songs like that, the music surfing on a light breeze from the Indian Ocean. There were no tourists, just plenty of African Rastas. Leo, Kimanze, and I were up on a dance floor that was encircled by lights and speakers strung between the palm trees. Leo's birthday was becoming one terrific and unforgettable night.

A few hangers-on kept trying to sell me useless Rasta trinkets. It is against their principles to be employed in a normal waged job; they must earn money solely by being self-employed. They clearly had no problem, though, with not being teetotal like a true Rastafarian. One of them, whom Leo had indicated was not an acquaintance, tried to steal a few coins from my pocket. I seized his hand, the others threatened him and he scarpered. By now, we were wilting with exhaustion.

After a breezy tuk-tuk ride back to the chalet at around 5am, and just as we were dropping off to sleep, the silence was ripped apart by loud wailing emanating from the minaret of the large nearby mosque.

'*Allah Akbar* . . . God is great . . . prayer is better than sleep . . .'

Maybe not, though, at 5am after a night out with the Rastas!

That morning was to be Kimanze's first ever sight of the sea in the full splendour of daylight. To relieve our headaches, the three of us had opted for a wash and a swim in the Indian Ocean, in a beautiful bay fringed by coconut trees. If ever I witnessed a person being in awe of anything, it was Kimanze at the waters' edge. For ages, he simply stood there in silence, staring out to sea. I could only try to imagine what was going through the head of that Akamba lad from the arid lands of the Kenyan interior.

It is one of my quirks when travelling that I have to go for a swim in any lake, river, or sea. The Indian Ocean was a new one on the list for me. I floated lazily on my back, rising and dipping in tandem with the warm gentle waves, thoroughly enjoying myself. The Indian Ocean felt almost unnaturally hot there. I could see the attraction for the European tourists. Gangs of local children happily floating around me were using empty plastic water bottles to keep themselves afloat.

I went to look at a few elephant carvings being sold, laid out on the sand, further down the beach, possible souvenirs to take back to Nancy, Sr. MM, and a few others in Kitui. By coincidence, the woodcarver was a young Akamba man from Kitui, and there was a lady with him selling rope. Akamba actually means 'rope' in Swahili, from the days when the Akamba traded rope at the coast, and the Arabs would ask for 'the rope people.' It is still a common sight to see women in Kitui stripping sisal plants in the hedges and plaiting them into ropes.

Suddenly, the respectable looking proprietor grasped my head and whispered urgently in my ear:

'Would you like the services of my sister?'

'No thanks, I'm alright at the moment, the carvings will do fine.'

'Are you sure, she really beautiful!'

He grinned, whistled, and made a perfect sign with his finger and thumb.

CHAPTER 3 TO MOMBASA WITH JESUS HITLER

'She promise you good time, and good price.'

This sort of thing happened to me a few times in really unlikely places as I was minding my own business. It was always 'my sister, she is for sale,' followed by a wide-eyed look of genuine surprise that I was not interested.

The touts, known as 'beach boys,' can be a real pest on some of Mombasa's beaches. So can the stunningly beautiful 'Mombasa girls.' It is not uncommon to see an old white man—or woman—hand in hand with a twenty-something African. It is rather disconcerting, but some might say it is a win-win situation; the African gets an up-market lifestyle, at least temporarily, and the *mzungu* gets . . . company. I could see the temptation. These women are charming, beguiling, arousing, and can be bought with a beer.

You do not have to be rich to be propositioned. The night of Leo's birthday was typical. While we were chatting with the Rastas and Kimanze at a bar, two young ladies came up, sat down beside us uninvited, and began caressing and fondling both Leo and me. There was some suggestion of 'marriage.' The Rastas were laughing at our attempts to repel them, and puzzled as to why we were not responding in kind. If we had succumbed to temptation, the Mombasa girls would most likely have departed with our wallets, and probably have left us with AIDS in exchange.

During the birthday weekend, there was a revealing and probably typical incident that reflected badly on the Europeans. A scruffy Italian in his thirties, whom Leo knew from his time in Mombasa, arrived for the birthday celebrations. A striking Kenyan woman accompanied him. During the evening, a roaring row started between them.

'You give me my money, you think you have your way with me,' she said. 'You won't get away from me, I want my money, you pay me now, you pay me my 10,000 shillings, give to me now.'

Kimanze leaned over and quietly asked, 'Is she a prostitute?'

'Think so.'

The couple left together, but the Italian rejoined us a while later.

'There are two things I hate paying for.' he proclaimed. 'One is water, and the other is women. I'm only paying for one of those today.'

'Is that carry-on not a bit dangerous?' Leo warned him, 'you might contract something nasty.'

'Don't worry,' he assured us, 'I took precautions.'

'Well, at least that's something,' Leo sighed.

'I took precautions alright—I didn't leave her my name and number!'

Mombasa was the first place in Africa in which I received marriage proposals. (I would later receive more serious ones from women in Kitui.) The 'Mombasa girls' would have married me straight away if I had answered yes. They mistakenly assumed I was loaded, like the rich tourists.

Just as we approached the bus depot to return to Kitui, Leo pointed approvingly to the road,

'This is the very first pedestrian crossing I have seen in Kenya,' he announced.

Such orderliness appealed to the Teutonic half of his personality. Assuming he had the right of way, he stepped out and was almost killed by a bus. A policeman who had witnessed the incident came over.

'They will only stop at zebra crossings if they see zebras crossing!' he joked.

Very droll, I thought to myself. If Leo and I were Akamba, we would have blamed it all on a curse having been placed upon him, instead of pure carelessness on his part. Luckily, he was more 'shook' than physically injured.

A few days after we had returned to Kitui on the overnight bus, we were rather astounded when Kimanze's best friend, Mwangangi, quite casually informed us that he had married his neighbour at the weekend while we were away. Mwangangi, a twenty-two year old mechanic at Nyumbani, was abnormally laid-back, even for an Akamba, and looked rather like a black version of Inspector Clouseau. He told Kimanze and me—and everyone else at Nyumbani—about his marriage only a couple of days after the event, which was the norm apparently. He was present for work on Monday morning as usual, not an iota of difference to his routine did it seem to make. We had not even known he was seeing his wife beforehand, or was even interested in her at all.

An Akamba marriage becomes official when the father of the bride drives home the cattle that constitute the bride price. The minimum Akamba bride price involves giving the parents of the bride a goat, honey, sugar, and flour. Everything above that is negotiable. An educated girl may, for example, fetch a bride price of a concrete water tank. An Akamba bride price, I was told, can be as much as twenty-eight cattle, forty-five goats and twelve types of homemade alcohol. A working daughter, after all, is a valuable asset and the bride price is a kind of compensation for the family's loss. Inevitably, marriage often has more to do with economics than with romance. I used to think I could have bought myself a wife or three with the bride price I would be able to pay out there.

Often in Akambaland, if the rains fail, money earmarked in families for school fees has to go on food. If a choice needs to be made between which children can stay in school, it will always be in favour of the son, and the daughter must drop out. Once the daughter leaves in these circumstances, she is pushed into marriage so that the parents can obtain a bride price for her. She often has no choice in her husband, who may be years older than her.

'Bush weddings' among teenagers are common, where they elope together, but rarely live happily ever after. The husband usually runs away again after a couple of years of marriage. Nearly everyone in Akambaland is married by twenty years of age. If an Akamba man is not married by then, there is something wrong either up above or down below.

Speaking of sex! On one occasion, Nzoki asked me,

'What time is it, Brendan?'

'Half six,' I answered.

She stared at me for a moment, 'Did you just say it's time to "have sex"?'

I was eighteen years old before I realised I had an accent. When I went to college in Dublin, nobody seemed to understand a word I spoke in my dulcet Donegal brogue. And yet, for some odd reason, non-native English speakers around the world seem to grasp my meaning better than native English speakers. In Kenya, most people who had any English could understand the rhythms and idioms of east Donegal.

Many Kenyans can speak four or five languages or even more—the two tribal languages of their parents, the language of the neighbouring tribe, as well as Swahili and English. Swahili is used as a common language between the tribes in East Africa, with English used as a *lingua franca* among the more educated people, especially in Nairobi. Many Kenyans I met, who had only attended primary school, could speak several languages. Multilingualism is a fact of life for them. They would put in the shade those of us who struggle to learn a second language.

However, in the remote area where I was living, a lot of people spoke only the Akamba tribal language (called Kikamba), with perhaps a few words and phrases in Swahili. The Akamba have a bit of a hang-up about speaking Swahili, going back to the days when the coastal Swahili people traded the Akamba as slaves to the Arabs. A minority of rural Kenyans can speak limited English, but hardly anyone living in the area around Nyumbani had mastered the language of the old colonial power. Most of the people with whom I became friendly were the ones able to converse in English, like Nancy, Nzoki, Kimanze, and Mwangangi among others.

Swahili is an easier language to speak than Kikamba, partly because of the range of learning materials in it. As it is understood throughout East Africa, I devoted myself to learning Swahili instead of the Akamba tribal language. As languages go, Swahili is fairly easy to learn, and I picked up quite a bit early on. Sometimes, others would tell me Kikamba or Kikuyu tribal words, and then they would laugh when I garbled three languages in one sentence by accident. The problem was that it somehow all turned into 'African' in my head.

After a month or two, I was conversing in simple functional situations entirely through Swahili. Often, when conversing with Kenyans, if my Swahili or theirs was not up to it, there would be someone else on hand who could translate between English and the tribal languages, or between English and Swahili. Sometimes though, I simply had to shrug my shoulders in bewilderment. At other times, the lines would be crossed quite literally. I recall an occasion when I was using an old 'wind-up' telephone. The operator kept me talking for ten minutes enquiring about my life history and, by the time I got through, the line was hopelessly crossed, making communication impossible in any language.

Time and technology move on, and mobile phones began to appear in the hands of Kenyans after I arrived. Nobody ever had any phone-credit in them, so they 'flashed' whomever they wanted to ring. When I first heard the term, I pictured a woman standing on a hill, lifting up her skirt and catching the eye of the friend she wanted to contact. In fact, 'flashing' means they wait until your phone beeps and then hang up—time after time, incessantly and rather pointlessly. Even without the aid of any phone-credit, though, every tiny bit of gossip races up and down and back again among the Akamba faster than a Nairobi taxi crashing a red light. They love to gossip; it is part of their amiable nature.

In Akambaland, I had discovered probably the only race of people outside Donegal and Derry who say 'yes' for 'hello.' It made me feel at home! They also said 'good morning' at any time of day at all—even as I was retiring to bed for the night. There were other examples of linguistic confusion. They would say strange things like 'I am coming' as they walked away from me, and used peculiar and perplexing English phrases such as 'I met you absent'—which means that you were not there when he or she called, and 'I walked the wrong number tomorrow.' Your guess is as good as mine as to the meaning of that one.

An Akamba wrote a letter to the *Daily Nation* newspaper (Kenya's *Irish Independent*) in October complaining that it was a conspiracy against their tribe that the English alphabet has a letter 'h' when the Akamba are incapable of pronouncing it correctly. Insecurity with the 'h' sound means they often say 'he' for 'she,' and 'she' for 'he.' Like the Japanese, they pronounce 'r' as 'l' and' l' as 'r'; also 'f' as 'p' and 'p' as 'f.' Because of this, I once heard Sr. MM's school caretaker shout to the students, 'No taking flutes at the liver.' After a moment of wondering what on earth he was on about, I deduced he must have been referring to 'fruits at the river.'

Whenever I met a Kenyan for the first time, the conversation typically went as it did with Mwangangi's portly uncle in The Paradise Hotel (that well-known misnomer!) in Kwa Vonza.

'Where are you from?' he inquired.

'Ireland.'

'Oh, what part of the U.S. is that?'

'The Europe part,' I informed him.

'Oh, you're beside Australia then!'

'Yes, of course I am.'

How long would it take me to explain that 'Whiteland' is not all the one big place? I just said 'England' from then on; at least they had heard of that, to which a cousin of Mwangangi's responded on the same occasion,

'So you are the same country as Canada'

These are the same people who speak, perhaps, four languages. Their geographical knowledge usually falls far short of their linguistic ability.

Keeping in contact with home was also difficult. It was an arduous four-hour cycle under the punishing sun to a landline phone. There was no coverage for my mobile around Nyumbani and no way to re-charge the phone because there was no electricity. Using the internet normally involved going to Nairobi for the weekend, and that was at least three or four good hours away in a vehicle. Getting to Nairobi normally started by jumping on the back (or hanging off the end) of an open-topped lorry, bouncing and swaying over the rutted dirt tracks for mile after juddering mile. There might be as many as forty Akamba packed onto the lorry. I found it thrilling. The alternative could involve sitting with the dangerously stacked luggage on the roof rack of an over-flowing, speeding clapped-out bus.

However, despite all the difficulties of transportation and communications, there were occasionally pleasant surprises. One evening in Nyumbani, as the orange sun descended over the scorched red Kitui desert, I managed to pick up Mícheál Ó Muircheartaigh on the BBC World Service radio, commentating on Tyrone winning the All-Ireland. Despite the static, I was able to follow the action. Croke Park seemed very far away though.

CHAPTER 4
THE BANANA REFERENDUM

IN THE MONTH OF OCTOBER, I gained an insight into the sometimes bizarre world of Kenyan politics. The talk of everyone that month, whether they were knowledgeable or not, was about the big referendum due in November on the proposed changes to the constitution. The main points of contention centred upon land reform issues and the powers invested in the President. President Kibaki (who was elected in 2002) and the smaller parties of his coalition were urging a Yes vote, while the largest coalition partner had left to join the main KANU opposition party in opposing the proposed constitution.

The symbol for 'Yes' was a banana; the symbol for 'No' was an orange. They had to have pictures of both on the ballot paper because so many are illiterate, even though some people of the remoter tribes in the northern deserts, like the Turkana tribe for instance, may have never seen either fruit before.

Kitui was 'No' country. The Akamba, just like many other tribes, feared that the Kikuyu tribe of President Kibaki was trying to take over the country to benefit themselves at the expense of the others. Bananas were being sold on the streets of Kitui village but nobody was buying. You could not for the life of you be seen eating a banana. I was innocently chomping on one in Kitui village shortly after coming back from Mombasa when a random Akamba passing by challenged me,

'Why are you supporting the Kikuyus?'

It would be prudent, I decided, to eat local fruits from then on. Of an evening, crowds of ragged men would cram into a bar in Kitui village to watch the news on a small fuzzy TV. They bought nothing, then exited the bar en-masse once the news finished. There was a certain tension in the air.

Because newspapers are only sold in villages that are perhaps sixty kilometres apart, and since most Kenyans outside Nairobi do not have a television in their own home, campaigning for the referendum was done at monster rallies all over the country. I ventured close enough to observe an Orange rally in Kitui village. On stage were colourful politicians dancing and enrapturing cheering crowds, working those assembled into a frenzy of jumping, singing, and waving leafy branches. It resembled a really colourful and noisy carnival. But there was a counter attraction in town. The local MP, the aptly named Charity Ngilu, who was Kenya's health minister and was supporting the proposed constitution, organised famine relief food to be distributed at the same time as the rally. So, near where the Orange carnival was in full swing, hundreds upon hundreds were queuing up at the home of nearby chiefs to collect their food, courtesy of the Banana faction.

During the era of President Moi, from 1978 until 2002 (for most of it as a corrupt dictator in a one-party state), Akambas sometimes had their individual voting cards exchanged for famine relief. Famine relief food was also being sold openly in some shops in Kitui village during the height of the famine in late

CHAPTER 4 THE BANANA REFERENDUM

2005. Some government official had evidently been bought. Notoriously, such corruption is endemic in Africa—at all levels.

Over a drink one evening at Sr. MM's home, I argued the merits of the proposed constitution with the veteran Akamba MP who had organised the Orange rally. Sr. MM knew him well. I decided to agree with him for two reasons; I did not really know the background history to some of the issues; and I remembered I was technically in the country illegally. I was on a tourist visa and should not have been near Nyumbani or Kitui.

At one monster Banana rally in the weeks leading up to the referendum, near Lake Victoria in western Kenya, four school-children were shot dead by Orange supporters. This incident shook the people of Kenya to the core. The country was pregnant with violence. I had travelled the whole way from Ulster, only to find it was 'Orangemen' involved in trouble in Kenya as well. The hanging shadow of tribal war weighed upon the population like a Damocles' sword about to fall. One incident, even an accident, could tip the country over the brink. We held our breath and mostly stayed indoors.

A bank holiday was declared for the day of the vote. Many people in Kitui took the opportunity to be drunk on moonshine by midday. The result of the referendum was duly declared; the proposed new constitution was heavily defeated. Everyone was anxiously awaiting the reaction of President Kibaki. He addressed the country on television in Swahili that evening. Sr. MM, another Irish missionary and I all listened attentively to him for thirty minutes in Sr. MM's home.

Eventually she piped up in her melodic tones,

'Sure, you would think we all understood what he was

saying!'

President Kibaki accepted the result against him, and everyone had a party. The legacy of the referendum, though, was a polarised country and a weak government that heretofore had been reforming and popular. The extent of tribal polarisation was apparent in the voting patterns; one Kikuyu constituency had a result of 30,417 Yes to 78 No, whereas a constituency in Luo tribal land near Lake Victoria recorded a vote of 163 Yes to 17,866 No.

Around this time, I remember writing a long email home, in which I described the tense build-up to the referendum. I felt it appropriate to finish it off with a verse of Sean McBride's well-known song:

Now the time has come that I must go, I bid you all adieu,
The open highway calls me back to do these things I do,
But when I'm travelling far away, your friendship I'll recall,
And, please God, some day I'll return unto the homes
of Donegal.

Before I departed for Kenya, my friends in Letterkenny had been joking that I would either be eaten by a lion, speared by a Maasai, die of hunger, be shot by guerrillas, or succumb to some tropical disease. I dismissed it all as nonsense born of stereotypes. They were nearly right, even more so if they had mentioned road accidents. Kenya was indeed more dangerous than I had envisaged. They were also well aware how my cavalier attitude tended to attract trouble's attention everywhere I had ventured in the world up to then.

The 'open highway' of McBride's song represented one of the greatest threats to a long life in Kenya. A typical journey on a Kenyan main road between cities is heart-stopping. It could involve three vehicles abreast; two overcrowded buses passing on either side of a lorry (on this occasion with me standing on the back), and two other buses coming towards us at breakneck speed. Add in a giant crater or two, a few people walking on the road and some donkeys in the middle of it all, with the bus driver lighting himself another cigarette from the one he is already smoking. The buses were all brightly painted with slogans like 'In God We Trust'—and I would be thinking to myself, whatever about God, I would not be putting much trust in the driver anyway.

In the second half of October in Kitui, I had the experience of being in a thirty year old Lada taxi, with nine other people somehow squeezed inside, driving up a deeply rutted dirt track towards Sr. MM's. Suddenly the door was flung open, leaving me hanging out for about thirty seconds—it seemed like an eternity—before the driver even noticed.

Sr. MM was not there, but a blond thirty-year-old man with an almost incomprehensible Cork accent and a pronounced limp opened the door to me.

'Howya, Kevin's the name.'

Introductions over, we nicked a few bottles of Tusker beer from Sr. MM's storeroom, and sat chatting for hours on the wicker chairs under the welcome shade of the verandah. Kevin told me he had been a social worker for the past two years in the slums of Nairobi.

'Sr. MM is like my Kenyan mother,' he explained. 'I come to Sr. MM's to get away from the hubbub of the city.'

'I come to Sr. MM's precisely to get a bit of hubbub,' I replied.

NO HURRY IN AFRICA

I was delighted to have met another young Irish person, and the conversation quickly switched to the Premiership, of which I had heard nothing at all. When I asked him what the slums were like, he regaled me with a flurry of stories in the singsong cadences of Cork. He was a volunteer through the V.M.M. organisation in Ireland, and he spoke a lot of sense about what volunteers like us could realistically achieve. The next day, he invited me to stay with him and see the slums for myself. With my curiosity whetted by his stories, I readily accepted his invitation.

The following weekend, the last weekend of October, was my first weekend in the capital, Nairobi,—or 'Nai-rob-you' as it is disparagingly known. It is home to nearly three million people and counting, the largest city between Cairo and Cape Town. It is officially the most dangerous city in Africa, and with good reason. On our arrival just after dark, as Kevin and I were opening the door of the taxi outside his building, we witnessed a carjacking at gunpoint about a hundred feet further down the road. The car sped off, its tyres screeching.

More recently, things are improving on that front, but you still need your wits about you. I met one Dutch volunteer in the city centre that weekend who had been slashed in the back with a sword by a random African in broad daylight.

'A mob nearly stoned my attacker to death before the police escorted him away,' he told me.

Early the following morning, I was introduced to a friend of Kevin's named Kyalo, an articulate, well-dressed twenty-five year old Akamba who grew up in Kibera slum but had gone to university and educated himself out of it. He took me on a guided tour on foot through the slum.

CHAPTER 4 THE BANANA REFERENDUM

'Kibera is the biggest proper slum in Africa,' he explained, 'with over one million people crammed into about one square mile. It was Nairobi's original slum, beginning around forty years ago. Soweto in Johannesburg was bigger, but it has large tracts of middle class communities nowadays.'

As Kyalo was busy introducing me to some of his childhood friends in Kibera, a black man wearing a 1992 Donegal football jersey from our only All-Ireland winning year ambled by, singing loudly. Africa is full of surprises!

All his friends were eager to meet me, and joking away with Kyalo in Kikamba. What really struck me was how welcoming the people of Kibera were. I felt safer there than I had done in parts of some American cities. Despite the dreadful poverty and dire living conditions all around, I found aspiration, ambition, and energy in these friendly people. Nevertheless, I was always mindful of the opportunists lurking around the place.

I was invited into several homes in Kibera. They had been neighbours of Kyalo, and were clearly elated to see him once again. One hut was only the size of a modest Western bathroom; it was dark, contained no furniture at all, and was home to *nine* people who slept on the uneven surface that was the floor. Another home to which Kyalo brought me seemed fairly well off by the standards of the slum—it was the same size as the others, but had a couch and a tiny television set run off a car battery.

'This is not entirely uncommon,' Kyalo explained. 'People sometimes choose to continue living in the slums even after they can afford to move out. There is a community here. They might even buy up other rooms in Kibera and become landlords.'

It was a pity that I was not fluent enough in Swahili (and that most of the people in Kibera could not speak English), because I was very keen to talk with them.

'You should become a professional tour guide,'
I praised Kyalo.

He was a class act.

'Ah Brendan, you could never bring a tour group into Kibera. Well, you could—but you wouldn't get back out, *bwana*,' he countered, smiling, and continued to enlighten me. 'The huts consist of walls made from mud and sometimes cow dung over a framework of sticks, with rusty corrugated iron roofs over that. Some homes here are over forty years old. It has really become a permanent slum with a permanent community.'

The foul lingering smells were sometimes overpowering as we strolled together. Children were playing in heaps of rubbish and beside open sewers full of a horrible grey toxic soup. There was delight in their faces all the same. After a good while hopping over sewers and meandering through the one-foot wide alleys in this vast impenetrable warren, we reached the only small piece of open land in the whole of the slum.

'Moscow has Red Square, New York has Times Square, and Kibera has this,' laughed Kyalo, waving his arm over the scene. 'This is the cockpit, the epicentre, the place where everything happens for a million people—football games, political rallies, religious services, celebrations, everything. If anyone attempted to build on that dusty land, they would be burned alive.'

I sensed he was not entirely joking.

Kyalo was anxious to show me another part of the slum. As we walked along, he kept pointing out the various sectors with their invisible but sacrosanct boundaries.

CHAPTER 4 THE BANANA REFERENDUM

'Each section of Kibera is dominated by a particular tribe—
for example, the Nubian tribe from Sudan, who were left over in
Kenya from when the British used them as soldiers before Independence in 1963. A lot of them didn't, or were unable, to make
their way back.'

After a bit, we arrived at a colourfully painted building made
of concrete blocks.

'I do my volunteer work here, Brendan. It is very worthwhile.
Children come here who have lost both parents and are fed by us,
and we educate teenagers on the dangers of AIDS.'

I liked that about Kyalo, and the people of Kibera. They
seemed to help each other. Maybe I just had not yet witnessed
the sinister underbelly where crime was a way of life.

The next day I ventured into Mukuru, Nairobi's slum of
slums, with two local youths from Kevin's centre as bodyguards.
Neither spoke English, so communication was though Swahili
and some hand signals. Mukuru is a much more recent slum
than Kibera, and a good deal smaller. It is a crammed labyrinth
of tiny never-ending passageways between simple corrugated iron
shacks, requiring the inhabitants to jump over open sewers and
dodge out of the way of the happy children who seem oblivious
to their squalid surroundings.

Altogether, Mukuru is a very interesting place. At one point, I
saw a man running past in the nip. I found this rather odd. Then
another followed him with no clothes on either, and yet again another, a couple of minutes later. A few bystanders were laughing
as all this happened. It turned out to be the lighter side to Nairobi crime. Evidently, they had turned a corner and were mugged
of everything including all their clothes. With all this serial strip-

ping going on, I was grateful I had my two bodyguards to make me feel a bit more secure. A definite hint of menace clung around Mukuru, though—more so than in Kibera.

Many Kenyans are overly friendly—the rural ones are usually genuine and try to give you stuff you do not even want; whereas the Nairobi people may be setting you up to be mugged. A generalisation, I know, but that was my experience. My favourite conman was a youthful one I encountered that weekend. His head was strangely rectangular; he had hunched shoulders, and he just exuded an aura of shiftiness at fifty paces. He operated on Nairobi's Kenyatta Avenue, the city's main street (named after the country's first president). He sauntered past me furtively, and about three minutes later was briskly trying to keep up beside me, walking in the same direction. As if it was the most casual remark in the world, he asked me,

'Gentleman, where are you from?'

As he cantered beside me, I just kept looking ahead and striding forward. But after he had asked me a few more times, I answered,

'*Ninatoka Kitui. Unaenda wapi bwana?*' (I'm from Kitui, now where are you off to, sir?).

This momentarily stumped him. He pointed up the street, and I could sense the permutations of possibility running around his mind. Finally, he piped up,

'But where are you from before Kitui?'

Continuing at a good pace, and knowing that I could usually handle these people on my travels, I told him,

'Ireland.'

I imagined that, like the Akamba, he probably would not have a notion where it was. But he became animated.

'Oh, really, I will be studying medicine at Trinity College in Dublin next year.'

Now it was my turn to be stumped. I asked him a few questions about Trinity, about Dublin, and about medicine courses, all the time looking ahead of me and trying to lose him as I ploughed straight through road crossings. Fair play to him though, he had his homework done and answered every one of them correctly. Then he became fed up with my interest in his supposed studies and he landed the punch line.

'But I am a refugee from Sudan and I need money to go to Tanzania before I can go to Ireland.'

'Sorry, but I have only fifty shillings left on me,' I replied.

This was the truth, and I opened out my pockets to show him, while still galloping onwards to the top of the street.

He seemed to be again momentarily confused, but quickly reverted to what he must say to everyone else when they ignore him or refuse his request. It was an interesting change of tack.

'But you don't like to talk to Africans, you don't like to give to needy Africans, you are a racist perhaps?'

'I give to the people in Kitui. They need it more than you. I cannot give to everyone.'

'And what about me? You are in my country, Kenya.'

'Are you not a refugee from Sudan, sir?'

The two of us grinned widely at this skit into which our encounter had developed.

'Just some shillings?' he pleaded, as he held out his hand in front of me to try and slow my pace.

'*Hapana, kwa heri bwana*,' I countered.

NO HURRY IN AFRICA

Hapana is a great Swahili word that means 'no, and that's the very last word on the matter,' while *kwa heri* when used in a certain tone is a firm but very polite way of saying 'get lost and good riddance.'

Nearly every weekend that I was in Nairobi after that, I met him again on the main street. I would now be from France or Israel or some such place and he would be studying veterinary in Toulouse or reading theology in Jerusalem. Each time he needed a couple of shillings to go to Tanzania before he could fly to his university. This happened about eleven or twelve times in total, and he never seemed to remember me once.

Much later, Sr. MM told me that a male Irish friend of hers, who was over visiting, was arrested by 'police' for talking to 'a known criminal.'

'He was taken to a back room of some dingy building. The police were demanding thousands of euros for bail money. He was completely traumatised by the event, poor man. Of course, the "police" and "the known criminal" were all in it together. It was a set-up to scam money from a white person,' she concluded.

Sr. MM began to describe the 'known criminal' towards the end of her tale—and he sounded uncannily like my friend, the Sudanese refugee!

'Most Nairobi villains take a simple approach,' said Kevin, after I told him my tale. 'They threaten to throw their excrement in your face if you decide not to comply with the request to empty your pockets. It happened to me once, in fact, when I was in the back seat of a car stopped at a junction in broad daylight. For some reason, most people faced with this option pay up! To stay relatively safe in Nairobi,' he continued, 'you just have to stay close to crowds of people most of the time. Mob justice means the thief will be stoned or burned alive if he tries to mug you in a busy place. Otherwise, thieves go to crammed prisons that are like battery hen-houses—indefinitely—for stealing as little as the equivalent of three euros.'

As a rule in Nairobi, it is inadvisable to engage in conversation when queuing or waiting with others, lest the conmen get useful information from you on your movements. It is best to walk around with just a few hundred shillings and no phone or wristwatch—or even spectacles, which oddly seems to be a favourite of Nairobi's thieves as well. Kiragu once recounted to me how, one time, he was flagging down a bus when a man just grabbed the glasses off his head and ran away. He knew lots of other people in Nairobi to whom this happened as well.

'You can't run after them when you can't even see them,' he chuckled.

I got the runs that weekend. By now, I was totally unused to the 'richness' of the normal food that I was eating with Kevin in Nairobi, after dining on the rather limited menu around Kitui. I took the opportunity to stock up on a few provisions that were not readily available near Nyumbani, such as toilet roll, a big bottle of drinking water, fruit, 'nice & good shampoo,' the *Daily Nation,* and, very importantly, batteries for my torch.

When I returned to Nyumbani after the bright lights of Nairobi that weekend, I began noticing how life revolves around light and darkness in Akamba society. Even the light of a full moon changes habits. For example, people may work at their crop or fetch water under a full moon. Moonlight—and there's a lot more of it in Africa—extends the Akamba day in the same way as electricity does in Ireland. Many of their tribal ceremonies are guided by the phases of the moon.

Even slight changes in the weather become more noticeable around the phases of the moon. However, when there is no moon (or a 'black moon' as some of them refer to it), active life abruptly ceases. There are no lamp-posts to keep the day alive. People tend to rise at dawn and go to sleep once the sun drops, their lives determined by the rhythms of the sun and the moon.

Many of our nights in Nyumbani were spent sitting on rocks around a campfire, just having the craic. There was nothing else to do; we were so remote. Leo, Kimanze, Kiragu, the others in the house, and I would spend hours under the star-filled sky simply chatting, occasionally singing, and indulging in some light-hearted banter in the warm air. The campfire was simply to keep any wildlife at a distance. The night after I returned from Nairobi, I bumped straight into Kimanze by accident outside in the dark. He was standing in a basin—in the middle of washing himself. I was forever bumping into black people at night, walking straight into them because there were no lights about. Quite literally, I could not see them in the dark unless they were smiling! It was a serious problem in a place where there is so little artificial light after the sun sets.

On Halloween night, at my suggestion, we had a bonfire that probably could have been seen half way to Sudan, possibly the only Halloween bonfire in Africa. It was massive, from all the vegetation that had been cleared for the farm and buildings. The wood was so dry it burned out fairly quickly, though. They do things differently in Bavaria, so I briefed Leo on the reasons behind the pagan Halloween bonfire. The irony was not lost to him. Here was I, who spent so much of my time visiting the Christian missionaries, creating a pagan fire supposedly to ward off the evil spirits let loose on that night, deep in the dark heart of Africa.

The watchmen duly arrived with their bows and arrows after the fire burned out. They thought our house had burnt down; we had forgotten to tell them about the bonfire. For all the use they would have been if the house really did burn down! Were they about to dowse the flames with their bows and arrows?

One of the joys of night-time at Nyumbani was watching the cosmic constellations, especially when there was no moon. With no light pollution, the stars actually twinkle, as in the nursery rhyme, and the Milky Way actually looks milky. Venus and Mars are clearly visible and the endless cascade of shooting stars is spectacular. The equator is perhaps the best place in the world to view the constellations, with billions of stars competing for space in the sky. Awe-struck, I used to stand on the highest point in the area, and for miles and miles around, I could see no artificial light from any car or home or streetlight, and hear no sound except the occasional shrill cries of birds. At times, it was the most complete silence imaginable.

Sometimes I would fall asleep up there. (Nyumbani later built a huge concrete water tank on the high spot that had been my observatory, and I would climb up on top of the tank and lie down.) On other occasions, I listened to the sounds of nearby drumming for hours and hours after dark. The rhythmic pounding was an accompaniment to the elders exorcising evil spirits from possessed people in their huts, in an Akamba ceremony that Mwangangi informed me was known as 'Kalumi.'

CHAPTER 5
SURVIVING THE FAMINE

THERE WAS A FAMINE IN KITUI district when I arrived in September. The situation was becoming more and more desperate, so that by early November it was even beginning to attract the attention of Western media. Officially—and somewhat euphemistically— termed a 'food shortage,' many people were going maybe three or four days between meals, and that probably consisted of cornflour. The problem, that many in the West do not realise, is that there is no such thing as social welfare in Kenya. It is left to the missionaries or aid agencies to provide help in times of crisis.

At the height of the famine during November and December, I was always amazed that people, who had no food to feed themselves or their children, would always make sure that I was fed, if I was visiting their home. This is a special trait among the Akamba; they are extremely generous and hospitable. I felt uneasy and slightly guilty eating their precious food, but knew they would be offended if I refused. They took great pride in hosting a white man. They would be the talk of the area for days and their children the talk of the school. I would always bring something simple like shiny stickers as a thank you. These were normally for their children, but the adults found great fascination with such mundane Western objects. It really was another world.

No Hurry in Africa

I found out that some people, whom I knew very well, could not even afford bread every day for their families. This included people like Nancy (who was still warning me about baboons); people who I thought were fairly well off for Akambas. I saw Nancy eating paper from a copybook that she said was for her 'iron,' and eating soil from a small mound created by ants on the corrugated iron for her 'calcium.' Nzoki told me this ant-soil is beneficial for a child in the womb. Nzoki still breastfed her child who was nearly three years old. I even witnessed a baby suckling his grandmother once. I would never know what it is really like to be living with such hunger, or the insecurity of finding the next meal. As a European in Kenya, I could always get to an ATM within a few days, or take the next available flight home.

People in Ireland sometimes ask did the famine affect me. It did not, insofar as I had the money to go to a shop and buy food, but it did, in that the nearest shop with any variety of supplies was four hours away, or necessitated a trip to Nairobi. I sometimes walked into a rural shop which was open (it was often only a ten foot square mud-hut), but had no stock save for Kenya's leading brand of biscuits 'Dotcom Biscuits,' and cigarettes sold singly for two shillings each (two cent). The people had no money to buy anything in the shops anyway because their subsistence farming lifestyle had failed without the rains.

For most of Kenya, the long rainy season lasts roughly from March until May, with a 'short' rainy season from late October until early December. In Kitui, for some reason, more rain normally falls during the November rainy season than the April rainy season. The temperature never falls below the high twenties Celsius at any time of year. By the time I arrived, every rainy

CHAPTER 5 SURVIVING THE FAMINE

season had largely failed since 1998. When the rains do come, as long as it is not part of a violent storm that washes away the soil, it generally makes life considerably easier for the people. The seasonal rivers flow and people can wash, fetch water, and bring their animals to drink.

Vegetation that is used to withstanding prolonged parched spells, amazingly quickly becomes green with leaves and flowers, allowing the animals to feed and fatten up. Right throughout the rainy season, people are up before dawn and work until sunset— ploughing, planting, weeding and, if they are lucky, harvesting. It is still dry and sunny during the afternoon, but the dirt roads, now muddy, become troublesome to navigate and it is harder to get around, with routes cut off by the newly flowing rivers.

Many days at Nyumbani, I ate a slice of bread in the morning and a bowl of rice on its own later in the day—and that was it. If the rice ran out, we ate nothing. I was not too bothered; we Westerners sometimes eat too much anyway. Sr. MM often gave me a pot of her homemade marmalade if I saw her at the weekend. This was like dessert to me; I ate it straight out of the pot. If I were in Kitui village at certain times of year when sugarcane was in season, I would buy freshly cut sugar-cane stalks and chew them.

'That'll make you go deaf and impotent,' warned Mwangangi.

Not the kind of warning to take lightly! I was not too concerned, though; it was really the only way to get something sweet. I remember reading in John Steinbeck's *Grapes of Wrath* how the 'Okies' from the 1930s dustbowls ate fried dough when times were really hard. Well, in Nyumbani, fried dough was our treat, known as *chapatti*.

NO HURRY IN AFRICA

Incredibly, I actually managed to put on weight during the height of the famine. This was despite hardly eating anything and despite cycling or walking everywhere. My friends at home jumped to the conclusion that it was really my eating which must have caused the famine! I eventually figured out that it was probably because the main staple, called *ugali* and which is made from corn flour, was pure carbohydrates. I had arrived fairly trim, and now, somewhat ironically, a potbelly was beginning to swell. I simply was not getting a balanced diet. *Ugali* is completely tasteless. It is like eating three-day-old porridge for lunch, supper, and snacking. I had managed to settle amongst one of the few peoples to have invented tasteless food.

Because of the famine and because we were so remote, we did not have any fruit or vegetables during the week; they were only available in Kitui village. That meant I had to cycle the forty kilometres from Nyumbani to Kitui, risking 'highway' bandits along the way. Eating native Kenyan fruits, I soon discovered, left me with either constipation or diarrhoea until I became used to them. Young people in Ireland have often heard their parents tell them how tastier the fruits used to be in their youth. I finally understood what they meant. The fruits are fresh off the tree that very day, have no chemicals or preservatives, cost two shillings each (about two cent), and are overflowing with juicy succulence and vitamins.

For a special treat, we might have had a bit of fat on bone, which was supposed to be goat meat. There tended to be no meat on the goats and hens since, because of the drought, they had nothing to eat or drink either, while beef or fish were unheard of.

I bought a few black hens to have eggs each day; black hens

especially, because I had never seen a hen that colour before in Ireland. Over time, I built up the brood until I would say I owned one of the largest hen broods in Kitui District. I had to stop my hens from their habit of laying their eggs under my bed and on top of my bed. One night I entered the bedroom in the dark (as there was no electricity), laid down my head on the pillow and found I had just squashed an egg into my ear and hair. The hens started laying indoors because their eggs kept being taken—anything from dogs to monkeys to rainbow-coloured lizards were blamed. Probably a few humans too, I suspect. They were welcome to them. I used to give away plenty of eggs to the Akambas—and occasionally some hens as well—as gifts.

If I wanted milk, I sometimes had to rise at dawn to milk the cows by hand, after being woken by Fog-Horn-Leg-Horn cock-a-doodling before the sun even rose. The cows produced hardly any milk anyway, because there was virtually no grass for them to feed on. I used to let someone else boil the milk, went back to bed, and drank what little there was at breakfast. Cooking was done outside over an open fire of sticks on a base of stones. The problem was that I could never start a fire. Luckily for me, we hired a striking twenty-three year old Kikuyu cook named Nyambura to do that for us. Like Kiragu, she was typical of the Kikuyu, assiduous and scrupulous, and always brightly and impeccably turned out. She spoke some English, and was really talkative.

On a number of occasions, our house went for a day or two without water, and being practically in the desert, Leo and I found it quite worrying. I usually stored one emergency bottle of water I never told anyone about. One time, to get a cup of drinking water involved Leo, Kimanze, and me loading jerry-cans onto the donkeys, herding them down to the dried-up river, (an alternative was a more inaccessible well), digging a hole in the riverbed, filling the cans with water, loading the heavy cans onto the donkeys, herding them two kilometres back up the dirt track, searching around for sticks for the fire, spending ages trying to ignite the fire, boiling the water (which was essential to destroy the germs), and waiting a long while for it to cool down . . . and hey presto, we had a cup of drinking water!

Eventually Kimanze, Mwangangi, Leo, and the others made good progress in trying to develop a water system to reach the focal points of Nyumbani. Construction of homesteads was also continuing at a good pace; community buildings were springing up where there had been 1,000 acres of wild bush only a few months before. Everyone was busy. Plans were afoot for further development in the next phase. About this time, I was preoccupied with proposals to find extra funding for the project. Kiragu was very encouraging. At the end of one of his lengthy monologues—we were still working close to midnight next to a tilly-lamp—he summed up the situation.

'We have all this money going out; now let's get some coming in.'

Our fame was beginning to spread. People were coming from as far away as southern Sudan to copy the novel block-making techniques we used, marvelling how the walls could be made without cement. The blocks were all manufactured on-site from materials sourced within Nyumbani. As a volunteer, I found it an exciting project to be working on; it felt like we were pushing the frontiers of ingenuity and improvisation. The whole concept of this village was an experiment in itself—one that, to our knowledge, had not been tried before.

There were many unanswered questions. We would be bringing orphans and their carers into a new environment in order to create a community for themselves with all the facilities already in place. What would happen to their existing possessions and homes? Would the people coming in get along together? How would they interact with the existing community around Nyumbani? How would we prevent the village from becoming an 'AIDS ghetto'? Would the existing community be allowed to have use of the facilities as well? What would happen to the children when they finished school, would there be still be a place for them here? Who exactly would own the produce of the farms, like new calves? How would the villagers govern themselves, and how much input would the existing Nyumbani management structures retain? Kiragu and the others were forever debating issues like these, making plans and revising them again and again. I also regularly contributed my views, my doubts and my ideas.

Nancy, Nzoki, and some other clerks were becoming adept at the computer by now. Nancy, in particular, was making very good progress. At the start, she was like a hen pecking the keyboard every ten seconds with her right-hand index finger. Now she could turn on the computer, type up something on Microsoft Excel or Word, and just have me polish it up for her. For Nzoki, I made a complicated spreadsheet that she was able to upkeep herself without my help, to show how much materials went into each batch of blocks, how many blocks were in each batch, where they were used, and how it all compared to averages. It would soon be time to begin teaching them the more complicated aspects of these software programmes.

I could see that modern technology could bring great benefits to these people who had so little of anything, including food. But I could not help wondering how they would adjust to our Western notions of progress. Would there be a price to be paid, in terms of them too hastily abandoning a way of life that had changed so little over centuries?

CHAPTER 6
THE MAGIC OF RAIN

DUST DEVILS—which are like mini tornadoes—kept sweeping through Nyumbani in the first half of November, often appearing suddenly out of thin air. Nzoki, Mutinda, Kimanze, pretty much everyone said it was a sign of rain coming. Then again, they always said everything was a sign of rain. Anything from a particular bird singing at a certain time of day, to the meandering trickle of a stream was a sign that rain was on its way. These dust devils, harbingers of rain or not, always stole my khaki hat.

In the end, the predictions of rain were proved right. Kitui's long rainy season belatedly got going in the middle of November. The whole place changed from dusty red to verdant green within a few days. I was amazed by this miraculous transformation. Wild seedlings suddenly punched through the crusty ground. Crops began to shoot and sprout. Leaves appeared all over plants that had seemed long dead. Families were busy ploughing their fields with oxen. My tentative weekend travel plans to other parts of Kenya were put on hold, because the rains made many of the dirt roads impassable at times. Some of these roads now had three-foot-deep gorges running down the middle of them. Each night there were apocalyptic lightning storms that illuminated the entire sky for hours on end, accompanied by monsoon force rains drumming menacingly on the tin roof of our house.

The rainy season in Kitui means there are heavy showers at night, with thirty degrees Celsius in the sunny daytime. I have never seen faces of people so happy to see a drop of rain when it finally did arrive; workers in Nyumbani started dancing elatedly outside under the monsoon showers, thrilled that finally it was raining.

But the rains always bring tragedy as well as joy in Kitui; they are simultaneously a blessing and a curse. Disease increases, Kitui village loses its electricity, and phone lines are down for weeks; roads are impassable whether you are driving, cycling or even walking. Several bridges in the district were washed away. Mwangangi and Kimanze told me of several incidents of locals perishing while attempting to ford the torrents that the dry rivers had developed into in that particular rainy season. It was later reported that over sixty people had drowned around Kitui. Some incidents were heartbreaking. Some children near Kwa Vonza drowned after wading out to rescue other children coming back from school.

'Many drownings are simply put down to witchcraft and curses,' Nancy informed me one day at our desk.

Then, after a week, the rainy season ended abruptly, stopping as early as it started late. It was followed by what I can only describe as a biblical plague of insects. Fortunately, all expired after about two days. Children would sit after dark on the roadsides with paraffin lamps catching 'sausage flies,' which they fried as a tasty protein-filled treat. However, with the early cessation of the rains, the long-term problem of drought and famine would remain a problem for the foreseeable future.

CHAPTER 6 THE MAGIC OF RAIN

Around Nyumbani, the rains had also brought a lot of sickness. When I greeted Mwangangi and enquired how he was, he replied in his own distinctive English idiom,

'I am very fine, and I am very sick with malaria'—all of this in the one sentence. He added, 'The mosquitoes were boozing (i.e. buzzing!) in my home last night.'

I pictured the mosquitoes having a few pints with him. The rains had brought the mosquitoes, of course, and with the mosquitoes came malaria. I was one of the very few to avoid malaria, because I was still taking tablets faithfully every day to prevent it—just as I had promised my mother!

'Malaria swells all your internal organs, it feels about four times as bad as flu, and leaves you bedridden for over a week at least,' was how Mutinda put it.

It fell within the realm of his medical expertise.

'It has to be treated early, and can be fatal if left untreated. The problem is, the initial symptoms are tiredness, a cough, and just about the exact same run of the mill symptoms as the common cold, the flu and a lot of other ailments.'

When I was in Kenya, one of Arsenal's players contracted malaria while on international duty in Africa. It was reported that all the other Arsenal players carefully avoided him on his return. That malaria is contagious is a common misconception; it is spread only by mosquitoes biting.

One night before the rains stopped, I was in the car with Sr. MM when we came upon two lorries that had toppled on their sides off the dirt roads in the rain and lightning, just outside Kitui village. For once, I was breathless with anxiety, fearing the curious crowds that had assembled in the darkness and the possibility of bandits among them, maybe intent on opportunistically looting the contents of the lorries—or passing vehicles.

We were on our way to visit the mission house of two convivial Irish Kiltegan priests, Fr. Frank and Fr. Liam. Fr. Frank and Fr. Liam were in their sixties, typical of the age profile of the Irish missionaries in Africa. We spent a long time that night on the verandah admiring the squadrons of glowing fireflies dancing in the rain. We were exchanging stories.

'There was uproar the other day when everyone in Kwa Vonza village refused to be confirmed,' Fr. Frank told us, in between puffs on his trademark pipe. 'They had heard about the Holy Spirit coming down upon them; they thought it meant evil spirits would possess them. It was time for a bit of basic theology.'

As the topic of conversation turned to witchcraft, the electricity suddenly went off in the mission house. We lit candles and pondered, as we always did, whether the electricity going off was caused by the rain, or if gangsters had cut the electricity supply for the village in order to raid a house. No one ever said aloud what he was thinking. Would we get a knock on the window?

Sr. MM had told me that, earlier in 2005, a gang of armed men called to the mission house one night when Fr. Frank was alone. All the missionaries have a watchman outside their homes during the night, but Fr. Frank's had a habit of falling asleep on the job. The gang was surprised when Fr. Frank opened the door to them, smiled and simply said 'Karibu' (you're welcome in). They had a good search round, and were disappointed to find nothing. Fr. Frank owns only a couple of changes of clothes, some books, his characteristic cap to protect his bald head, and an old ink-ribbon typewriter that he lets some of the villagers use.

CHAPTER 6 THE MAGIC OF RAIN

He gives everything else away.

If Sr. MM was like my aunt, then these two were to become like uncles to me. Yet they were so different in personality. Fr. Frank was a calm, contented, jovial and robust hardworking man from the Dublin Mountains. Whereas Fr. Liam, from Tipperary, was eager, energised and animated behind his big glasses; his generosity and conscientiousness were testaments to his character. Both had a sharp wit and could tell a good story. Fr. Frank was, on occasions, to be seen clad in a big heavy jacket in the afternoon heat, alighting from his battered old motorbike after doing his priestly rounds. Fr. Liam preferred the bright safari suits his parishioners had sewed for him while he attended to his duties.

Fr. Frank was known to one and all as *Mnambo,* the Kikamba word for lion. He either did not know why or was too modest to say—although I heard a rumour that he had started it himself decades previously. As he and I were driving to Mass, very early the next morning after the rains, to an out-station near Nyumbani, his small jeep became stuck in the mud of the dirt track, half way up a slope. Not a man to give up lightly, Fr. Frank revved and revved, then finally yelped,

'Uh oh!'

Gently, almost in slow motion, the jeep toppled over sideways—with us inside. We abandoned it and trudged through the muck to reach the out-station, carrying all the paraphernalia for the Mass in our hands.

All the Africans we encountered along the track were delighted with the recent rain, telling us about the amount they had captured in barrels and buckets. They did not seem to mind the effort involved in hauling the oxen and carts through the deep mud. We greeted all the barefoot schoolchildren we met along the way. They were carrying copybooks and pencils, as well as some sticks for a fire in school—they found it cold after the rain. I was sweltering still. I took some photographs that the kids were thrilled to view when I showed them back on the digital camera.

Before the November rains, I had been cycling to the mission house one day after leaving Sr. MM's home. I had to pass over an ancient concrete bridge that was cracked and broken, and about to collapse. I decided to crawl down onto the riverbed (as it was dry at the time) and cross that way for fear of falling through the gaps in the bridge. Just then, forty or so children were walking home from school, coming in the other direction. As they were walking over the bridge, they spotted me below. Not one of them would get off it until I took a group photo of them on the rickety bridge. Quite concerned, I gestured to them to keep moving, but they insisted on a photo. I was terrified it would collapse as I took the shot. I could just picture how that would go down with everyone in Kitui—and in Ireland! The bridge got washed away completely the week after, and that photo is a piece of local history now, I suppose.

Often when I was taking a photo of Akambas, they would tell me to wait, then disappear into their homes, and come back twenty minutes later dressed in their Sunday best. Fr. Liam, a trained photographer, possessed a collection of more than 40,000 photographs he had taken of the people of Kitui—a priceless archive dating back to the 1960s when things were even more primitive.

'Back then,' he recalled, 'most Akamba didn't wear the conventional clothes they do now.'

Whenever I travelled around before, I always regarded the camera as a necessary nuisance. I preferred to enjoy the moment instead of capturing it for posterity. I still do, but I became a bit more snap-happy in Africa. But for all the photos I took, some of the most vivid images in my memory are photos that got away. Perhaps it was inappropriate to take a picture, it was too dangerous, the moment passed too quickly, people noticed and ruined the spontaneity, people refused to be in the photo, the camera was broken, the camera was forgotten, the batteries did not work, there was no memory space or film left, or else I thought I would see the same scene again and of course I never did. In any case, a camera can never capture the kaleidoscopic colours of a 360-degree African panorama, full of exotic sounds and smells.

A truly bizarre experience, which I failed to capture on camera, occurred shortly after the rains abated. Kimanze had taken a break from work and was resting on the ground near the river. I was a distance away, on higher ground, when I heard a commotion. He had suddenly jumped up, screaming urgently. People were rushing over towards him amid a hullabaloo of shouts. He had nearly been completely wrapped up by a giant twenty-foot black-green python that had slithered up behind, unnoticed. The others nearby were desperately throwing stones at it. After a short frantic time, they were able to beat it off with their farming implements. Had there been no one around, it is possible Kimanze could conceivably have been killed. I had often wandered down to that exact spot on my own, not even aware of the python's existence up to that point.

The really odd thing, however, was the almighty rumpus that

ensued immediately afterwards. Nearly everyone was gesticulating vigorously and shaking their heads, or had angry expressions on their faces as they made their point in Kikamba. Kimanze would not speak about it to me afterwards; he never did in fact, not about any of it. It took me two days to get it out of Mwangangi what it was all about. It was like a confession, the way he explained the incident in a slightly bashful tone.

'Brendan, not everyone believes; it is just some people. That particular python lives under a *mikuyu* tree on the riverbank right next to where Kimanze was sitting. It is a species of tree associated with evil or magic.'

In my head, I was comparing it to the fairy trees in Ireland.

'A few days before that,' he continued, 'some people here sacrificed a goat to this python. They placed a circle of blood around the tree and left the goat for the snake to eat.'

There was obviously more to this than I had ever imagined.

'It is forbidden to break the bones of the goat being sacrificed. During that ceremony they asked the snake for more rain,' he explained. 'The workers of Nyumbani told Kiragu that they would not dig wells near this python—unless a sacrifice of a goat was made first.'

Could this be the oddest reason I would ever hear for a workers' strike, I wondered.

Nyumbani is a Catholic charity, so the nearby Catholic outstation sold one of its goats to Nyumbani, which in turn donated it to be sacrificed to the giant python in return for the rains—and few people seemed to see any irony in this whole set up!

'The loud row occurred because some people thought the snake should not have been attacked and chased away,' Mwangangi went on. 'It goes against their witchcraft beliefs. They predict the snake will punish us by withholding the rains.'

As we sauntered past the same spot late that afternoon on our way to Mutinda's home, Mwangangi relayed more evidence of the prevalence of witchcraft among the people.

'Yesterday, another goat was sacrificed to appease that python after two men came to fisticuffs within sight of its den in the *mikuyu* tree. Akamba custom forbids fighting within sight of the python's lair.'

The strength of the people's belief in witchcraft was brought home to me much later, in July 2006. The papers reported that in Kisii District near Lake Victoria, several families were burned out of their homes, and some people were burned alive by lynch mobs who accused them of being witches or witchdoctors. After some days, the witch-hunt evolved into being used as an excuse to settle old scores. It was effectively Salem, Massachusetts, transported to Kenya 2006.

We met Kimanze just past the *mikuyu* tree, where he was fixing pipes for the water system long after others had stopped work. He was unusually conscientious for an Akamba.

'Come on Kimanze; it's time you finished!' I urged him.

He looked up at the sun and realised the time of day. It was quite an accurate method, because being on the equator, the sun maintains a constant pattern throughout the year. I told him we were off to visit Mutinda, so he decided to join us. Kimanze grabbed my hand a few seconds after we set-off, as if we were a couple on a stroll. This was one Kenyan custom, just like the witchcraft, that I still found different at this stage. Men held hands with each other even though they were not that way inclined. However, one never saw a man and a woman holding hands or hugging in public, or indeed ever saw a man dancing with his wife even though one might see him dancing with every other woman around the place. At the beginning, I did not know what to think each time a man took my hand when I was walking in Kitui, until Mwangangi told me it meant you are just good platonic friends. If you would not hold hands, it was a very negative signal that you did not want his friendship.

We were sharing all sorts of stories on that walk to Mutinda's home. The one taboo subject of course was Kimanze's close encounter with the python, now that he had joined us. I told them about a recent scary experience of my own. Cycling back from Kwa Vonza, I had passed a skull by the roadside with money inside it. I did not delay long enough to confirm if it was the skull of a baboon or a human. After all the witchcraft I had heard about, I fairly kept on cycling, not entirely sure what it was I was frightened of.

'It was a human skull, Brendan.' Kimanze put me in the picture. 'But two brothers from Kwa Vonza came and stole that money. They bought beer with it.'

He did not elaborate any further as to what happened to the thieves.

But it reminded me of another tale. Fr. Liam told me that he had his bible stolen once. Some Catholics would hope to retrieve it by praying to Saint Anthony. The witchcraft way of getting it back is to place the tail of a goat on the spot where it was stolen, and put a curse on whoever stole it. The Akamba are so scared of such a curse, once they hear it has been performed, the stolen object always mysteriously reappears. Fr. Liam recalled with

CHAPTER 6 THE MAGIC OF RAIN

amusement how he got his bible back.

'I placed a goat's tail on the spot my bible was stolen from. I omitted to perform the curse, of course, but word must have got around, because my bible reappeared within hours.'

An outsider such as myself has to ask whether witchcraft really does work, or instead works because the people believe it works, with a faith as strong as any belief in supernatural powers. I have an open mind tinged with scepticism on such matters. I could not be persuaded, for example, that a python could bring rain upon Kitui—no matter how many goats you fed it. However, there was plenty of evidence of the efficacy of witchcraft practices. For example, I saw shops with the doors left open at night in Kwa Vonza village, through which no human or even a dog would pass through, or indeed *could* pass through if the witchcraft was working. There was also an African priest I was friendly with, who told me that whenever he passed through Kwa Vonza village on his motorbike, a dog would chase after it and try to bite him. The priest complained to the owner. The dog never even looked at the passing motorbike again, let alone chase after it. I could think of several rational explanations for that one, but they would not count for much. The owner was widely known to be practicing witchcraft, and that was enough.

However, there were some black-magic-related beliefs that seemed downright incredible to me. I reminded Kimanze of the man we had seen in Mombasa who was chopping down a tree laden with bananas.

'That's right,' Kimanze recalled. 'He said, "I am cutting down my banana tree because it is producing too much fruit. I'm afraid a genie will come in a few years and ask for something big from

101

me in return . . . Like my son." '

Where would you start with a man like that? I thought.

As we approached Mutinda's home, the conversation turned back from superstitious beliefs to traditional customs, specifically to naming children. I explained that in Ireland many people tend to name children after relatives or after Christian saints. Mwangangi told us his sister had named her newborn baby 'Mothune' because it had been a difficult childbirth; the Akamba name simply means 'a problem.' I thought the American psychologists would have a field day with that one! I was often surprised, though, at how some Kenyans possess rather un-African names, and I am not talking about the missionary influence. I was used to meeting people with names like Boniface, Hamish, or Innocent (the latter I thought was a good name for a Nairobi child who can turn to the police when caught and go 'I'm Innocent').

I told the two lads a story that Sr. MM had told me recently about twins born in Kitui that year called 'Toyota' and 'Corolla.' Sr. MM had driven her banger of a Toyota Corolla to hospital with their mother once she started contractions, and the mother named the children after the car, of all things! Even Kimanze and Mwangangi thought that one was silly, and were still laughing when we reached Mutinda's home.

As a medicine man, the 'magic' that Mutinda practiced was of a different order from what we had been discussing earlier. I was certainly prepared to give him the credit for curing my ladybird headaches. We found him sitting on a small wooden stool in front of his hut when we arrived. He stood up to shake hands with each of us. He was delighted that I had had no recurrence of the headaches. Mwangangi shared a joke with him in

CHAPTER 6 THE MAGIC OF RAIN

Kikamba inspired by the conversation about names that we just had. Mutinda looked at me and chuckled, and then continued in the same vein, for he loved telling me about this type of thing. He had a wealth of knowledge on tribal lore.

'A more tribal custom, Brendan, is to name the infant after an ancestor who made a sign they wanted to return to earth in that infant,' he explained. 'Even a deceased child can make a sign in a dream, and the next child is named after the deceased child because it has the same spirit. Sometimes they believe the spirit of the deceased child is good; if evil, the elders must rid the spirit in order to avoid recurring child mortalities.'

Mutinda went on to describe how the Akamba believe the spirits of these ancestors to be the intercessors between them and their one transcendent God.

'Normally though, Brendan,' he continued, 'Akamba children are named after an event surrounding their birth. You know Nzoki's son "Wambua"; his name means "born during rain," or Wambua's friend "Muthoki"; his name translates as "long awaited one." That would explain why we now have a little Toyota and a little Corolla in our community!'

We listened with fascination to the tales of this gentle and good-natured man for an hour or more.

Before we left, Mutinda insisted on being updated on the Village project. I told him that Nancy and Nzoki were picking up computer skills remarkably quickly. Kimanze described the progress that he and Leo were making with the water supply. They now had a system of delivering water to a central point, but as yet did not possess a really reliable source of water. So the well-digging continued apace. Mwangangi explained that enough bush had been cleared to have the outlines of a farm, and that many of the community buildings, such as the police station and health centre, were beginning to take shape.

'And how is Kiragu?' Mutinda asked.

'Well,' I said. 'He is still coming up with new ideas all the time, and ways to improvise and improve.'

'That sounds like Kiragu,' he chuckled.

That night, Mwangangi and I got a lift to Kwa Vonza on the back of a rattling old truck. Kimanze could not join us; Leo wanted his help with something. We spent hours drinking warm bottles of Tusker beer at The Paradise Hotel. The pub could only hold about thirty people, but I knew most of those streaming in and out. They worked in Nyumbani or were neighbours (and suspiciously often 'relations') of Mwangangi. Most of them came over to us for a chat. I was pleased at how much Swahili I had picked up at this stage. I think it is known as 'deep immersion' in language circles.

Well after midnight, Mwangangi staggered outside into the dark to relieve himself, then stepped back in and, to my amusement, tripped over the dog lying on the ground just inside the bar. We were the only two left by now. I ordered another round. The barwoman brought it over and I paid. Then she took off the bottle-tops and poured a bottle straight over each of our heads.

'You have had enough, time for you both to go home,' she roared as she threw us out.

Her methods were surprisingly effective.

It was a moonless night. So, standing in the darkness (and I could not see Mwangangi even though he was only a foot or two away), Mwangangi pondered how could we get back to Nyumbani. He was not keen on walking.

'Too many snakes, Brendan,' he pointed out.

'Oh for a Toyota,' I cried.

'Or even a Corolla,' he laughed.

Then he had a *eureka* moment.

'It would be best if we could find a motorbike.'

So, at about three in the morning, we knocked on the door of his cousin's wife's uncle, or something along those lines. A large man wearing pyjamas opened the door. I did not think it was a good idea to be knocking at this time.

I could not have been more mistaken. The man even called his wife out (appearing topless before she spotted us) to make *chapatti* for us. His small children appeared too, and stared sleepily at the strange *mzungu* who had appeared in their home in the middle of the night. Next, he fished out a bottle of homemade hooch from his bedroom, one he had been specially saving for just such an occasion when a stranded *mzungu* would call to his house at 3am on a moonless November night. A bewildered expression met my decline of his offer. I had shipped too much Tusker already. Then he brought out the motorbike from the back, and after a good few attempts managed to start it.

'OK, Brendan, you will drive,' ordered Mwangangi.

I was not convinced that that was a good idea.

After the disappearance of the rains, it became too hot to cycle on the boneshaker to Kitui, so I had borrowed a motorbike from some of the priests a few times. You rarely met anything on the dirt tracks other than a few wild animals and some people herding goats or donkeys. But, in truth, I was still a novice biker at this point. I hesitated, but Mwangangi cajoled me into agreeing. Confident we would not meet anyone, we headed back over the dirt track at a steady pace in a happy Tusker-induced daze.

Mwangangi was seated behind me with his arms out like wings, looking up towards the stars, which thankfully had now appeared. Caracal cats and other unidentified creatures were jumping out in front of me as I drove. The road from Letterkenny town out towards home was never like this, I kept thinking. One kilometre before reaching Nyumbani, we ran out of fuel. It was quite an effort to push the bike the rest of the way over a sandy track.

I woke up the next morning realising how dangerous it had been; never in a hundred years would I even dream of contemplating such a journey in Ireland. It was like the time Leo and I staggered the fifteen kilometres back one other starry night without the benefit of a lamp.

Kimanze told us a cautionary tale the following morning.

'One of the Nyumbani workers was walking home one night full drunk. He fell asleep, out cold on the side of the road before he could make it home. He woke up to find a hyena eating off his left buttock.'

Kimanze was not joking.

CHAPTER 7
THE MISSIONARIES OF AFRICA

ARCHBISHOP TUTU OF SOUTH AFRICA once famously declared, 'The missionaries came with their bibles, and taught us to pray with our eyes closed. When we opened our eyes, we had the bibles and they had the land.' That happened in the late nineteenth and early twentieth centuries; it is a bit different now.

I always had a childhood picture in my head of missionaries walking around, throwing holy water over naked spear-wielding black people. The reality proved very different. The Catholic missionaries in Africa are remarkable people: priests wearing colourful shorts fluently conversing in an African tribal language with a Kerry accent, perhaps; or elderly white nuns riding motorbikes over treacherous dirt tracks. As well as spreading Christianity, they do a tremendous amount of practical work to improve the lives of Africans; setting up schools, health centres, water projects, and creating employment opportunities. They are outstanding people whose extraordinary efforts are rarely acknowledged at home.

The Irish Catholic missionaries in Kenya install the infrastructure for entire communities, for Catholics and everyone else indiscriminately; infrastructure the government would not or could not establish. For example, Fr. Liam introduced me to a nun from Leitrim who was largely responsible for eradicating leprosy from Kitui District in the 1980s. The disappearing old-style missionary, who has lived amongst the community for decades in much the same basic conditions as the people themselves, does great work, albeit affecting the cultures of entire tribes in the process.

This has always been a prominent topic for African writers, such as Ngugi wa Thiong'o in *The River Between,* and Chinua Achebe in his novel *Things Fall Apart.* These two authors brilliantly narrate the life stories of fictional African characters against the background of the arrival of missionaries, and chart the growing tensions within the tribe, the village, and even within families between those who embrace the culture of the white people in matters such as religion, schooling or medicine, and those who continue to affirm their indigenous tribal traditions.

What cannot be denied, however, is that all of the Irish missionaries in Kitui are doing tremendous work for the poor. I became acquainted with many of them fairly soon after arriving. OK, I had mixed motives; in remote places, they are the only people with a few Western comforts—like a functioning shower, albeit a cold one from their tank of rainwater. All of them, without exception, immediately welcomed me as one of their own, and we instantly became friends. It was the Kiltegan Fathers (Saint Patrick's Missionary Society), with whom I had stayed on my first night in Kenya, who brought Catholicism to Kitui in the 1950s. Around a fifth of Kitui District is now Catholic, and the Diocese celebrated its golden jubilee in 2006; there was an Irishman at its helm even then. These ageing missionaries may vanish over the next decade from Kenya, to become a part of Ireland's, as well as Africa's, history.

I used to have an uncle working amongst the Zulu tribe in South Africa and an aunt living alongside the Ibo tribe in Nigeria, working as missionaries for many decades. As a child, I would listen, mesmerised, to their tales of life in Africa, and be fascinated by the exotic carvings they would carry as gifts whenever they came home for the summer on a break every three or four years or so. I never pictured their lives properly until I came to Kenya. There is a character in Brian Friel's play *Dancing at Lughnasa* who arrives back to live in Ireland after spending decades working as a missionary priest in Uganda. After a while, it becomes obvious that he had gone native and is suffering from malaria-induced delusions. He feels more at home in Africa.

Many of the missionaries I met would feel perfectly at home in both Ireland and Africa, but a great number of them soon discover they have a greater commitment to Africa. They have adapted well to life in Africa, and feel they belong more in Africa than in Ireland. These missionaries seem to stay exceptionally active and nimble as they grow older, tirelessly working long after people of their age would retire in Ireland.

The newer-style missionaries, mainly from America, might stay for a few weeks and, arguably, not do a whole lot of good. They often hand out a load of money to some local and hastily recruited African pastor to build a church. The money may be the conscience money of some televangelist. These local pastors are sometimes reported as embezzling money; many spout an intolerant 'saved' brand of Christianity. This may sound a bit cynical, and they are not all like this, by any means, but I saw evidence of harm done by a few of these fly-by-night operators, however well intentioned they might have been.

Indeed, one could argue that there is too much 'religion' in Kenya. In Ireland, most people talk down their personal religious commitment, whereas in Kenya they talk up how religious they are all the time, like when applying for a job, for instance. On occasions, I became frustrated when some people would not help themselves, lazily using religion as a crutch. 'God will help us,' they would tell me, when they should have been giving God a hand. Sometimes, admittedly, they told me this in sheer desperation.

Some of the buses run by the cool dudes in Nairobi even had a Pioneer Total Abstinence Association symbol brightly emblazoned across the side of the bus. It was not necessarily a pledge of Christian abstemiousness! I was in a truck once with Cecil (our Akamba Nyumbani driver), who like every other Kenyan lives by the philosophy of *'polé, polé'* (slowly, slowly). Except, that is, when he got his hands on any kind of vehicle. Like most Kenyan drivers, he treated the road like an airport runway. Cecil and I were sometimes bombing it down a narrow, gravelly track near Kitui village with a steep embankment on one side. Every time I asked him to slow down he replied, 'God cares for us.' I did not share his confidence that God would necessarily keep us alive if we plunged over into the ravine.

Religion and church are so much more relevant to the people of Africa than Ireland. It provides them not just with hope, but also with practical support, education, health, and employment. The larger mainstream churches in Kenya—such as Catholic, Anglican, and Presbyterian—also act as the only honest brokers in a country where the people are rightly suspicious of government, profiteering charities, and some meddling international organisations.

As is typical in any Kenyan village, everybody walks to Mass at the mission house church, some for many kilometres, and they love socialising outside afterwards. The people, many of whom wear tattered clothes for much of the week, dress up in their best second-hand suits or in elegant bright dresses and hats. Masses are so jammed that children sit around the altar and crowds of people listen from outside the church, while looking in the windows. They possess the zeal of new converts. A Mass can turn into a disco of sorts: entire congregations singing loudly and dancing in the uninhibited African fashion. Every Mass is a celebration of music and colour. It lasts for hours, and is nothing like the sober monochrome Sunday mornings in Ireland. Catholicism has a more liturgical focus that is truly African. I always had to look twice each time I saw a black Madonna or a black Christ on the cross. The African priests are often men in their thirties; the African nuns so young I found many attractive! It is a vibrant, relevant Church in Africa, and growing rapidly.

Kitui is perhaps two-thirds nominally Christian at this stage—but almost 100% animist at the same time, at least to the extent that witchcraft appears to be pretty much universally believed in. It is in some respects like rural Ireland right up to the 1950s: Christianity co-existing with 'pagan' beliefs and superstitions regarding curses, charms, fairies and so on.

'In Kitui, Brendan, to pass your own bad luck on to your neighbours, you singe your corn black, and spread it along the path for others to pick up on their feet,' Mutinda told me. 'They pick up your bad luck and walk away with it.'

NO HURRY IN AFRICA

In Donegal, I heard similar tales from older folk of tossing a ram skull backwards over one's shoulder with a pitchfork into a neighbour's field, or placing three hen eggs in the neighbour's haystack, in order to pass on the bad luck. Of course, many Akamba deny witchcraft even exists, and a *mzungu* will only pick up hushed references to some of the practices.

Of the two-thirds nominally Christian, some people might be Pentecostal one month, Anglican the next, Catholic shortly thereafter. Some may set up their own church for a time and practice some witchcraft while they were doing all this—depending on what school their child needs to go to, or simply for the sake of it. Christian zeal in Kenya was also responsible for my lack of sleep on many occasions. Fundamentalists used to roar over loudspeakers in Swahili until 2am opposite the Catholic mission house, where I sometimes stayed at the weekends. When I had finally nodded off, I would be woken up again at 4am by an evangelical call to prayer blaring over a megaphone—in imitation of the Muslims, presumably.

An old Irish priest (the same one who grabbed the boy for calling him British) once furiously left the mission house and pulled the plug out on their equipment to get some sleep. Fr. Frank had a different method. The preachers were roaring abuse and condemnation of Catholic beliefs in Swahili, backed by the obligatory passages from the bible. Fr. Frank calmly strolled over, and in perfect Kikamba, quoted about three times as many bible passages to contradict every single bit of abuse they could come up with. But they started up again a few days later anyway. Kenyan TV is full of these pastors, performing 'instant miracles' on members of the congregation by 'curing' their HIV or AIDS.

CHAPTER 7 THE MISSIONARIES OF AFRICA

They gesticulate a lot, ask for generous donations, and lay on healing hands with tell-tale fancy gold watches gleaming on their wrists. I could not help contrasting that with the frugality of Fr. Frank and the others.

Sr. MM is an institution around Kitui; she has been there so long. Every single Akamba seems to know her and hold her in high regard. There is a theory that the world has six degrees of separation, but I always maintain Irish people have only one degree of separation. I discovered that Sr. MM knows my uncle in New Zealand well. Fr. Paul, a much younger and very diligent priest from Dublin, was the Diocesan Administrator (acting Bishop) during my time in the District. Like Sr. MM, he too has a high profile locally. He is extremely clued into the bigger picture of the needs of the people of Kenya, and Kitui in particular. He was my initial contact for Kitui.

It was Fr. Paul who suggested to me that we go to a party for an African nun who had just been professed. I pictured a sober gathering of elderly nuns and me sipping water. An Akamba Archbishop had been invited. Fr. Paul drove us in his jeep to a compound a bit outside Kitui village where the convent was situated. I was very quiet and polite walking in, greeting each one of them reverently. Fr. Paul introduced them all individually to me,

'This is Brendan. He's just come from Ireland.'

'You are very welcome, Father Brendan,' they chorused.

'Pleased to meet you Sister, but I'm not Father,' I corrected them.

They giggled at their mistake. There were so many to greet, several dozen African nuns, and none of them appeared to be older than thirty.

There were bowls of snacks laid out on the tables for us to help ourselves. Whilst thus engaged, I spotted two young white faces at the back of the room. Surely this could not be two young white nuns in the heart of Kitui; 'young,' 'white' and 'nuns' not being words that you would normally find in the same sentence.

'Head over and introduce yourself, Brendan,' Fr. Paul encouraged me with a wee wink.

'Ah, actually, I've met them already . . . earlier on today after the nun's profession Mass outside the Cathedral.'

I gave him a discreet thumbs-up and bounded over to them.

They were two Dutch girls, both twenty-two years old. Like me, both of them were just out of college. We were probably the only young white people between Kitui and Nairobi, 150km to the west. I was delighted they were Dutch. Out of all the nationalities I love to meet when travelling, the Australians and the Dutch have to rank as by far the best companions. One was called Ilsa, the other Yvonne, and both were extremely genial. They had arrived in Kitui three days after I had, and would be spending the next six months volunteering at a centre for street-children in Kitui village that was operated by these nuns. Just for the record, the Dutch girls were not nuns at all; in fact, one was not even Catholic.

It had not been very hard to spot each other earlier that day. We had been throwing quizzical faces towards each other during the Mass that went along the lines of . . . what are *you* doing in Kitui? . . . and why on earth are you at a three-hour long profession of a nun? We got talking outside at the end. Both were terrific mimics of Fr. Paul and of some of the nuns, of all their speech and actions and mannerisms. They were living in a cottage on the edge of Kitui village, they told me. Like most Dutch, they spoke perfect English. Yvonne's long blond hair contributed to her typical 'Dutch girl' image. Ilsa, on the other hand, did not look Dutch at all. She was very petite, with brown hair and dark skin. She told me the reason for her colouring.

'My great-grandparents on both sides settled in Indonesia when it was a Dutch colony. One of my grandparents married locally, but my parents moved back to the Netherlands once I was born.'

I ambled up to the nun who had just been professed and warmly congratulated her. She was all decked out in the bright blue outfit and veil of her order, and was very young and quite bashful. I was very formal.

'Congratulations sister, I hope your vocation may be extremely rewarding and fruitful.'

She beamed a proud smile at me.

'Thank you very much, Mr. Brendan. You are very, very welcome here. Thank you, Mr. Brendan.'

We had all started off very reserved that evening, but the real informality of the professed nun and the rest of the convent surfaced once we had finished eating.

The nuns suggested a game of musical chairs—a giant game with over forty people playing. Big Archbishop Lele of Mombasa, Fr. Paul, Ilsa, and Yvonne all joined in too, and I messed with the Dutch girls. Three nuns banged an African rhythm on the drums. Every time the music stopped, half the chairs went crashing as people dived for them or hurtled over the top of them. Archbishop Lele, who for a laugh had decorated himself in a shawl wrapped around his waist, was wriggling his behind just as the Akamba ladies did when they danced. He would invariably end up being the one without a chair, so he always excitedly grabbed a nun off a chair and jumped on the seat.

'Could you imagine an archbishop in Ireland at that carry-on!' I shouted over to Fr. Paul.

'Par for the course out here, Brendan,' Fr. Paul laughed back, 'he loves a good time!'

The nuns were just as bad themselves; I have never seen so many ways of cheating at musical chairs. It was hilarious at times. I got knocked out of the game when I slipped onto the floor off the side of my chair; Archbishop Lele snapped it up. The festivities continued with dancing—the Akamba version of the conga, and other eccentric African dances in a circle formation. I joined in. I was showing off for the benefit of Ilsa and Yvonne, of course. I was having great craic, and was in my element right up until Fr. Paul signalled it was time to head on home. I never guessed I would enjoy a party with nuns and an archbishop so much. As I was heading out the door, Ilsa, who at this stage was tired out before the nuns were, whispered to me,

'My friends in the Netherlands won't ever believe this if I ever tell them.'

I knew what she meant.

Many times afterwards, I would again find myself in the company of priests and nuns. It was like living in a *Father Ted* series at times, I could not help laughing at some of their stories and antics. One missionary used to tell me before siesta, 'I am off now for some horizontal exercise.'

I could never bring myself to say that 'horizontal rest' would be less ambiguous.

The missionaries are so scattered throughout the District, I might be lucky to bump into one or two of them in Kitui village from time to time. There was only one decent café and one decent shop that we all frequented. I could usually spot that one of them was in town; their small jeep would often be the only vehicle on the street.

One late afternoon, a few days after the party, many of us met up again to celebrate the milestone of Sr. MM being forty years in the Ursulines. We occasionally got together at a weekend or evening if there were a special occasion such as this. Fr. Paul, Fr. Frank, Fr. Liam, myself, and a few other missionaries from as far as a few hours away assembled for a proper meal and a party. Sr. MM was the hostess again.

Sr. MM's convent house had a red corrugated roof and was built with mud walls, but it was the same inside as a middle class house in Ireland that was furnished around the time the convent was constructed, in 1957. For instance, she had a piano, probably the only piano in an area of Kenya half the size of Ireland. An odd key was out of tune from the heat and the complete absence of piano tuners, there not being much demand for their services.

Nonetheless, as always, we loved singing along to it. That was the evening I treated them to my own long rendition of Phil Coulter's *The Town I Love So Well*. The rest of them could all strike up a good tune and sing along to the likes of Percy French's *Phil the Fluter's Ball*. Fr. Frank was a master of the harmonica and Fr. Paul was nifty on the guitar. Two of Sr. MM's Akamba friends told me bluntly the following morning, 'Your music sounds boring.' They never took to the sound of the piano or to our Irish songs at all. Maybe, I thought, I should restrict myself to the short version of Coulter's iconic song in future!

Surveying the scene that evening—the African cook dressed in a khaki bush-jacket, us drinking on the verandah as the sun set, the sight of white faces enjoying ourselves—it felt to me like we were briefly living as the settlers had done during the colonial days. The early settlers of Kenya were often equally scattered; they would only have seen each other occasionally just as we did.

As a small lizard—known as a gecko—scampered up the wall preying silently on mosquitoes, the conversation at this dinner flowed seamlessly over a variety of topics: from us laughing along to Fr. Liam's hilarious account of a misadventure that happened to an African we all knew, to Sr. MM relating the seriousness of the plight of a family nearby, to Fr. Frank revealing a secretive part of Akamba culture, to Fr. Paul recounting a lucky escape from a dangerous situation earlier, and back again to laughing at some more of the antics of the Kenyans or my own interactions with them.

The following afternoon, I found myself sitting on a wicker chair on the sunny verandah with a whiskey in my hand (call me *Bwana!*), reading old news from a three week-old *Irish Times* that was doing the rounds. I was really lapping up the grand old-style colonial feel, and remained for ages under the shade of the verandah, admiring the choir of birds performing in glorious harmony until the fiery setting sun turned the red soil of Akambaland a deeper shade of vermillion.

But most of the time, and of necessity, we all lived frugal lives in Kitui District. The missionaries were always immersed in— and sometimes nearly swamped by—the troubles of the Akamba people. That is how it has always been.

'There were many missionaries whose daily routine was morning prayers, followed by a full day's toil helping the poor, and then bed—day after day, year after year, decade after decade,' Fr. Paul had explained at that party.

It was far from glamorous, and it had not changed that much. Which is why Sr. MM's home was occasionally and temporarily transformed into an oasis of escapism.

CHAPTER 8
A DATE AT NANCY'S

BY EARLY DECEMBER IN KENYA, the bizarre seemed mundane and the mundane still seemed bizarre. Surreal things happened to me all the time, such as when a man in a wheelchair passed me out as I cycled downhill, or when I saw a man walking around Kitui village, selling socks that were perched in a two-foot-high pile on his head. Passing a man cycling with a bed tied onto the end of his bicycle had the same effect. Then there were all the times a goat, a hen or a deer was unhygienically slaughtered in front of me and I ate it for dinner an hour later—because the only way to keep it fresh was to keep it alive. That I spent my time dodging poisonous snakes when walking in the dark did not seem out of the ordinary. Eating with my hands in a restaurant seemed normal, and I no longer saw anything strange when a troop of angry baboons walked in front of me as I rode an ox and cart. But it still took a bit of getting used to the children running away scared from me, simply because I was white. And I never ceased to marvel when I spotted ostriches, giraffes and antelopes by the roadside on the way to Nairobi.

One day in the first week of December, a crowd of barefoot children mobbed Kimanze and me as we went to fetch water from a well near Nyumbani. Kimanze asked them, in the Kikamba language, to tell us their names. They all politely identified themselves, and I feigned enthusiasm until one boy replied,

'Bush.'

'That's a bit of an odd name for him, Kimanze.' I spoke in English, surprised.

A minute later, after a few more called out their names, another boy replied,

'Osama.'

Kimanze exploded in a fit of laughter. It transpired they were twins born on 9/11. In an extraordinary twist to the ancient Akamba practice of naming children after a significant happening around the day of their birth, there are now two twin brothers in a remote part of Kitui who have to live forever more with being called 'Bush' and 'Osama.' I recall riding a bus named 'Al-Qaeda Troop' from Kitui village that week, the name decorated prominently along its side. Some things I would never stop finding unusual.

I also found it strange that women can marry each other in Kenya—but are not lesbians. Fr. Paul, who is something of a social reformer, bemoaned the social and economic circumstances underlying this custom.

'Some women who cannot bear a child will pay a bride price of cattle to the parents of another woman who then marries her,' he explained. 'This woman, who has effectively been bought, has children by any man other than the husband of the first wife. The first wife then "owns" the children of *her* wife.'

'That sounds similar to slavery,' I suggested.

'Exactly, Brendan.'

That week, Mwangangi enlightened me further.

CHAPTER 8 A DATE AT NANCY'S

'Men will not let women ride bicycles,' he told me, 'because the men believe it damages their wife's ovaries.'

I had expressed surprise that I had never seen women on bicycles. Moreover, I had seen men spending ages trying to soup-up their bikes by fitting them with radios and extra mirrors and brightly painted slogans. It is the women in Kenya who seem to do not just the housework, but the farm work as well. They often eat separately, sometimes after their husbands have had their fill. I used to be amazed at the sight of women struggling with big drums of water and other heavy loads, while the men were playing draughts under a tree. It is very definitely a man's world.

If a man owns enough farm animals, he is able to afford dowries for several women's parents—he may subsequently have two, three, or even four wives. Each wife has a separate compound with huts, where her own children and grandchildren live around her. A *clochán* type settlement develops. The husband spends a couple of nights at a time in each compound, where a voluntary communal system exists.

Women are not allowed to own land in Kenya. It is only now that Akamba women are speaking out against these practices. Even the Catholic Church in Kenya, which helped ignite this change of view among women, will bless polygamous relationships but not marry the people concerned in church. Viewed through Western eyes, women are very definitely treated as second-class. Yet there is a need to tread cautiously where such long-standing customs prevail, and the Church seems to accept that.

Economic empowerment of women is perhaps a more pressing problem than any disease in Kenya, or indeed in Africa. Women will always be beholden to a man until they achieve an income of their own. Many women are only too eager to be educated and work productively in a job. So much is heard about the exploitation of Africa's natural resources, yet the deep potential of Africa's women is largely untapped. This was glaringly obvious at Nyumbani, where women were hired for every type of job, and entrusted with real leadership positions—thanks to Kiragu's inspired leadership. They all became very successful in their respective roles. It became clear to me that Africa is held back because her women are held back.

The more homes I was invited into around Nyumbani, the more conditions seemed almost neolithic at times. Around the beginning of December, Nancy asked me to spend a Sunday at her home. She had been eager for me to meet her family for some time now. It was a hard job finding the place though, because there were not even dirt tracks near her home, just barely discernable paths through the dry vegetation. Getting nowhere fast, eventually I gave up, and went looking for help. The ever-reliable, ever-obliging Mutinda escorted me there. As we made our way, I spotted a tortoise hidden amongst the dry undergrowth.

'Ah, this will make a nice gift for Nancy's family,' Mutinda said as I lifted it up and handed it to him.

'I suppose her children would enjoy it as a pet,' I suggested.

'Her husband will really love eating it later this week!' Mutinda declared.

Nancy lived with all her cousins in a compound of about a dozen round mud-huts, each with a cone-shaped thatched roof. The huts, with their wattle and daub walls, were clustered together and corralled in by a boundary of heaped, dead, thorny branches. This encircled the cows, goats, hens, and children inside the corral and stopped them wandering off; and it kept out any animal predators or (theoretically) human bandits.

When we finally reached her home, Nancy rapturously welcomed Mutinda and me. She began by introducing me to her husband—proudly, as if showing me off.

'This is Bradan, he is the *mzungu* who is teaching me so much,' she beamed.

Then she brought me round to greet her grandmother, who was sitting churning milk by hand at the time, as well as her own mother, her cousins, and her second cousins—all living in the compound. Nancy's father was staying at the compound of his second wife and would not be returning to them until the next day.

Nancy's father has two wives, and spends a few nights in the compound of one wife, then a few nights in the compound where Nancy lives with her mother. Such arrangements are typical. In Akamba culture, the wider family is central to the life of the community. Indeed, it is reasonably common for the first-born grandchild to be brought up by their grandmother, the grandchild then caring for her into old age. I am told that similar arrangements were not unknown in Ireland in the past.

'Where are your children you are always telling me about?' I enquired.

I could spot about a dozen children under ten years old hiding behind a neighbouring mud-hut, shyly peeping out every so often, then running back in behind again.

'They are fearing you, Bradan,' Nancy chuckled, 'they have not seen a *mzungu* before.'

She ambled over to them, and with that real motherly reassurance she effortlessly exuded, Nancy held their hands and led them over to me. A couple of them were braver than the others and radiated cheeky, toothy grins. One pinched the white skin of my arm while the rest cowered behind Nancy's legs for protection for another while. She has five small children, but only showed me her four daughters. I knew she had a six-year-old boy too.

'Where is your only son, Nancy, will I meet him?' I was curious.

'Ah Bradan, he is gone, gone away, I don't know where he is, he left this morning. But he will come back, Bradan, no fearing, he is around, exploring, all the time he is exploring.'

She did not seem at all concerned.

By now, we were all seated under a tree on the tiny one-foot high African-style stools that are carved out of a single block of wood. The meal consisted of *ugali*, with purposely-soured milk to sip. The goats, hens, dogs, and cats were fighting it out in competition for the scraps we threw onto the dusty red earth. Nancy's kitchen was a round mud-hut with a conical thatched roof, filled with smoke inside, the only light originating from the open doorway. It contained an iron pot boiling over a fire of sticks burning between stones on the clay floor. I watched her grind the millet in the hut by continuously pressing a long stick into a tall wooden cylindrical box carved from a hollowed-out trunk. When I showed great interest in what she was doing—so run-of-the-mill to her—she and Mutinda were busy swapping jokes in Kikamba, amused by my fascination at old-time practices that had died out in Ireland long, long before. Just as I was often amused, I suppose, with the Africans being so utterly fascinated by things like my digital camera.

CHAPTER 8 A DATE AT NANCY'S

Nancy showed me an ordinary looking stick resting against the wall of the kitchen hut. She lifted it up, and I could see it was hooked at the end, shaped like a thumb and index finger.

'You know what this is for, Bradan?'

'No.' I was expecting something profound. 'What is it used for?'

She hooked my right leg with the stick and, hopping on one leg, I nearly lost my balance.

'This is for a husband to trip his wife if she tries to walk away from him. Every home has one of these. But my husband, no, Bradan,' she exclaimed with a confident expression, 'he knows not to use it on me!'

When we stepped back out into the sunlight, her husband was walking towards us with three cups of drink for Mutinda, himself and me. Homemade alcohol was normally plentiful when I was around any Akamba home, brewed from just about anything, which is why I usually politely declined, even though it was regarded as a bit of an insult to them. It would be produced for me at any hour of the day or night.

I took a sip; it was very palatable. It was one of the more popular concoctions, a form of beer made with honey. I had feared for a second he had brought chang'a, which is a poitín type drink that can be poisonous, even lethally so; it is made from fruits and millet and just about anything they can find. At first, I wondered if these potions were why Kenyans seem so happy despite their hardships, but I soon discovered cheerfulness is more in their nature than in their potions. Mutinda and Nancy's husband spilt a drop of alcohol on the ground before drinking to quench the thirst of their ancestors—just as the ancient Romans poured libations of wine to their gods.

Soon, hordes of children from nearby huts arrived to stare at me, and some adults came around to Nancy's throughout the afternoon just to gawk, when word quickly spread that I was there. The children now took turns running their hands through my straight fair hair, pulling the hairs on my arms and giggling. I must have been like a one-man circus act coming to visit. It amazed me that I was the first white person many had seen in the flesh—and I am not just referring to the children. Ironically, their grandparents' generation, who were young in the 1960s, would have been more used to white people; at that time, the numbers of Irish missionaries were at their height in Kitui, and the British were just leaving. In terms of multiculturalism, there has been a regression. There were never any British settlers in Kitui District as the land was far too poor for agriculture, but some civil servants and soldiers were stationed there.

Men looking not much younger than a mature oak tree, and just as gnarled, who I wrongly presumed had never even made it as far as Kitui village, were in fact army veterans.

'Many Akamba men were cajoled into the British Army to serve in World War II in Burma, Singapore, India, and Egypt,' explained Mutinda. 'These men brought back a sense of orderliness and cleanliness that was drilled into them in the army.'

The Akamba tribe still has a reputation for such virtues in Kenya nowadays—as well as for being lazy, of course. The Akamba language, I was proudly informed by one veteran who was related to Nancy, was used as a secret code during World War II to pass messages among the British troops.

When I was visiting people like Nancy, old people sometimes

CHAPTER 8 A DATE AT NANCY'S

told me that I was the first white person ever to set foot on their farm or their 'townland.' Some of these were very, very old.

'I buried a 110 year old woman today,' Fr. Liam told me around that time. 'She had great-great-great grandchildren at her funeral.'

Many in Kenya live to a very advanced age, being quite sprightly well into their nineties, and are still walking great distances and carrying loads on the farms even then. They never suffered from the excesses that a Western lifestyle entails.

I was bidding a noisy farewell to everybody before the evening sun sank when, out of the corner of my eye, I noticed one small boy hiding. It was Nancy's young son.

'He is fearing you, Bradan.'

I lifted him in the air and sat him up inside a domed hut (these are made of dry yellow grass and stand on stilts of wood). The boy immediately scrambled to the protection of the back of the dome.

'Next time Bradan,' Nancy assured me, 'he will not be fearing the *mzungu.*'

Mutinda and I finally set out on our return journey. Like the Pied Piper, there was a swarm of children silently trailing us, albeit at a discreet distance. It had been a tremendous day. Later that week, as she sat at her desk in Nyumbani, Nancy informed me proudly:

'There has been a stream of neighbours coming to my home for days now, wanting to look at the *mzungu.*'

Those children pulling at my hair that Sunday—it had been such an attraction—made me think about getting it cut. The scruffy long-haired look that I had favoured on most of my travels before now proved quite impractical in Kenya, what with the heat, not to mention the insects I kept finding in it each time I scratched my head. So, a week after my visit to Nancy's, I hopped on the back of a creaky lorry with Mwangangi and about fifty other Nyumbani workers and grabbed a lift down the track to Kwa Vonza village.

The barber sat outside, under the shade of a tree, at the side of the track near the village. He was using a car battery to power his clippers. Mwangangi had his head shaved first; like all the Akamba, he had it shaved right down to the skin. I had a job explaining in Swahili how this would leave me with a badly sunburned head. The barber could not grasp how the sun could burn skin. Mwangangi did not really twig it either. So the barber trimmed very little in the end. He charged us each twenty shillings (about 20 cent).

Mwangangi and I flagged a lift on the back of bicycles being ridden by two random people cycling in the direction of Nyumbani. As usual, they were brothers of the wife of a cousin of Mwangangi's wife, or something like that—everyone was related to Mwangangi somehow. As the bicycle careered downhill over bumps and potholes, my whole body was vibrating as I clung on. About two kilometres before Nyumbani, I yelled out,

'Stop! Do you see that?'

It was a huge brown tortoise, easily over a foot and a half high.

The lads could not get over the size of the creature, a giant even by African standards. It retreated into its enormous shell when we investigated further. One of the cyclists had a large sack with him and we wrapped it around the shell. It took three of us to lift it. We were probably nearly two hours walking back those last two kilometres; we kept resting every few minutes, it was so heavy. Mwangangi had suggested we keep the monster as a pet. He came up with the bright idea of confining it inside one of our empty Kenyan-style henhouses (made from branches hammered into the ground). Of course, as happened with most of Mwangangi's bright ideas, the tortoise escaped the first night and was never seen again. I was not entirely displeased; keeping such a magnificent creature captive would not have been right.

CHAPTER 9
TWO CHRISTMAS PARTIES AND A FUNERAL

I CELEBRATED CHRISTMAS in Kitui on the fifth of December. Ilsa, Yvonne and I were sitting chatting in the gloaming in the dappled shade of a red-flowering bougainvillea tree. A big red sun was slipping below the horizon. When it finally set, we lit a couple of hurricane lamps. We were celebrating early because apparently Santa Claus comes to Holland on the fifth of December. Ilsa explained,

'Sinterklaas—he is Saint Nicholas—is the patron of children. Sinterklaas wears a red bishop's robe and hat and comes on a big lit-up steamboat into the port at Rotterdam every year. He steps ashore on Saint Nicholas's eve with presents for all the children. The eve of Saint Nicholas is the fifth of December. It is truly wonderful . . . '

I could see she was feeling nostalgic, perhaps a bit homesick. Yvonne took up the story.

'The Dutch colony of New Amsterdam kept the tradition going even after it became New York. He became Santa Claus over there.'

Fr. Paul, a few Kenyan priests and nuns, a young Akamba man, the two girls, and I had enjoyed a great time earlier that afternoon, sharing food and jokes and presents. The girls had made Fr. Paul a present of a painted cardboard bishop's mitre that he was forced to wear throughout. He let on he did not want to wear it. Yvonne handed me my ingeniously disguised present in turn, telling me,

'Sinterklaas used to have lots of helpers known as "Black Pete" to wrap everything for him. He doesn't anymore, because it would be seen as racist now to have lots of black people helping him for nothing. So he wrapped this one himself for you.'

It was a clown horn for the handlebars of my bicycle so I could beep at everyone who kept walking in front of me. Sinterklaas had also composed a comical poem about me—with a little assistance from Ilsa.

Sadly, just a day after that, the two girls contracted severe malaria. This was despite taking anti-malarial tablets, which incidentally had been giving Yvonne hallucinations of five-foot high grasshoppers jumping on her bed. Such delusions are not uncommon with anti-malarial drugs. The malaria weakened their systems so much they suffered other illnesses, and were bedridden until the 'real' Christmas arrived.

People around Kitui seem to believe that illnesses, ill fortune or accidents never just happen by chance; they would insist it was a curse or a hex put on a person following some dispute. One of the few people they did not associate with this kind of thing was my good friend Mutinda, despite him being a 'hocus-pocus' herbal doctor-cum-vet. In view of what was about to happen, I would soon find this very ironic.

On the Monday morning following the girls' early Christmas party, I cycled the four hours back to Nyumbani, setting off before dawn had broken properly and waving wildly to early risers working on their farms along the way. I was in a cheerful mood and graced them with shrill hoots of my new clown horn. They were all surprisingly amused by this. None of them had thought to soup-up their own bicycle with a similar klaxon. Reaching my destination, I spotted Kimanze working at the gate of Nyumbani and let out a few raucous quacks from the horn. I dismounted and shouted a breezy 'Good morning' to him.

'I hear you lost Mutinda,' he spoke almost casually.

'What, I lost Mutinda?'

I was perplexed. It sounded to me as if he thought I had misplaced Mutinda and could not find him wherever I had hidden him. Kimanze straightened up from his work to pause for a moment and then said gravely,

'Mutinda, he is dead.'

My blood froze in every vein. I felt the insides tighten, and the hairs on my arm stood on end. I was short of breath, the colour draining from my face. It was a knockout punch that had come from nowhere.

I had been speaking with Mutinda the previous Friday and he was in great form, just as he always was. Kimanze told me what had happened.

'Mutinda had gone to Nairobi on business for Nyumbani. He decided that, instead of staying overnight in Nairobi, he'd get a late afternoon bus to Kitui. After it grew dark, there was a lorry in front of the bus with no rear lights and lots of thick black exhaust coming from it. The bus driver was speeding and was far too close to the lorry. When the lorry braked suddenly, Mutinda went flying forward. There were six others killed as well. Still more are unconscious in Nairobi hospital. It's very sad . . . '

I slumped onto the dusty ground in disbelief, trying to take it all in. Despite our age difference—Mutinda was in his mid-fifties—he had been one of my best friends in Nyumbani right from the very start. After some time, I wandered down to the office, feeling deflated. Nancy noticed me arriving.

'We all loved Mutinda. We will miss him, every one of us,' she spoke tearfully. 'I cried and I cried and I cried, Bradan. My husband could not stop me crying all of yesterday.'

I nodded, unable to find the right words; I could hardly grasp it yet. A good while later, Nancy broke the silence.

'He will be better off in heaven. We must celebrate his life. He touched so many of us deeply. But God loved him more.'

The mood was one of dejection in the days that followed. Mutinda had been one of those characters known to everybody, whether important or anonymous. He was a popular leader of one of the 'community groups' on the Project, as well as being in charge of a part of the farm. He had a great sense of humour, not beyond a bit of harmless devilment, and had such a hearty laugh. I regretted all the irreplaceable knowledge in his mind that was now irretrievably lost.

I will never forget the day we buried Mutinda. It was two weeks later—this was to allow time to collect a contribution from everyone to pay for a big funeral, as is the custom. It was a typical Akamba funeral and quite a spectacle, lasting from dawn until darkness away up in the hills, at the settlement of round thatched huts that was his home place.

On the morning of the funeral, we duly set off from Nyumbani in a convoy of four lorries crammed with people standing in the back. The Akamba in each lorry were singing burial songs together as we journeyed. But it was not an entirely solemn occasion. Everybody cheered loudly each time one lorry passed another. In Kwa Vonza, we all had to wait for the truck carrying Mutinda's coffin to arrive from Nairobi. It was a typical hot and dusty village where nothing much was happening. We were sitting for hours in what little shade was available. A child occasionally rolled a tyre with the end of a stick along the street, puncturing the stillness.

After a long time, the boredom was relieved when a car limped into Kwa Vonza, its bonnet dented and front windscreen smashed up. Apparently, the driver had just collided with a cyclist. Hundreds rushed up to surround the car. A lynching looked on the cards—only to be prevented at that very moment by the coffin of Mutinda arriving on the back of a pick-up. There were seven or eight people sitting on top of the white coffin, the pick-up decorated with ritual red ribbons.

When we set off again, the mourners resumed the funeral songs. We were now into the mountains, not far from where Sr. MM lives. It was here the track ran out; we all had to walk in procession the last few kilometres to Mutinda's home place; a vehicle could get nowhere near it.

As is the modern Akamba convention, he was lowered into the red earth outside his front door to the accompaniment of much song and dance and many lengthy speeches. Mutinda's walking stick was brought along, with its distinctive carved lion as the handle. I recalled how he used to carry it as he strolled around— the more decorative the stick the greater the status, according to Akamba tradition. Mutinda was a great man for tradition. He knew all the stories of his tribe, as well as being an expert on the medicinal plants and time-honoured remedies for both man and beast.

As the sun went down, I was still sitting, lost in thought, on a tiny African stool under a lemon tree, looking across to the round thatched mud-huts on the hill opposite. Suddenly, I was mobbed by a gang of children who swarmed around me while others timidly hovered just out of view. And in amongst them, also hiding, was an African wearing a Dublin GAA jersey! Life goes on, I thought, heading back to the lorry and a lift home.

It was around the time of his funeral, just before Christmas, that I decided, for a variety of reasons, to take a longer break from Nyumbani. I tapped on Kiragu's door, and he looked up as keen as ever to see me and share his latest ideas.

'I need a break,' I told him, 'I want to explore other parts of Kenya. I will return when my enthusiasm comes back. I promise you that.'

He knew the causes; I had no need to explain, he had no reason to ask. He wished me all the best, and assured me he looked forward to my return. I did not really let on to anyone else what I planned to do, but gave a few hints to Nancy, Nzoki, Kimanze, Mwangangi, Nyambura, and a few others. When the time came I would prefer to slip away unnoticed.

As with everything in Kenya, internal politics and splits had become rife, often running along tribal lines. I somehow managed to stay out of it, as I always instinctively tried to do; everyone still got along with me. However, on some occasions, the atmosphere was poisoned. Like many young volunteers whom I met in Kenya, even those working for organisations like the American Peace Corps, idealistic notions were sometimes swamped by disillusionment. The pity was that only a couple of short weeks earlier, I had been so passionate about the Project; it had such wonderful potential.

It was around that time that I began to suspect that a financial accountant in Nairobi was either incompetent, or—as more often than not is the case in Kenya—guilty of fraud. My hands were tied. I could not start whistle-blowing, because I was on a tourist visa and would have risked being deported. Of course, I also did not know how many others, if any, might have been involved. Though having learned a bit about auditing, and through sheer intuition, I had my suspicions.

The most obvious red flag was the late arrival of the wages every month. I had nothing at all to do with this delay, but I was the accountant they saw around everyday, and I suspected many workers presumed I had a hand in them not being paid on time. A young engineering volunteer from Letterkenny named Niall McMenamin had been shot dead in southern Kenya in the mid-1990s for much the same thing—something that was beyond his control. A teacher told me his tragic story one day, when I was reading the caption under his picture hanging in St. Eunan's College in Letterkenny. The worry of a similar incident happening to me sometimes lodged itself in the back of my mind. One is automatically the outsider for being white. Anyway, the whole project was also being held up because the government would not officially release the land deeds. Apparently, some senior official in Nairobi was looking for a bribe.

Leo, still universally referred to as 'Jesus Hitler,' had decided to leave the week before Christmas to work on a project in Mombasa. He had originally intended to go there before he left Germany. I became lonely as the only *mzungu* remaining in

Nyumbani. Then a good friend from College committed suicide back in Ireland. I received this news by text message, of all ways. There was nothing I could do but pray; I had nobody to talk to. Mutinda was also dead. Suddenly, after nearly four months in Nyumbani, I felt really alone. I was punctured. The isolation had finally got to me. Sometimes, the only way to communicate a message was to wait until someone was cycling in the right direction to pass it on; and then you had to wait on a reply until someone was cycling back. It could take days. That, and surviving on plain rice every meal of every day. Frustration all of a sudden became exhaustion.

That was also the week that Mwangangi and I became stuck down a thirty-foot deep well, when we were trying to collect water. The rope that was tied onto the bucket broke, and we climbed down the ladder to fetch the jerry-can resting in the water. One of the well-spaced iron rungs fell out as we were climbing down, and we could not reach the one above it to make our escape.

'Here we go again,' I laughed ironically.

While we were patiently waiting to be discovered, Mwangangi slipped into conversation.

'Could you loan me a few shillings for a new dress for my baby girl?' he asked.

'Sure, no problem, how much do you need?' I replied before wondering, 'Wait a minute Mwangangi, how old is your baby?'

'About one week old,' he replied, matter-of-factly.

He had not even bothered to tell anyone he had become a father. Mwangangi could be secretive that way, just as he had been about his wedding. It took over an hour for us to be found down there, and another hour to fix the replacement rung into the concrete to enable us to clamber out. That incident further fuelled my intention to escape.

Coming up to Christmas, the famine was becoming acute. Some farmers had planted two or even three crops of maize— but with the rains so disappointing, they had harvested nothing. The other tribes always say that only the Akamba could survive in that region. The famine had also made life uncomfortable for me. In my own mind at least, I was now a sitting duck for bandits who might mistake me for a rich *mzungu,* as I cycled alone the four hours through the parched bush to Kitui village at the weekends. The only consolation was that there was no longer any need to wade up to my waist across swollen rivers to get there.

However, my situation was far from being as dire as that of the local people. Some families now went from three to seven days between meals. The Catholic Diocese of Kitui was feeding over 250,000 people at this point. The situation deteriorated so badly that in one village, when relief food was being distributed, a troop of baboons ambushed children and grabbed their relief food. Some children had to attend hospital after the assault. The baboons were starving as well, and attacked the humans in an effort to survive. I recalled Nancy's warning.

It took two trips to Nairobi just before Christmas to have my visa sorted out at Nyayo House—an infamous government building where the public were interned and tortured in the basement during President Moi's periods in office in the 1980s and 1990s. It is still fairly infamous among the white people, but for a different reason nowadays. Each time I entered, various immigration officers would tell me to do something different; they would contradict each other. I was sent from counter 9 to 1 to 5 to 2 to

NO HURRY IN AFRICA

7 to 3, up to the fifth floor, round the back, and back down to Counter 9 where we started all over again. I told them that I was still touring. Eventually they took my fingerprints, stamped my passport, but computerised none of it.

One is supposed to receive an alien's card after this process. Its main use to me would be for much cheaper entry to the country's game parks (it was finally ready for collection three months after this!). At least I did not have to endure the requests to slip a few shillings to the officials that Leo experienced when he went looking for a visa. It was astonishing the amount of bureaucracy and corruption one encountered.

The real stroke of luck on this trip to Nairobi was that, by pure chance, I found out about an ascent of Mount Kilimanjaro planned by an Irish organisation known as Childaid. An ascent of 'Kili' had been top of my wish list long before I even landed in Africa, but up until now, I did not really have a group to climb with. I had 'met Fr. Jimmy absent' (as they say in Kenya), an industrious Irish Kiltegan priest with whom I stayed on occasions when I was in Nairobi. To pass the time whilst waiting for his return, I went for a cup of tea with some Irish Mercy sisters living nearby. It was there that Sr. Mary (not to be confused with Sr. MM) told me out of the blue about Childaid's sponsored climb to raise funds for her Nairobi slum projects. When I pricked up my ears at this information, she encouraged me to get in touch with them. Everything happens for a reason, as the Africans believe.

On my last day at Nyumbani until I would return from my break, Mwangangi introduced me to another distant relation of his whom, as it happened, I had found myself sitting next to on a bench outside the offices. He turned out to be a former minister in President Jomo Kenyatta's governments of the 1960s and 1970s. Now a weather-beaten elderly man, he lived near Kwa Vonza. He was sporting a big brown trilby hat and was resting his arms on an artistically carved walking stick. He rather resembled a fading mafia godfather, I irreverently thought. With great pride, he told me his story.

'I was originally a freedom fighter at the end of the colonial era,' he began. 'Back in 1960, I flew to London as an Akamba representative for the independence negotiations with the British Prime Minister, Harold Macmillan. Macmillan had recently delivered his famous "Wind of Change" speech, signalling Britain's intention to withdraw from Africa.'

Mwangangi interjected at this point,

'He helped draft the "Lancaster Constitution," you know, the one that the referendum this year was trying to supersede.'

I could see a touch of the politician in the retired minister yet, as he emphasised points with his hands and spoke with pride and conviction.

'Kenya's population has risen from eight million, at the time of Independence, to thirty-five million now.' He paused briefly. 'Name me one country in the world that has the capability to keep up with that,' he challenged me.

Nancy and a few others ushered him away on a tour of inspection. He had come to Nyumbani to have a look around and see for himself what was going on. It was these random encounters that happened when living in Nyumbani that I would miss, as well as the camaraderie and close friendships I had with many Africans working there.

NO HURRY IN AFRICA

Because I was preoccupied with other things, the only reason I was even aware Christmas was nearing, was because Ilsa and Yvonne asked me to dress up as Santa Claus for the street-children of Kitui at their Centre on Christmas morning. I was delighted to agree, I loved that kind of tomfoolery. We went searching for anything that could be cobbled together into some manner of costume, but without much success. Around Kenya, there were no decorations to be admired, no Christmas tunes to be enjoyed, no exchanging presents, certainly no snow—absolutely nothing of a seasonal nature. The street-children did not even know who Santa Claus was. Most Africans had never heard of him. Reluctantly, we scrapped the idea.

The Diocese threw a big outdoor Christmas party (probably the only one in Kitui) on the 23rd. We passed the night dancing, or in my case, trying to. All the young African nuns and priests were moving around a lot more rhythmically than I was. Fr. Paul struck up a few songs on the guitar towards the end of the night. My friends in Ireland, I was to learn later, were speculating that I was not coming home for Christmas because I had a few black babies on the way. The story was that I was too busy starting a tribe of my own.

I spent the afternoon of Christmas Day with the street-children. It was comical to hear me talking with the children of Kitui village, making full use of my limited Kikamba. There were lots of misunderstandings. It was not always just a matter of language. One young boy told me he was eleven years old, and when I asked him the same question a while later, he said he was nine years old. Half of them can only guess even the year in which they were born; indeed nobody knows for sure. What these children do know is how to survive—by whatever means. I sometimes paid a street-boy a few shillings (around ten cent) to keep my bicycle from being stolen on the street in Kitui. Of course, it was himself I was bribing not to steal it!

I had my Christmas dinner in the shade of a mango tree at the street-children Centre, eating with a spoon out of a bowl as I sat on a shaky wooden bench. It consisted of goat's liver—a 'specialty' they had reserved for me. Slaughtering a goat for Christmas dinner was a big deal in these parts. In truth, I was utterly tired of having tough sinewy goat meat by this stage. (The Irish missionaries slaughtered some scrawny chickens for dinner that night, the only alternative to goat, and not much more appetising.) All afternoon, there was dancing with the two Dutch girls, six young African nuns, Fr. Paul and fifty very excitable street-children—every one of them outside gyrating rhythmically to the lively modern 'bongo flava' music of Kenya's favourite singer, Mr. Nice. Not in person, of course, but on tape. It was shaping up unlike any Christmas I had ever experienced or was likely to experience again.

The missionaries' Christmas dinner was being hosted that evening in the Mercy convent where two long-serving Irish nuns called Sr. Nora and Sr. Helen ran a school and a dispensary near the mission house. Eighteen of us were gathered. After praying grace at the start, the craic was like something out of *Father Ted*. The missionaries were animatedly reminiscing about funny things that had happened over the last forty years. Any yarn I could tell paled in comparison. We were all in stitches throughout the stories; sometimes there were several narratives going on at once. They were spraying punch lines thick and fast, like bullets from Al Capone's machine gun. I really wish I had been able to remember some of them or written a few down, but I had consumed slightly too much whiskey for the details to register. It had been a Christmas dinner to *try* to remember.

At the time, it struck me that life in Kitui District was much the same as it was in the Nativity story; the same desperation many families suffer, and the way their farm animals are omnipresent. The people's empathy with the Nativity story was obvious in their sheer joy at celebrating the Christmas Vigil Mass. However, in every other respect, it was just another day to them.

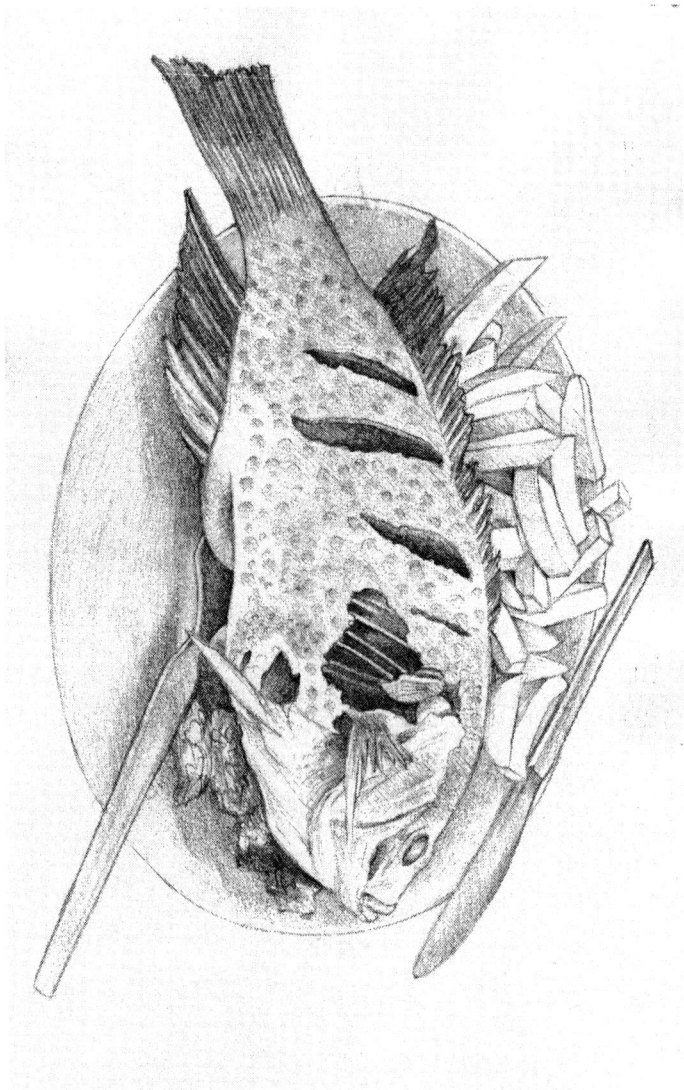

CHAPTER 10
RESCUE ON THE HIGH SEAS

ON SAINT STEPHEN'S NIGHT Ilsa, Yvonne and I enjoyed a memorable bus journey down to Mombasa on the coast, where we were planning to take a break for the next week. We were aboard a bus called 'Bush Senior,' perhaps a clue to its age. Some passengers were singing along to the catchy African tunes on the radio and dancing in the aisle in amongst their goats and hens. Passing through Tsavo Game Park about half way to Mombasa, they fell silent; by now, it was dark and we were hurtling straight through a herd of elephants. Somewhere near the town of Voi, the driver knocked down a zebra. All the while, a number of passengers were sitting on the roof of the bus. It was like a night-time animal safari. Zebras up close, by the way, look just like stripy donkeys.

We were staying in a simple chalet at Tiwi beach, ten kilometres south of Mombasa. The accommodation was fine, although it came as a surprise to find *saltwater* flowing from the taps. Tiwi beach is everyone's image of Paradise—long stretches of fine white sand, warm turquoise sea, coconut trees, and empty of people. We had it to ourselves; the big resort hotels are ages from Tiwi. To top it all, there was European food. It never felt so good to eat potatoes, pizza, and lobster. In the morning time, loitering monkeys stole breakfast straight out of my hand as I ate crackers on the porch with the girls. They were rampant colobus monkeys, whose most distinctive features are the bright sky-blue testicles of the male. By this stage, I considered them pests just as the Africans did.

Off Wazini Island, a small island an hour south of Mombasa down near the Tanzanian border, we organised a trip on an Arab sailing dhow. Hundreds of years ago, this island was the main centre in Africa for trade between the Chinese and Arabs. Our particular interest was snorkelling with the dolphins at the coral reefs. I loved it. The boatmen threw us overboard without bothering to ask could we swim. There were no life-rings on the boat, or lifejackets, or indeed any other paraphernalia remotely connected with safety. Swimming among all the varieties of exotically patterned fishes, and the tremendous coral formations themselves, was exhilarating. It was just the tonic I needed after recent days at Nyumbani.

The girls were eager to walk around some of the city while we were in Mombasa. So was I, for I had seen relatively little of it that weekend with Leo and Kimanze. The following day, Ilsa, Yvonne, and I had just finished touring the historic old town, and the fairly imposing 400 year old Fort Jesus (built by the Portuguese) when, directly below the Fort we spotted a place where some young locals were swimming in the narrow channel that cuts Mombasa Island off from the mainland.

'You two should have a race across,' I dared the girls, light-heartedly.

'How far do you reckon it is?' Ilsa asked, warming to the idea.

'About half a kilometre probably,' suggested Yvonne. 'Come on, we'll go for it!' she said, to my surprise.

CHAPTER 10 RESCUE ON THE HIGH SEAS

Of course, I had to join them. We dived off the wall into the inviting water. When we were some distance from shore, one of the ferries took a different course from all the other boats sailing up the channel that day. It was coming straight for us.

'We're about to get mowed down!' I shouted a warning to the girls.

We swam like the clappers to avoid it, and just about got out of its way in the nick of time. I do not know if they had seen us before that, but one passenger gave us a friendly wave, apparently oblivious to the danger we were in. It was not the first time for me. Something similar happened to me once at Arranmore Island off Donegal, and once in Croatia as well.

Ilsa and Yvonne had decided to return to Kitui by bus on the morning of New Year's Eve to ring in 2006 with the street-children. After waving them off, I set out to meet Leo at Bamburi beach, just north of Mombasa, where I would be spending the night. However, just then I 'met the ATMs of Mombasa broken,' as they say locally. So with my last few shillings, I bought a bus ticket home—to arrive in Kitui on the second of January—with just enough money left to purchase some fruit at the heaving markets down the backstreets. The place was full of dodgy-looking characters. Mombasa is a bit like Cairo, chaotic, bustling and raucous. In the narrow streets and among the crumbling colonial era buildings, goats were competing with the hand-pulled carts and getting in the way of the three-wheeled tuk-tuk taxis, whose incessant horns were drowning out the prayerful cries from the Mosques. The prevailing aromas were of exotic spices and goat droppings. It is certainly a bit different from Letterkenny on New Year's Eve, I thought.

Then something rather unusual happened. I walked into a shop to buy a pen, only to be greeted by a man wearing a sarong-type skirt who had been kneeling on a mat, presumably praying to *Allah*. Having established where I came from, he began conversing with me in Irish! His grammar was a bit ropey, but this is roughly how the conversation went:

'*Ca h-áit a d'fhoghlaim tusa do chuid Gaeilge?*' I enquired, with a dumbfounded but pleased expression.

'*Blianta ó shin, bhí mé ag obair ar feadh tamaill le sagart Éireannach. Táim líofa go leor go fóill, nach bhfuil? In aon chor, cad atá de dhíth ortsa anois?*'

Apparently, he had once worked for an Irish missionary priest who had taught him Irish.

'*Ba mhaith liom peann gorm le do thoil, má tá ceann agat?*'

'*Fan bomaite, chífidh mé.*'

At this point he whipped out his own pen from his breast pocket (ever eager to spot an opportunity for a sale), and I handed him a few shillings for it.

'*Slán go fóill, chífidh mé arís thú,*' he concluded, as I left his shop.

With his long dreadlocks, Leo was easy to spot on the beach. I crept up behind him and gave him a gentle fright. He was in high spirits and we were delighted to see each other again. I had to update him on Nyumbani and on his good friend Kimanze. Leo was along with another young German volunteer named Torsten and, being Leo, a few Rastas. We just chilled out in the heat, and had great fun messing with a beach ball in the waves.

'I have started at another children's project near here, Brendan. It is starting from scratch,' he told me in his concise German manner. 'There is a lot of work. But I like it very much. Torsten though, he has just had his bag stolen this morning. His passport, his camera, and his wallet are all gone.'

He hit the closed fingers of one hand onto the palm of the other, clearly annoyed. Then he carried on matter-of-factly,

'We will forget about that until tomorrow. Tonight, my friend, we will have fun.'

'I'm up for that,' I smiled, remembering our previous visit to Mombasa.

Nearby, local fishermen were wading in the shallows, casting their nets searching for fish. As the sun was going down for the very last time on 2005, I spotted a young Kenyan woman being swept out to sea, clinging onto an inflatable ring. She was drifting further and further out. Bamburi beach was packed with tourists looking forward to celebrating the New Year; they did not notice her. Her African friends were laughing at her from the shore and clearly did not realise the seriousness of what could unfold. Maybe they were from the interior. Having worked as a lifeguard on a beach while a student, I have a sixth sense honed over a number of summers for spotting potential danger.

I briefly looked around me. Mombasa had obviously never heard of hiring lifeguards. I pulled off my clothes, raced into the sea, and frantically swam out to pull her in. There was indeed a strong current, but finally I reached her, and towed her back to shore fairly promptly. She was clearly shaken by the experience. Looking both embarrassed and relieved, all she said was,

'My name is Francesca, thank you.'

And we parted, just like that . . . By now, it was quite dark, and the sun was disappearing for the last time that year.

NO HURRY IN AFRICA

We spent the night of New Year's Eve on the beach, at one of the many bonfires. Camels were sauntering on the sand. Fireworks shot up tumultuously all along the beach and for miles along the coast in both directions. Rockets were being launched at any angle, some whizzing dangerously past our ears. Children chased after one another gleefully, and hawkers praised their merchandise,

'Looky looky is free. Good price my friend. You speak Swahili, local price for you.'

Leo, Torsten, and I were now the only *wazungu* amongst the horde surrounding the bonfire. The tourists had long since retreated to the safety of the hotels. As the stroke of midnight approached, everyone around me counted 'one, two, three . . . ' *up* to ten, and not from ten backwards. The stroke of midnight released a blissful holler of welcome to the New Year, and the crowd proceeded to sing a chorus of . . . 'Happy birthday to you'!

The three of us stayed awake for the first sunrise of 2006, and then we fell asleep on the beach. As I had paid over the last of my money to book the bus ticket back to Kitui earlier in the day, I had to spend the night outside anyway. I always do a New Year's Day swim in the arctic-like waters off Donegal, and I continued that tradition in the Indian Ocean, having been woken up by the incoming tide soaking me. A bit more pleasant this year though.

Back in Kitui, the famine worsened. The morning after the night-bus from Mombasa, I was sitting alone in front of the mission house when a woman arrived carrying a baby on her back that was snugly wrapped inside a bright shawl. She addressed me in Kikamba.

CHAPTER 10 RESCUE ON THE HIGH SEAS

'*Waja?*'

'*Aa*,' I responded telling her that I was fine, and asked in kind, '*Uvoo waku?*'

'*Nimuseo*,' she replied, indicating she was well also, before launching full steam ahead into a torrent of indecipherable Kikamba.

However, I understood her message from her eyes. The baby possessed a disproportionately large head, and its ribs were showing. One has to be careful about setting a precedent in these situations, at the risk of sounding heartless. I did not want to bring every beggar from the village immediately down upon the mission house, which would inevitably happen. So I handed her twenty shillings (about twenty cent), enough to buy her and her child breakfast.

Suddenly she took off her skirt and began gyrating. It is heartbreaking what some are prepared to do for food. This particular woman may well have spent the money on drink; she came back to me every day I was near the mission house afterwards. Fr. Liam told me she had a history.

'That same woman once dropped another baby of hers on the lap of Bishop Dunne from Westmeath some years ago when he was Bishop of Kitui, right in the middle of an ordination ceremony. As you can imagine, Brendan, the gesture wasn't really appreciated.'

The problem was, as much as I wanted to give them what they wanted—and it was often only pennies in Irish terms—one can only ever meet a small part of their needs. Sadly, in many cases, their needs centre on the next bottle of Kenyan *poitín*. Yet I was always strongly conscious that, when weighing up whether to donate money, in genuine cases some people might really be close to death. The missionaries face such dreadful dilemmas every day, especially difficult when it is hungry mothers with starving children.

During that first week of January, I stayed for a couple of days in Fr. Paul's cottage. Also staying there was a twenty-five year old Akamba friend of Fr. Paul's named Katuta, whose family Fr. Paul had been supporting. A somewhat philosophical fellow with a neat moustache, Katuta displayed a worldlier outlook than most Akamba, having lived in South Africa for the previous two years. Fr. Paul set off at the crack of dawn each day, his labours taking him around the far-flung Diocese. So with the two of us at a loose end, we scrounged the loan of a motorbike off an Akamba priest without being entirely truthful about our destination.

Having filled the tank with petrol in the village, we embarked on an 'easy rider' motorbike trip over the high hills the other side of Kitui village, sending up clouds of red dust in our wake, the breeze in our faces, not a care in the world. The weather was perfect. We stopped now and again to admire the dramatic scenery. Our destination was a famous local landmark, a colossal yellow half-mile-wide rock sprouting 300 feet vertically up from the ground. Katuta explained the legend associated with it.

'If you walk around this big rock seven times without blinking, or without looking behind yourself, then you will change sex. You will become a woman, Brendan,' he chuckled loudly.

'I think I'll risk going around it fourteen times,' I declared.

We clambered up to the top of it. Katuta was out of breath with the effort involved.

'You're just not fit,' I teased him.

The view, however, was truly memorable. I could see for miles, even over to Nyumbani over four hours away. The small buildings of Kitui village seemed almost camouflaged, the ochres and reds mimicking the surrounding landscape. Once he got his breath back, Katuta pointed out something of considerable interest.

'Do you see that orange rock face over there?'

'Aye, what about it?'

I was straining my eyes, but it seemed a fairly routine rock face to me.

'Look closer,' he urged. 'There is a home built into that rock. Can you see? Two people live in it with their two children. Their grandparents first hacked it out of the soft rock years ago. It keeps cool inside all day. I visited them once with a friend who is related to them. It is quite homely inside. What is the word in English for those people?'

'Troglodytes,' I suggested.

I could just about make out three miniscule figures milling around the cave entrance. They could have been figures in a Stone Age tableau; Katuta reminded me that East Africa is known as the 'cradle of humanity.'

Katuta and I carved our names into the leaf of an aloe vera plant on the summit, and then rode back on the motorbike over dusty dirt tracks, edging through clusters of people and animals—and in the process becoming downright lost. It was long since dark by the time we made it back. Our earlier bluff had been called, unfortunately, and we received a minor telling off from the Akamba priest.

'I suppose boys will be boys,' he shrugged.

Katuta wanted to return home for a few days to visit his family in a place called Nuu. That night Fr. Paul, who had been stationed in Nuu when he first arrived in Kenya, suggested that I should go see this place as well. He made it sound very remote and isolated.

'You know Brendan, Nuu translates as "end of the road," isn't that right, Katuta?' said Fr. Paul.

'Yes,' Katuta agreed. 'It is situated right at the outer edge of Akambaland, beyond which is a barren desert with nothing for hundreds of kilometres the whole way to Somalia.'

'I really loved it there though. It is my favourite place in Kenya, really special,' Fr. Paul enthused.

'Yes, a cruel paradise,' was Katuta's contradictory verdict. 'You should come with me Brendan, and experience it for yourself, and meet my family too.'

Ah, sure I may as well, I thought to myself. I'm not pushed for time, I don't really have much else planned.

'It's Nuu or never!' I punned, and thanked him for the invitation.

'Oh, that was bad,' laughed Fr. Paul.

Heading for the village of Nuu the following morning, we made the cardinal mistake of taking the back seat of the bus. We were continuously being bounced up a foot or two off our seats, nearly somersaulting at every bump and pothole as the kamikaze driver flew down the dirt road. After hours driving deep into nowhere, the bus nearly toppled on its side at one point.

'Oh crap!' (or words to that effect) I screamed to all and sundry as I tightly clenched my fingers around the seat in front.

Luckily, the bus just managed to right itself after a very long, very hairy moment. At times like this, you might ponder on human mortality. On the roads of Kenya, you have a lot of moments like this. The passengers sitting outside with the luggage on the roof-rack of the bus were even luckier to be alive.

Nuu proved to be every bit as remote as Katuta had claimed; it is well over eighty kilometres from the nearest post office or newspaper seller. The daily approach of the bus is a big deal in such an isolated village. On arrival, a giddy and curious crowd of people, young and not so young, greeted us. As a white man, I was of special interest to them. Everyone kept energetically shaking my hand and beaming, 'Hello Father,' because they so rarely see a lay *mzungu*. I never let on otherwise, until one came looking for money from 'the priest.'

Just then, about twenty women performed a boisterous Akamba dance around us—though it was actually for Katuta rather than me, to welcome him back from South Africa after two years. Later we feasted on the local specialty of goat's liver and goat's stomach. The animal was specially slaughtered for the occasion. Not so much the fatted calf as the scrawny goat!

The whole village appeared to have turned up at the family's corral of thatched mud-huts, a good walk from Nuu along paths through the bush. Katuta had come home for the celebration of his older brother's graduation from college. He was the first person from the village ever to graduate. For ages, the afternoon was enlivened with colourful and typically animated dancing. Different people formed themselves into groups and danced in a snake formation which wound its way up to Katuta's brother; they danced in a circle around him, and then one by one placed a few shillings onto his palm. It is an Akamba custom to donate money to the person at the centre of a celebration.

NO HURRY IN AFRICA

The whole place was in a joyous mood. With feet stamping rhythmically and upper bodies shaking vigorously and almost uncontrollably, the dancers burst into brilliant high-pitched singing in the inimitable African manner. There were ecstatic yelps of joy piercing the air. It became one of my favourite memories of Africa. I loved dancing in the tribal fashion. I had picked up a feel for it over the months. Everybody in Kenya loves to start dancing at any time; they do not need an excuse. It is really spontaneous and infectious. Sr. MM claims it is what keeps them going.

Etiquette at these events requires you to first search out the oldest man present, and then try to greet everyone from oldest to youngest. I imagine I often guessed wrong. I was amused, as I usually was on these occasions, at the inevitable and rather ridiculous speeches—until, unexpectedly, I was called up out of the blue to make my own speech. The first thing I did was to find a translator, then improvise as best as I could. Every third sentence or so, I threw in a few superlatives and invoked God's blessing upon them—and they loved it.

'Wonderful speech!' Katuta's brother assured me.

Kenyans always made me make speeches for them, and they really liked them long and drawn out. I was always praised. They also loved saying grace before meals, versions that seemed to last sometimes for over ten minutes. I used to silently laugh when one of them would crank up his neck, turn his head to the sky, close his eyes, and begin praying interminably, thanking God for everything under the sun.

After my gripping speech, I had to take a siesta in a tiny grass dome-hut normally used as a granary. Four children regularly slept in it at night, Katuta informed me, with their goats tied underneath to the wooden stilts upon which it rested. As I dozed off, I was thinking how fortunate I was to be welcomed into the homes of these kind and hospitable people.

The following day was market day in Nuu. It was a lively affair, full of hustle and bustle and banter. The place was packed with haggling men weighing grain on their old-style scales, and jammed with colourfully dressed women sitting on the ground selling fruit that was laid out neatly on rugs. The women were continually hitting out at the donkeys, shooing them away from eating their produce. There appeared to be a fair amount of food at the market in this remote place, even though I knew it had been severely hit by the famine. I was wondering how patchy its effects could have been across the region when it suddenly dawned on me: I was almost certainly the only white person for several hours journey in any direction.

At the end of market day came the perennial problem for a European running out of hard cash in rural Kenya; there is often zero chance of getting anywhere near a bank. Even if you do make it to one, then the bank often does not have an ATM, but if you are lucky and it does have one, then it is invariably broken. While I was in Nuu, I wanted to call on Sr. Goretti, a lovely Irish nun stationed there whom I had met at Sr. MM's home one weekend before Christmas. Unfortunately, she happened to be on her annual trip to Kitui village the very days that I was in Nuu.

CHAPTER 11
BEYOND THE BEYOND IN TURKANA

WHEN I ARRIVED BACK in Kitui a number of days later, I passed two days running rings around the street-children at football, and trying my best to sing Akamba songs with them. At this point, I was contemplating not returning to Nyumbani at all, even though it had been my original intention to go back after some weeks. I had set up computing and management accounting procedures that Nancy and the others had shown they would be able to operate. I was pondering my options. One was to volunteer full-time with the Kitui street-children. Through the volunteers' grapevine, I had also been invited to assist in an accounting role with three other projects in various parts of Kenya. But first, Ilsa, Yvonne, and I were planning to spend a fortnight in Lamu, the historic Swahili island up the coast towards the Somali border. I had long been itching to visit this famous centre of Arabic culture in Africa.

Before we could go to Lamu however, I had to return to Nairobi once again in early January for two days to sort out my work visa. On the plus side, as ever, a half-palatable dinner was available in Nairobi, and it cost under a hundred shillings (about one euro). Nairobi has many faces—and by now, I was seeing the city in all its rich diversity: from the city centre skyscrapers, to the smelly teeming slums, to the upmarket and gated mansions, to the dickensian cast of characters along River Road.

It was not uncommon to see the Maasai all dressed up in their traditional red blankets and staffs going about their normal business in the middle of Nairobi. Visitors certainly take a second look at these tribesmen, with the distinctive decorative holes in their elongated earlobes, herding cattle on the roadside in front of the suburban mansions of the wealthy Europeans. You see them too with their livestock in the middle reservation of the dual-carriageway on the way out to the airport.

The footpaths of Nairobi are crowded with shoe-shiners doing a roaring trade, fire and brimstone preachers, tourist touts, beggars, businessmen in pinstripes, madmen and vagrants. Everywhere there are hawkers walking around with their wares on their heads, badgering people to buy. One has to haggle for absolutely everything; if it was a small amount I never bothered, even though there is always the 'white premium'; they stick the price up once they see your skin colour. We called it being 'mzunguled.' For bigger items, I would bargain with them. The banter would often be good; I relished the craic of it all, until it went on and on too long and about half an hour later the African was still asking an inflated price. Many times, they started at well over twenty times the normal price.

The bargaining process could be either enjoyable or frustrating. Sometimes I just paid what I knew was a rip-off price as my way of donating to an obviously struggling person, letting them think they earned it instead of being given a handout. For all the ones ripping me off, many others treated me with a kind of colonial deference simply for being white, treating me better than they treated their own, giving way to me in queues and allowing me endless credit. I hated that.

Some Europeans, especially Germans, make the mistake of bargaining them too low, so the African hands them a dud or cuts back the service. I took the view that even if I paid way over the odds of what an African would pay, that if I were prepared to pay it, then that was the price of it. There is a lot to be said for price tags though!

On my second day in Nairobi, just as I was leaving Nyayo House, once again confounded and frustrated by bureaucracy, the Dutch girls phoned to say the Lamu trip was off. I was more than disappointed; it just was not my day. But my luck changed. An exceptionally droll Kiltegan missionary from Limerick named Fr. Tom, whom I had only met the previous day in Nairobi, said to me that evening,

'I'll be driving up to Turkana on my own tomorrow, why don't you come along and we'll keep each other company? You can visit people you've met when you are up there.'

I had intended for sometime now to visit the remote, alien, barren, northern region called Turkana. A couple of friends of Sr. MM had strongly encouraged me to go sometime. However, nearly everyone flies to Turkana in a light aircraft, if they ever need to make the journey; not too many choose to drive there from Nairobi. *Carpe diem*, I thought—my motto as always; seize the day. I gratefully accepted his invitation.

'*Giorraíonn beirt bóthar, Tom, nach fíor sin?* Sure, we'll go with the flow, sounds class. Thanks a million.'

For all the inopportune events that catch me on the hop, an incredible amount also just fall straight into my lap.

Fr. Tom has been living in Turkana since the colonial days before Independence. He was one of Turkana's original pioneering missionaries in 1961, venturing into uncharted hostile territory far beyond the boundaries of both comfort and Christianity. When I inquired how he ended up in Africa, and living in Turkana of all places, this genial and modest man in his sixties replied,

'There was an inspirational priest who gave us a talk in secondary school about his life in Africa. I had never considered a vocation before then. Eventually I was assigned to Turkana. Four of my class in school are missionaries in Kenya still.'

'Any regrets?'

'Not at all! My enthusiasm for the work is still as strong today.'

I did not doubt it; he was relentlessly positive about everything.

Fr. Tom was not one for celebrity. It was left to another Irish priest in Nairobi to show me a passage in Bob Geldof's book about Africa in which St. Bob sings the praises of Fr. Tom. This was accompanied with a bit of gentle ribbing. Duly embarrassed, Fr. Tom responded.

'Ah yeah, Bob stayed with me in my home in Turkana for a few days. A gentleman while he was there. Sure, maybe you too can write a book and give me a mention when you're famous,' he joked.

Fr. Tom was tall, almost lanky, with tidy grey hair fringing a face that rarely betrayed emotion; he was as laid-back in attitude as any Akamba. He spoke with a lazy brogue, but his mind was flint-sharp and he could keep a conversation eternally fluid without effort or strain.

The first I ever heard of Turkana and its tribespeople was when Mutinda had described a tribe of 'savages' (his word) living far north in the Northern Frontier District. Nowadays, this primitive wild region, which is in the extreme northwest of Kenya, is officially called Turkana District. Fr. Liam, Sr. MM, and her visiting friends described Turkana to me as 'the Donegal of Kenya'—purely for geographical parallels, you understand!

Five days after we left Nairobi, Fr. Tom and I were almost 1,000 kilometres away in Lokichokio where he lives; it is the last village before the border with Sudan. I did not even have a change of clothes with me because I only intended being in Nairobi for two days. In fact, I really only had my toothbrush with me. With no change of clothes, I used to wash them at siesta time, and by the time I woke up again, they would be dry. Only once did an African woman catch me without my clothes on. It embarrassed me, even if she was not put out at all.

My journey to Turkana beside Fr. Tom that second week of January was riveting. The rocky road north passes up through the ever-changing panoramas of the Great Rift Valley. This is the Kenyan section of the rift system that stretches 6,000 kilometres from the Dead Sea in the Middle East to Lake Malawi in southern Africa. We were constantly climbing the valley side through a profusion of wildlife in which zebras were predominant; and then dropping back down the escarpment, as amazing and dramatic vistas opened up before us. When we crossed the equator on the second day, I spent the obligatory two minutes with a foot on both hemispheres. It was fairly cold, because we were at considerable altitude above sea level. I was really surprised to find myself in a landscape surrounded by pine trees, not the blistering sandy desert I had always imagined the equator to be.

'I actually have a certificate at home in Lokichokio to say I crossed the equator,' recalled Fr. Tom as he was taking my photo. 'I had spent well over a month as a passenger on a ship that left London back in 1961, when I first came as a missionary. That's how long it took to get here back then! The ship docked in Gibraltar and Cairo, and sailed through the Suez Canal before we landed at the port of Mombasa. It was a big deal at the time for anyone to have crossed the equator; everyone was issued with a certificate.'

On the third day out, when we reached Kitale, a town north of the equator near the Ugandan border, I visited Sr. Mary Dunne of the Medical Missionaries of Mary. Sr. MM had told me about this Donegal nun who lived in Kitale, and I was keen to meet her. Sr. Mary was running an impressive AIDS project there, having spent more than thirty years living in deepest Turkana prior to that. Sr. Mary and I agreed at the time, with a fair degree of certainty, that we were the only Letterkenny people living in the whole of Kenya then—we were the two 'Letterkenyans.'

As it happens, I knew her nephew Fr. Paddy well at home; he taught me in school. Just like Fr. Paddy, Sr. Mary was as lean as the Africans among whom she worked. She welcomed me, with a soft high lilting voice, into a modest former colonial home that now housed the Medical Missionaries' convent. Quite soon, we were doing what all Irish people do far from home; discussing all the acquaintances we had in common—in our case, around Letterkenny. Half way through our cups of tea, an African nurse from her centre interrupted us, and I had to smile when Sr. Mary spoke to her in Swahili with a strong Donegal accent. It was the first time I had heard Swahili spoken in my own accent; how the Kenyans understood a word of either of us I do not know.

As our conversation turned to the subject of AIDS, she told me,

'Some of the people attending this centre contracted AIDS through the custom whereby the brother of a woman's husband who has died (sometimes from AIDS), still demands his right to marry, or just sleep with, the widow of his recently deceased brother. The tribes who live around Kitale believe it brings bad luck upon them if the deceased husband's brother does not sleep with the widow.'

'It's the same with the Akamba people,' I pointed out.

'Naturally, we missionaries are trying to educate the people out of such customs in an attempt to prevent the spread of AIDS.'

She also told me something of the history of Kitale. It is an old white settler town built on the site of an Arab slave trading post. It is sited in the north Rift Valley and it is where the South African Boers made their last-ever great trek in ox-carts in the land rush of the early twentieth century. A hundred years ago, over a hundred families with as many wagons and horses set sail from Durban and Mozambique and landed at Mombasa. Their patriarch, J.J. Van Rensburg, had recruited families at public meetings in eastern Transvaal. Some were enticed by the exciting dream of what was said to be wild open land; others like Van Rensburg were being intimidated out for collaborating with the English during the Anglo-Boer war.

After temporarily setting up a camp in Nairobi, they faced the daunting Rift Valley terrain once they reached the Eldama

Ravine. As there were not even dirt roads to follow through the valley back then, it took them seven days to cover just ten kilometres in their wagons, cutting their way through dense forests and trudging through reptile-infested swamps. Individual Boer families continued to arrive after that, despite stricter conditions brought in by the colonial governor regarding the development of land holdings. It was an attempt to discourage further mass treks. These Boer settlers regarded themselves as 'God's Pioneers,' entering the Promised Land in which it was their divine right to settle. I was gaining insights into the colonial mindset.

'There are only handfuls of them left around Kitale nowadays,' Sr. Mary explained.

I got speaking with a few in a shop and with others while waiting at the post office. They struck me as an untamed, gungho race, or at least happy to portray themselves as such. They boasted about driving broken jeeps off cliffs—but jumping out just before the jeep disappeared into the ravine; and, more ominously, about shooting trespassers on sight on their farms. One African friend of Sr. Mary's, after she saw me conversing with them in the post office, assured me with a smile,

'Those people, they are crazy!'

I was able to appreciate their industry and stubborn persistence as I passed by fields rich in ripening crops—flat unending fields, fertile as any in Meath, which they had ploughed and harrowed out of the virgin landscape a century before. They had stuck it out through the turbulent *Mau Mau* guerrilla uprising, the uncertainty of Independence and what black rule would bring, the anxiety during the President Moi era, and the insecurity of the present day. They are still frontiersmen in a way.

CHAPTER 11 BEYOND THE BEYOND IN TURKANA

Kitale is also in many ways the last outpost of civilisation, the last frontier of the modern world. Onwards we drove through the high, narrow, twisty mountain pass beyond Kitale, our journey at times requiring *Dukes of Hazzard* style manoeuvres. I recall passing over the remnants of a bridge, forty-foot above the river-bed, that on my way back a fortnight later, I found had collapsed entirely. A lot of the concrete had been eroded in places at the edge of the structure leaving a slippery and treacherous mixture of pebbles and dust in the fragile central strip. At one point, the outer half of the wheels on both sides of Fr. Tom's pick-up were over the edge, as he struggled to get a grip on the pebbly surface. I heard a 'hmmm' sound coming from Fr. Tom as the peril of the situation struck him, followed by a resigned 'oh dear.'

It was only when we successfully reached the other side and had stepped out for a look that we exhaled a heartfelt 'phew' in harmony. Surveying the bridge from this angle, it was clearly in a much worse condition than we had realised. Looking down we noted that a lorry trying to cross the riverbed was well and truly stuck in the water below. After that hair-raising escapade, we had to strike out cross-country, partly through a parched and desolate desert landscape without even a track to follow. By now, I realised why most people choose to fly to Turkana!

At the pass into Turkana District proper, the police had placed a barrier across the road. Here we sat for a good ten minutes until one of the policemen noticed their only customer of the day had arrived. No hurry hereabouts!

On our long journey north, Fr. Tom was able to tell me something about the region. Situated in a wider section of the Rift Valley, Turkana District is bordered by the mountains of Uganda to the west, Sudan and Ethiopia to the north, and the 250km long Lake Turkana to the east. Around three million years ago, the lake area was particularly fertile, making it a centre for early humans. Richard Leakey, the famous, white-Kenyan scientist, conducted numerous anthropological digs in the area, leading to many important discoveries. In 1972, a two million year old skull uncovered was originally thought to be *Homo habilis,* but has since been assigned to a new species, *Homo rudolfensis.* In 1984, the 'Turkana Boy,' a 1.6 million year old complete skeleton of a *Homo erectus* boy was discovered (the forerunner to *Homo sapiens* or modern humans). More recently, Maeve Leakey discovered a 3.5 million year old skull there, named *Kenyanthropus platyops,* meaning 'The Flat-Faced Man of Kenya.' During the next fortnight or so that I would spend in this 'cradle of humanity,' I could not help thinking at times that the current inhabitants did not seem to have advanced much since then.

My first encounter with the Turkana people was when Fr. Tom and I were taking a break under a lone, forlorn tree in the vast lunar landscape near where we had been stopped by the police. It appeared as if there was no life at all between the distant horizon and us, save for two far-off camels. Fr. Tom was pretty sure they were wild camels. I could not get over my first sight of these camels; I was pointing like an excited child. Fr. Tom, slightly bemused by my excitement, smiled.

'Sure aren't wild camels as common a sight around here as sheep are to a Donegal man,' he quipped.

At that moment, seemingly out of nowhere (for there were certainly no people within view when we stopped at the tree), there appeared a man dressed in just a red blanket. He strode towards us, carrying an AK-47 behind his head. Behind him came a woman wearing only a goatskin skirt and adorned with multiple decorations, her head painted red. A tall bony man carrying a spear and wearing a cap apparently made from mud with an ostrich feather on top, followed up. With him were two completely naked children. To indicate our friendly intent, I reached one of the young children a banana. He bit straight into it; he did not know it had to be peeled first. He had evidently never seen one before.

Indicating they wanted a lift, as we made to go after a few minutes, they all hopped into the back of the pick-up for a few kilometres, in what may have been the only vehicle that passed that way the whole day. When they were alighting, I took out my camera to take a photo. I was keen to get a shot of these people in their natural environment, and to capture a scene that was timeless—apart from the AK-47!

Just then, as I composed the shot in my viewfinder, I had two stones hurled at me. It was the man with the spear. Unsurprised by this and in his unflustered manner, Fr. Tom explained,

'Probably best to put the camera away, Brendan. Some Turkana think a photo can hurt them.'

The words 'to take a photo' in Swahili (*ninataka kupiga picha tafadali*), inconveniently, can also mean 'to hurt.'

'They have a suspicion going back decades that a camera can also steal part of their soul. Some simply have an inherent suspicion of cameras and will not even let a fellow Turkana take a photo for this reason. At the same time, some don't mind— watch this, Brendan.'

Fr. Tom took out ten Kenyan shillings from his pocket for the man with the gun. I took a photo of them together, no problem. The Turkana were in awe when I showed them the digital image of themselves. Unlike the Akamba who enjoy being snapped, the Turkana often put aside their fear of losing their souls and ask for a few shillings to allow their photo to be taken. Talk about 'selling your soul!'

We had to keep on trucking another couple of days towards Fr. Tom's home in Lokichokio. Bouncing painfully over the hardened ruts and corrugations of the track, our progress was slow, not helped by the fact that we were loaded down with relief food in the back of the vehicle. Every so often, we were grateful for an odd patch of asphalt the Norwegian government had laid down in the 1970's, but which was never maintained. Violent sandstorms engulfed us periodically. Forty-foot high thin red columns of ant-hills were a common sight.

As we advanced further into Turkana territory, I noticed that most men seemed to be wandering around aimlessly, holding AK-47s horizontally behind their heads. I was hoping we would not encounter any of the bandits for which this frontier country is famous. Generally, though, they just smiled and waved at us, then just kept on walking to nowhere obvious in the middle of the sweltering desert.

The Kenyan government has little effective control over this area. Many Turkana people do not even grasp that they belong to a bigger country. One asked me in Swahili, a few days later,

'Did you come from Kenya, how is Kenya?'

The central authorities seem as unaware of what is going on in Turkana as the locals do about Nairobi. A colleague of Sr. MM was murdered in Turkana some time ago; she told me the court case was stopped because the police genuinely could not trace where the serving policeman at the time of the murder had been transferred.

In this searing desert landscape, Fr. Tom's home village of Lokichokio is a twenty-first century oasis—for one simple reason; the UN and every aid agency for southern Sudan is based there. Even so, the nearest decent shops for most of Turkana District are two days away by vehicle in Kitale. This is still in many respects a stone-age society. The Turkana tribespeople are mostly nomadic even today, building only a small igloo of thatch called a *manyatta* for a home.

'A common practice is that if an adult dies in the *manyatta*, the body is left there, and the whole family set up a new compound of *manyattas* some distance away,' according to Fr. Tom.

The Turkana are a war-like people; they raid the Samburu and Pokot tribes to the south for camels, donkeys, and goats to pay their dowries for marriage, usually killing a few Pokots as they go. A Turkana, who was being translated by Fr. Tom, informed me that the standard Turkana dowry is a hundred camels, fifty donkeys, and fifty goats. It sounded a bit of an exaggeration; maybe something got lost in translation! A number of times in Turkana I saw herdsmen directing herds of over a hundred donkeys. Fr. Tom was a rich source of information.

'The Pokots are afraid of the Turkana; the Turkana in turn are terrified of the Merille tribe to the north from Ethiopia. When the Merille raid, they have to take back proof that it was a male they killed—imagine, Brendan!'

I preferred not to imagine in any detail. During one particular incident in 2006, over two hundred raiders killed nineteen Turkana

NO HURRY IN AFRICA

herdsmen, and made away with 6,500 animals.

Even though they are starving, the Turkana will not kill their animals because it lessens their prestige among their own people. Since all their wealth consists of cattle, camels, and donkeys, their livestock act as their bank. Only four percent of all people in Turkana District have a cash income, and even those people are probably, for the most part, the very rare non-Turkana in the District. After his long decades in the region, Fr. Tom was like a social anthropologist with his wealth of local knowledge.

'The Turkana never thought to fish the 250km-long lake on their doorstep during all their famines, until shown how to fish by missionaries four decades ago,' he said. 'It had been taboo in Turkana society to fish before the 1960s.'

The Nile perch, a fish that grows to over six feet, is caught—I was told—by throwing pepper from the shore and making it sneeze when it jumps, so that it conks out on the rocks. I was somewhat sceptical! Away from the lakeside, the Turkana people drink blood from their herds—not uncommon among primitive peoples. Occasionally they drink urine from their cattle in a milk mixture; it is said to lower cholesterol. I did not fancy that, and I also declined the donkey meat offered on one occasion.

Turkana women are mesmerisingly beautiful. They walk tall with a majestic poise even when carrying thick five-foot long branches on their heads. Dressed in their colourful blankets and lavish adornments, many seemed to enjoy singing under trees, apparently having nothing better to do. They are decorated with extra beads and necklaces at each stage of their lives, such as marriage and child bearing. A Turkana marriage involves the mock kidnapping of the bride for a number of days. Married women have their heads shaved and painted red with ochre. When you meet them, they reveal a shy smile.

At the opening of a dispensary, I had lunch with Bishop Patrick Harrington of Turkana Diocese. He is a Society of African Missions priest from Cork, and a cousin of the golfer Pádraig Harrington. I asked him about his work.

'Keeping busy, Brendan, every day something different. Yesterday I opened a centre for the disabled built by the Diocese on the shore of Lake Turkana. Incidentally, there was a terrible tragedy on the lake very recently. Five Germans had flown to the small island in the middle of the lake to study the estimated 15,000 crocodiles living there. Their plane could not take off again. The rangers who set out in a boat to rescue them drowned in a sudden squall . . . Today, as you know, was Confirmation day, and now the new dispensary.'

Earlier, I had watched Bishop Harrington confirm a number of Turkana women and men. Despite the scorching heat, he was in his full ceremonial robes, complete with episcopal mitre and crosier. The Turkana men were dressed in their conventional diagonal blankets; they were bearing wrist knives and carrying a single piece of carved wood (ingeniously used as both a stool *and* a pillow). Some women had nearly a foot of bright beaded necklaces around their necks. In the hours of dancing and captivating tribal singing that followed, I was overawed at the spectacle of the Turkana with head decorations of feathers, leaping in their distinctive way. Their style of energetic dancing more resembles that of the Samburu or Maasai tribes, and is quite unlike the Akamba style of dancing with which I was familiar.

At Mass, the Turkana women had presented a very live and

very stubborn goat decorated in flowers to Bishop Harrington at the offertory collection. This was the kind of image of the African missionaries that I had in my head before I came to Kenya.

Whilst in Turkana I had hoped to visit Sudan, but I never made it. One reason was that the road north of Lokichokio had been cut off by flash torrents in the area. Instead of building bridges in Turkana, they lay upside-down concrete 'bridges' upon the floor of the dry sandy riverbeds. It is a lot less expensive, but they become covered over when a torrent gushes after heavy rain falls—and the rainfalls are as heavy as they are rare. For some reason, in this godforsaken corner of the world, these are called 'Irish bridges.' Fr. Tom speculated that the name might have originated because some smart-aleck thought the concept of an upside-down bridge to be 'a bit Oirish.'

As we were crossing over one of them, on our way from the dispensary to meet an Irish lady who would provide me with a lift south, Fr. Tom told me a cautionary story.

'A couple of Irish nuns were driving here when a surging flood came out of nowhere—from your left-hand-side there—on a sunny day like today,' he said as he gestured with a wave of his hand. 'It had probably rained up-country in Sudan the day before or such like. Happens occasionally. It swept their Land Rover down river a few kilometres. They survived though. One lives in Lodwar now, the other escaped to Kitale! Sr. Helen is her name; she lives there with Sr. Mary. You might meet her when you are passing through Kitale again.'

Just before Fr. Tom and I finally parted, he guided me around Kakuma Refugee Camp, situated about 100km south of Lokichokio. It is a UN Refugee Camp of some 90,000 Sudanese,

Ethiopian, and Somali refugees. I was engrossed by the sight of a vast city of tents, corrugated-iron shacks and stone buildings, with so many people living on top of each other in cramped conditions. It also made me think on how the great work of Fr. Tom and his like in such places is virtually unknown in Ireland, and on how he and Bishop Harrington probably lead a more exhilarating existence than most of us. Theirs is a fulfilling vocation, with a fresh adventure each new day.

Fr. Tom dropped me off and told me that I could get a lift going south with Deirdre, a medical doctor from Dublin, who was working at the refugee camp. It was dark by the time she arrived out of her surgery.

'Sorry, but it's too late,' she apologised. 'I won't be going anywhere tonight.'

So now, I had no way of getting out of the place, and nowhere to stay. An American priest, Fr. Peter, charitably took me in for the night at the refugee camp, where I stayed in his guestroom. Monstrous spiders were spending the night in it as well; it was no place for an arachnophobe. Fr. Peter, who speaks Arabic fluently, had fled Sudan a number of years before, during the fighting. Nowadays, his ministry is entirely for the inhabitants of the refugee camp.

Kakuma Refugee Camp has been in existence so long that some teenagers regard it as home, having been born and reared in the camp. Ironically, the refugees are better off than most Turkana outside the camp because they have food, clothes, and get a primary education. The camp still resembles a slum though, albeit a slightly better-off slum. There are a number of permanent buildings in the camp, and Fr. Peter, Dr. Deirdre, and I went for a meal that night where an entrepreneurial refugee has established an Ethiopian restaurant serving typical dishes from that country.

'The UN is having trouble getting the refugees to return home to Ethiopia, Sudan, and Somalia,' Fr. Peter informed me. 'There is relative peace is south Sudan at the moment. However, the refugees know they are guaranteed food, a small allowance and, most of all, security in the camp.'

I tried to imagine what life must be like for these displaced people. For that matter, what is life really like for the average Turkana? When I had negative thoughts about them—I was not too enamoured by the aggressive attitudes of many of the men in particular—I realised it comes down to the harsh environment in which they struggle to survive. Their problem is that the Turkana landscape in its barrenness resembles the moon; the side of the moon exposed to the merciless sun. I had landed in January, the very hottest time of year there. It tops fifty degrees Celsius in Turkana in daytime and is not a lot cooler at night. Many people, even the whites, sleep outside under the stars because of the heat. Even without a blanket, I found it was still too hot to sleep. I used to lie there at night, sweltering, listening to the shrill calls of unidentified animals, counting the falling stars and glimpsing, perhaps, a lone outdoor fire flickering in the far distance.

After getting a lift with Dr. Deirdre the next morning, I met Sr. Cecelia, a young Kikuyu Ursuline nun who had been recently transferred to Turkana from Kitui. She invited me to stay with her for several days. She lived in a tiny and exceedingly remote settlement deep in Turkana's interior, a place called Lorugumu. I ended up being stranded in Lorugumu for five days, a couple of days longer than I intended; I had no means of getting back out. But at least I had some time to explore.

Sr. Cecelia showed me the only 'attraction' in the featureless landscape around Lorugumu: the river. Wherever I went in Turkana, 'the river' always featured in conversation. When I would get to the river, it always turned out to be a dried-up sandy, stony bed where the river should be. On one visit to Lorugumu's river, I encountered a group of Turkana warriors. Some were wandering around, others just sitting under the biggest tree engaging in nothing more energetic than spitting. All were wearing wrist knives and carrying spears or AK-47s. A number of them were decorated with tattoos on their right shoulder, signifying that they had previously killed a man. I must confess that I was feeling a little uneasy.

While we were sitting there, a schoolgirl in obvious distress came along the riverbank to find Sr. Cecelia. The schoolgirl appeared to be very weak. Sr. Cecelia explained to me that she was suffering from the effects of a DIY abortion that had been induced using some concoction that included tea leaves (of all things). Sr. Cecelia arranged to meet me back at the school later, as she hurried away to deal with this potential tragedy—a not uncommon one, apparently.

Up at the school, I got chatting with the principal, who described some of the other problems they encountered. There was one, in particular, that I thought we would not come across at home.

'A government official visited this school to give out compulsory ID cards to everyone over eighteen,' he explained. 'Some students protested they were over eighteen, and admitted that they had lied to us that they were a younger age in order to be allowed attend. "Hard luck," they were told by the official, "that is the age on your school cert and that is the age that you will stick with the rest of your life.'"

Bureaucracy is bureaucracy, I thought to myself, even beyond the beyond.

Once Sr. Cecelia rejoined us, she complained, 'Some Turkana people are keen enough on education—but they want me to pay *them* for the privilege of me teaching them at the school.'

I agreed that this did seem a bit upside down.

'And I am an embroidery teacher,' she laughed. 'These people don't even want to wear clothes!'

At the beginning of a Mass late that afternoon, some of the congregation stood up when I entered from the back because they thought I was the priest. I was amused at the mistake, as I always was. A teenage Turkana boy, two rows in front of me, fainted during the Gospel, either from the heat or hunger, I presumed. Towards the end of the service, a Turkana woman outside began throwing stones onto the tin roof of the church. It made quite a din. She had been refused communion for reasons I was not privy to.

The following day a crowd of children in Lorugumu, half of them absolutely naked, followed me around doing impressions of me walking and talking. All of a sudden, I did a cartwheel on the sand and they fell about laughing. This happened a few times. On one such occasion, a twelve-year-old boy wearing only an AK-47 and nothing else at all warned them to leave me alone. I had been enjoying the fun, but I was not going to argue with a naked twelve-year-old wielding a loaded AK-47.

CHAPTER 11 BEYOND THE BEYOND IN TURKANA

In amongst the gang of boys was one named Séamus—of all names! I could only attribute it to the Irish missionary influence. Sr. Cecelia knew most in this trailing pack, which by this stage had expanded to over fifty children.

'The parents of many of them died of hunger,' she explained. 'They are now orphans being looked after by cousins.'

It was not only the children who were stark naked. I observed a surprisingly large number of adults just walking around in their pelts at certain times of day. I appeared to be the only one who even seemed to notice.

On my third night in Lorugumu, there was another of those surreal scenes to which I was becoming accustomed. Outside, under a glorious sky full of bright twinkling stars, I was listening to Count John McCormack evocatively singing *Oft in the Stilly Night* on a tape recorder. Suddenly, silently, there appeared out of the darkness five Turkana people, three of them naked, another one wearing skins and a half-foot of colourful beads around her neck, and yet another dressed in a purple blanket and carrying a staff and wooden headrest. All had come to listen rather be- musedly to this strange music. The great Irish tenor can rarely have had such a bizarre audience.

Through Sr. Cecelia, who was translating, they began telling me that they had discovered that morning the footprints of a thief in the sand. They had cupped the footprints in their hands and put a curse on each one so that the thief would writhe in pain until he returned what he had stolen the night before. This I knew well to be true, as I had heard of similar witchcraft prac- tices on many occasions, especially around Kitui.

Perhaps charmed by the music, they had become very talkative. They went on to tell Sr. Cecelia that if they see a snake, a scorpion or a spider at night, then someone has sent it with a vendetta against them. They disclosed that human sacrifice was not unknown among the Turkana up to the recent past. My scepticism kicked in, however, when they suggested that the human who was being sacrificed regarded it as a privilege. An Akamba in Nuu had told me a similar story about human sacrifice before. Thankfully, it seems nowadays to have vanished among the animist tribal religious practices. However, stories do appear in the Kenyan newspapers now and again of humans being sacrificed by devil worshippers in caves.

I met some real characters among the missionaries in Turkana—like the gigantic German priest who famously tamed a wild camel and now follows the nomadic people on it, as they in turn follow their animals; or the Irish nuns who pilot light aircraft full of sick patients. The Irish missionaries are nearly the second biggest tribe in Turkana. Some nationalities, such as the Germans or Americans, often like to 'go native,' and attempt to live in the exact same manner as the Africans. The Irish on the other hand will always act and dress as the Irish always did, sometimes sporting a pipe and flat cap; but arguably, they go native more genuinely by being long-term residents who learn the tribal languages and understand their customs. I could risk a generalisation: some other nationalities act African for a while; the Irish missionaries interact with the Africans over decades.

The Irish missionaries in Kenya have nearly all developed a peculiar but gentle humour at the expense of the Kenyans, because Kenyans would always take our irony seriously. I heard Fr. Tom teasing the Kenyan accountant of the cash-strapped mission-hospital in Kakuma,

'Is the hospital still running at full capacity . . . are there people still getting sick?'

The rhetorical question, God knows, did not require a literal answer. But the accountant in all seriousness began telling us about cholera and the like, instead of twigging he was really being asked if there would ever be enough money to run all the services.

The accountant led us to another room in the hospital where three people were having tea, and as I shook hands with them, the accountant introduced me to each one.

'This is the manager . . . and this man is the director . . . and he is the administrator.'

'Ah, it's the holy trinity. Who's actually in charge here?' Fr. Tom wondered mischievously.

'I am,' came the affirmation in unison from all three.

We both smiled.

I indulged myself with a bit of irony on occasions. Kenyans cannot grasp that people might want to go walking for leisure, something I often liked to do in Kenya, especially to wander in the relative cool of dusk. So when they asked in Swahili,

'Where are you going?'

'I'm walking to Nairobi,' I used to reply for amusement.

'And what time will you arrive?' they would then ask.

Nairobi is close to 1,000km away from Turkana. The light in Turkana, incidentally, played tricks on my walks at dusk, making the desert appear cloaked white with snow. That was pretty surreal, given the temperature at the time.

Despite this tendency to make fun, the Irish missionaries

command genuine respect in Kenya. In this remote northern region, they are often the only people helping the Turkana for hundreds of miles around. One of the exceptions was a gung-ho Dutch priest who drove me to Lodwar, the capital of Turkana. After five days in Lorugumu, I had finally managed to arrange a lift in his pick-up. Before setting out, Sr. Cecelia had entrusted me with a letter to deliver to Sr. MM when I returned to Kitui, whenever that would be, as there is not really a postal service in Kenya worth speaking of. I promised I would, thanked her for her superb hospitality, and we bade farewell to each other. Sr. Cecelia was a remarkable young woman who manifested many of the best qualities of her Kikuyu tribe: industry, ingenuity, resoluteness and a can-do attitude.

With what seemed like half the population of Lorugumu in the back of the pick-up, we headed east across the sands with hardly any track to follow. Lodwar is a few hours east of Lorugumu. It is also, I concluded, at the centre of the end of the earth.

I planned to stay only one more day in Turkana. Considering it was only bright between 6am and 6pm, and I could only move around before 8am and after 5pm because of the heat, and considering that I never woke up before 8am, you could say that Turkana forced me out. The heat was utterly debilitating. It felt like the hottest place north of the South Pole. At times, it was so hot you could not think straight. I briefly became confused with the date when I bought a *Daily Nation* in Lodwar, before being reminded that whatever date is on the newspaper in remote places, it is never today's!

I managed to get locked in the post office that day in Lodwar. I had been writing away on an aerogramme at the back of the building and was unnoticed when they locked up. Nor did *I* notice they were locking up. But I figured someone would be along presently.

'*Unafanya nini hapa?*' (what are you doing in here?), was the shocked reaction of the postmaster when he returned from a long break.

He shook his head; I waved the aerogramme at him with a grin. At this prompt, he remembered me coming in. He apologised, laughing loudly. My imprisonment had been as much my fault as his.

Upon my release from the post-office, I hired the rusty taxi parked beside Lodwar's only petrol station.

'*Twende bwana,*' I urged the driver (let's go, sir).

He took my fare before we started out so he could fill up with enough petrol to see him through until his next fare, even though it was only a five-minute ride. On the way, I enquired about the bus out of Turkana back to the twentieth century in Kitale (the twenty-first century would have to wait until I reached Nairobi).

'And at what time does the bus leave?' I wanted to know.

'Six in the morning . . . well by midday anyway!' came the reply.

On my way back down to Kitale, on the rickety bus heading south through the Rift Valley and over the tight mountain passes, I had time to reflect on my Turkana experience. I did not fully understand all the stories I had heard about Turkana until I ventured there myself. The place is indeed enthralling. But the land is harsh, the lifestyle primitive, the character of the people savage—the product of a truly savage environment. The Turkana, albeit in my limited experience, were not a pleasant people at all.

NO HURRY IN AFRICA

There were too many Kalashnikovs. Some were aggressive to me, as they are to their own and to neighbouring tribes. If someone is too weak to keep moving in the desert, they are said to abandon that person rather too hastily for the sake of their own survival. There is, reportedly, no word for 'thank you' in their language, and nearly every one of them greeted me with 'accaro' ('hungry' in the Turkana language), while holding out their hand. I became fed up with this constant begging; so when I was convinced they said it automatically, I would shake their hand and reply 'accaro' back, as if it meant hello. That really confused them.

Now, heading south again on the bus towards a more civilised world, I could turn my thoughts to other, more pleasant things. I was always intrigued by the unusual names on the shops in Kenya. I had to wonder about the gender of the owner of the shop named 'Mama Harry' that we stopped at. We ate lunch at the 'Coastal Dot Com Shop,' an establishment without electricity right in the middle of a remote inland desert. It was serving 'Bosnia Chips.' Whatever else these people lack, I thought, not for the first time, imagination is not one of them!

CHAPTER 12
WAKING UP IN THE 'WHITE HIGHLANDS'

IT WAS NOW LATE JANUARY. Returning from Turkana, my mobile phone picked up a signal near Kitale; I received a call from Kiragu. He enquired how I was getting on.

'Will you be returning to Nyumbani?' he asked, and then, inevitably, 'Your services are still needed.'

'Yes, of course. I'm on my way back to Kitui,' I explained. 'My travels are going well, the perfect remedy for the way I was feeling. So how is Nyumbani?'

'We are still progressing on many aspects of it. An American engineer joined us yesterday as a volunteer. You will get on well with him, Brendan.'

He was being persuasive, but I did not commit myself to a date for returning just yet. He wished me well for my travels in Swahili.

'Nenda salama.'

'Asante, tuonana (thanks, see you again),' I gave the stock reply.

I had allowed myself time for a bit more touring before returning to Kitui. Maybe another couple of weeks or so—it was up to me really. I wanted to travel and see more of this remarkable country, but I was also eager to volunteer again. I had no definite plans as such, and was taking it easy, one day at a time.

NO HURRY IN AFRICA

There was so much variety to Kenya; everywhere I chanced upon was different. It was like several countries in one, a rich mosaic of very diverse cultures and landscapes. I was always inquisitive, eager to explore and to venture further. I wanted to grasp every opportunity on offer.

I stopped for a couple of nights in Kitale again on my way back down south. There I met Bishop Maurice Crowley of Kitale Diocese, an impressive, heavily built, Irish Kiltegan priest, a man with obvious leadership qualities. He spoke to me enthusiastically about developments in Kitale, despite the chronic lack of resources in the Diocese. He was proud of the number of schools and health centres and other projects they had managed to develop and operate to meet the pressing needs of the people. He was not just proud of their achievements to date, but full of ambitious plans for the future as well.

Bishop Crowley's cathedral in Kitale, a very modest structure with makeshift benches, must compete strongly for the title of the smallest cathedral in the entire world. Another Irish priest, Fr. Gabriel Dolan, was celebrating Mass that day. When it came to the collection, I saw people handing up everything from pineapples, to a sharp knife, to old golf balls, to a bicycle bell.

I got talking to Fr. Dolan, a feisty young Kiltegan from Fermanagh, who had narrowly avoided prison and deportation on several occasions for speaking out on behalf of Kitale's poor. Just before I departed for Kenya, my parents had pointed out an article about him in the *Irish Times*. Having protested courageously on behalf of some of his deprived parishioners, he had to leave Kenya for his own safety and lie low in Ireland until the fuss died down.

CHAPTER 12 WAKING UP IN THE 'WHITE HIGHLANDS'

At an impromptu dinner that evening to celebrate the birthday of one of the other missionary priests, Bishop Crowley recalled the incident.

'An MP for Kitale sent in the army in an attempt to grab land for himself that a slum had been built on. Gabriel led a protest, which developed into a riot. He had to dodge tear gas and bullets and be hidden in people's homes in the slums for a few days while the police searched for him. He handed himself in at the end.'

'Sure I was let out after a couple of days,' Fr. Dolan interjected, slightly embarrassed by being cast in a heroic role.

But it was pointed out that white priests have been 'bumped off' before in Kenya, allegedly in government sponsored 'accidents,' after remonstrating too loudly for the poor.

'That was during the governments of President Moi in the 1980s and 1990s. It wouldn't happen now, I think,' said Fr. Dolan.

He paused for a moment.

'Do you know, though, the most bizarre bumping off in Kenya probably occurred in 2005, when the white Bishop of Isiolo was murdered,' he recalled, at the prompt of Bishop Crowley. 'Two of his own African priests have since been brought to court charged with his murder.'

I started thinking that there must be a lot less perilous lifestyles than being a missionary in Africa.

The next morning, I decided to call in to see Sr. Mary Dunne again.

'You look a little shook, Brendan,' she greeted me anxiously. 'Are you alright? Sit down and I'll bring you in a cup of tea.'

'I was on the back of a *boda-boda* (bicycle-taxi) flying down the hill to your place when a donkey suddenly walked out in front and caused a six-bike collision. It sent about twelve of us flying,' I explained.

These are not even bicycle rickshaws, mind; this is simply sitting pillion on the back of a Chinese boneshaker. The man pedalling my *boda-boda* had been attempting every trick going to persuade me to take a ride.

'It's an air-conditioned bicycle,' he announced rather implausibly, 'especially for the *mzungu,* twenty shillings only.'

'Oh, and how much is it without the air-conditioning?' I teased him.

'It doesn't have any. I was cheating you. Thirty shillings is still the price.'

Well that little joke backfired, I mused. He had upped the price after taking out the phantom air-conditioning from the offer. I hopped on the cushion on the back of the bicycle but had barely a chance to grip the saddle before he started off again.

'God showed me in a dream two weeks ago that I must found my own church to spread his message. I had a vision, that you, a *mzungu,* would ride my bicycle today, and that I must show you the way to save your soul.'

He was puffing continuously as he pedalled uphill.

'The Lord has provided me with this opportunity to help you,' he gasped. 'I must direct you to the light of God . . . puff, puff. . . Do you want a place in heaven, *mzungu?* . . . puff, puff . . . Are you ready for Jesus?'

By now, we had breasted the hill and were picking up speed on the way down when, providentially perhaps, the donkey walked out in front of us.

CHAPTER 12 WAKING UP IN THE 'WHITE HIGHLANDS'

'I'm feeling better now though, thanks,' I assured Sr. Mary. 'It was just a slight shock.'

Sr. Mary was letting out several little yelps of laughter throughout this story as I was telling it. The conversation took a more serious turn when she added,

'As it happens, the train in Kitale killed one *boda-boda* rider crossing the tracks a few days ago.'

'Sure they probably stoned the train,' quipped another Irish nun named Sr. Helen who had joined us, as lynching is the custom whenever a car knocks someone down.

I told them about witnessing a near lynching in Kwa Vonza when we were waiting for Mutinda's coffin. Sr. Helen too had witnessed something similar; indeed she had had a close shave herself only recently when a *boda-boda* rider had cycled out in front of her.

'I'm a white woman; anything could have happened. It's very frightening,' she concluded.

Sr. Mary offered me a lift from Kitale to Eldoret about a hundred kilometres to the south, when I mentioned I was heading that way; she had some business to attend to there. Sr. Helen came with us in the car. The latter was a well-spoken Munster woman in her sixties who had been working in Kenya as a nurse for decades. The two of them took turns regaling me with stories of their adventures when they used to fly a light aircraft around Turkana treating sick patients.

'We sometimes had to land the plane in the dry sandy riverbeds,' Sr. Helen recalled. 'It was the only safe place to land a lot of the time. In all the years though, there was only one time I crashed it, trying to land it at night. Mary here and Fr. Tom—

you know him, don't you, Brendan?—had their two jeeps on the ground at either end with the headlights on to show up our makeshift runway in the dark. But there were about ten camels in the way that none of us could see. To avoid them I hit a tree and broke the wing off.'

'We still saved the lives of that woman and her baby though, do you remember Helen?' Sr. Mary recounted with pride. 'She was giving birth, and we were supposed to airlift her to Lodwar. We treated her successfully in her home instead, with the few medicines and instruments we had to hand.'

'We didn't save the plane. It was a write-off,' Sr. Helen reminded her.

'Aye, but it was due retirement anyway. Sure that plane must have been older than us,' Sr. Mary chuckled. 'You know, Brendan, you think Turkana is like the Stone Age, and it probably is in some of the parts you were in. But you should have seen it forty years ago before they had ever encountered a person from the outside world. You would really have been amazed. The place could be reached only with the greatest difficulty. It took weeks on camels even to get there. Every single one of the Turkana people was in animal skins—or wore nothing at all. They only had spears back then, though; there were none of the guns around. Even Lodwar . . . Kitale was London by comparison. But Turkana was so special in its own unique way.'

I could hardly begin to imagine. I had nothing but the greatest respect for these spirited women, on life-saving missions for so many years landing a light aircraft at night in the desolation that is Turkana. As we finally parted, I knew I had been fortunate to share the company of two extraordinary women. I thanked them

CHAPTER 12 WAKING UP IN THE 'WHITE HIGHLANDS'

for the lift, they wished me well, and with fond goodbyes, I set foot in the metropolis (comparatively speaking) of Eldoret.

Eldoret is Kenya's fifth biggest town. It is in mainly Kalenjin tribal lands. The town was founded on that particular site simply because one particular white settler did not take up his allotted land. As the settlement expanded, it became the urban centre for the white colonists of its hinterland, a fair number of whom remained on scattered farms after Independence.

There is an elderly Irish missionary in Eldoret, Fr. Brennan, who is still working hard in Kenya since he landed off the boat in Mombasa way back in 1951. When I was introduced to him, he jocularly lamented,

'I would have been the very first Kiltegan missionary in Kenya, but for the fact that my only comrade on the boat managed to race off the gangplank in front of me!'

That was over half a century ago. A lot of rival missionaries in Eldoret have been very busy in the meantime, however. I noted the following establishments in town; there was 'The Growth Church,' 'The Friends Church,' 'The Happy Church'—and my favourite, 'The Winners Church.' I suspect I know who the real winners could be, I thought, before banishing such a cynical thought from my mind.

Since I started touring at the end of December, I had been discovering vital facts about life in Kenya. All sorts of facts. I was to learn more in Eldoret. For instance, the prostitutes are Kenya's best pool players. And an extraordinary number of them seem to be called Brenda! Some of them had great difficulty accepting that my name was Brendan.

'Stop trying to make fun of me, *mzungu*,' one Brenda scowled one night in a bar in Eldoret.

I was having the craic that evening with three American Peace Corps volunteers. Every girl in the bar seemed to be moonlighting as a prostitute. In reality, as I knew from Mombasa, nearly all of these women are opportunistic 'good-time girls' who spot the chance for a bit of extra money, and are not full-time 'professionals' at all. They can be very demanding and very persistent, though. Noticing that the 'Brendas' were put off by my revealing my name, one of the Peace Corps commented light-heartedly,

'If only it was that easy to lose the attention of all the rest of them!'

He went by the nickname Top Cat, a slightly geeky lad with many piercings. Not one of the four of us actually beat any of the girls at pool the entire evening, no matter how hard we tried to rig the rules in our favour.

A weighing scales in Eldoret revealed a further, somewhat ironic fact: somehow, unbeknownst to me, I was still getting heavier! Contrary to what my friends at home claimed later, this fact was in no way related to the famine. One of the Peace Corps named Amy, a blonde girl from Alabama who was 'All-American' in looks and personality, was surprised to hear I was gaining weight.

'Have you been at the dog food?' she asked, enigmatically, and then explained. 'In Kapsabet village, where I am normally based—it's about twenty kilometres west of Eldoret—the people recently fed their dogs instead of their children,' she told us. 'You see, Chinese workers were coming to build a road in Kapsabet, which was being paid for by the Chinese government. The Kenyans heard that the Chinese loved eating dog meat, and they thought they would make good money from selling their plump dogs. The Chinese when they came did not buy a single one. The Kenyans were left with fat dogs and bony children!'

I met up with her and the other Peace Corps in Eldoret more or less by arrangement; I had met them previously when they stayed for a few days in Kitui before Christmas as part of their training for their two years of service. They had invited me to stay with them if ever I was passing through Eldoret. It was great to have the company now and again of young white people; they were such a rarity in these parts.

The third Peace Corps volunteer, a gangly, shaven-headed drifter from Chicago by the name of Matt, immediately took up Amy's story about the dogs.

'It's ironic, but around the same time in early January,' and here he showed me a cutting from the *Daily Nation,* 'a New Zealand pet-food factory owner sent over a plane full of dog food to this same region as a contribution to famine relief. The people were eating away at the dog food until the government told them to stop.'

I spent the first fortnight of February in the Eldoret region, touring around the scenic Highlands region of the west. They use donkey-and-cart in this region instead of ox-and-cart as in Kitui, and a number of times I was coaxed into taking a lift on one when I was walking around. I was always delighted to accept, and I would find myself leaning back against the heavy ricks of hay overflowing from the carts. On the subject of donkeys, Matt made me read another one of his rich collection of outlandish newspaper cuttings. I read about an organisation in London that, in their wisdom, had decided to donate £100,000stg in January to stop cruelty to donkeys in Kenya, right at the very height of the famine.

'The English are great animal lovers, yeah?' was Matt's comment.

Top Cat warmed to the theme of injustice and complained, 'Fields of sugar-cane and other crops were lying unharvested in the Highlands because there was no market for the cane, while other drought-stricken regions like Kitui could not grow a thing and people starved.'

In fact, throughout the famine, there was food and money in the country, but it was all centred on Nairobi. I was able to draw parallels with the situation in Ireland during the Great Famine of the 1840s.

This region of Kenya became known as the 'White Highlands' during the colonial era. No Africans or Indians were allowed own land there—only Europeans could. The 'White Highlands' roughly stretched from Kitale in the north, to Kisumu in the west, Naivasha in the south and Mount Kenya in the east. It straddled both sides of the Great Rift Valley. At the beginning of the twentieth century British aristocrats, adventurers, speculators, fugitives, and former soldiers flooded into this region as settlers, because of its agreeable mild climate and fertile soil. The best part, from the settlers' perspective, was that they often found it empty of human habitation—and dense with relatively tame game animals for hunting. Unfortunately, what the Europeans did not know—or perhaps chose not to find out—was that the African pastoralists used the land on a seasonal basis; the pastoralists' livestock was their only wealth and without animal dowries, they could not marry. Moreover, the game animals were quickly being exterminated as well.

The settlers peaked at over 80,000 in the 1950s, and were led by the eccentric Lord Delamere. Princess Elizabeth awakened one morning in a safari lodge in these highlands back in 1952 to be informed that her father had passed away, and that she was now Queen Elizabeth II of the British Empire (what was left of it). The current Lord Delamere is still one of the biggest landowners in Kenya with an estate of 100,000 acres in the Rift Valley. Only the former President Moi, a native of the Eldoret area, owns more land than Lord Delamere.

There are only around 25,000 whites in the whole country today. There was a voluntary mass exodus in the years immediately after Independence in 1963. However, President Kenyatta had the foresight to appoint a white Minister for Agriculture in his first cabinet, thus avoiding an economic meltdown as happened in Zimbabwe in recent years, when Robert Mugabe commandeered the white-owned farms by force.

Matt, Amy, Top Cat, and I took a trip by bus to Iten, about an hour north-east of Eldoret. Iten is a rather nondescript one-street Highland village that just happens to be the centre of Kenyan long-distance running. The athletes have the advantage of growing-up at high altitude and of training there as well. This area is home to the Kalenjin tribes who account for nearly all of the famous Olympic long-distance runners from Kenya. Up in Iten, a small Kenyan girl kept running after us with a dirty battered Barbie doll.

'Amy, she thinks you are the Barbie doll!' Matt laughed. 'She is trying to give it back to you.'

The village's other claim to fame is that it sits on a precipice, with a 2,000-foot drop straight down to the floor of the Kerio Valley below.

While we were up there, one of the locals told me about an Irish missionary who trains some of the elite Kenyan athletes. Cork-born Brother Colm O'Connell is a world celebrity in athletic circles. He is headmaster of St Patrick's High School where several Olympic athletes have had their talent spotted and nurtured; he has given them the opportunity to excel on the world stage. Among his many protégés are Peter Rono (Olympic 1500m champion, 1988), Wilson Kipketer (800m world record holder), and Boit Kipketer (former world steeplechase record holder).

I called at Brother O'Connell's home but, unfortunately, he was not there that day. I could not help but notice that he had made his garden to be almost identical to a rural Irish garden—except that his hydrangea bushes and chrysanthemums and other plants were in full bloom in February. An African priest gave me a cup of tea. Later that afternoon, he also offered the four of us a lift back down to Eldoret in his thirty-year-old Peugeot.

The Peace Corps were working on various projects around Eldoret. Accompanying them gave me a feel for the town. Eldoret town centre is alive, dirty, chaotic, and exciting—if one hits the right places. It is a town where pigs meander randomly around the shoe-shiners in the town centre, and where men sit outside sharpening knives on foot-powered stone-wheels.

'Anyone fancy camping in Kakamega Rainforest for the weekend?' Matt enquired as we sauntered through the streets. 'It's only a few hours west of Eldoret. It is the only piece of rainforest left in Kenya today.'

We all immediately jumped at the idea; the rainforest

sounded exotic.

'I'll call a few others and see if they're interested. I've been dying to go there,' Matt enthused.

There were seven of us who went in the end. The first day we went trekking with an African ranger from Eldoret that Matt knew, who pointed out different kinds of monkey that apparently live nowhere else in Kenya. A lot of them looked the same to me, but my favourites were the black and white ones with the feathery tails. There was such a profusion of wildlife. There were elaborately festooned birds and a snowfall of thousands of white butterflies dancing in the sunlight. When the forest birds and animals spotted us, they tended to scamper, making any photography difficult.

We were all supposed to cram into the single tent we were sharing. But we stayed up all night; no one was ever going to get to sleep in our tiny two-person tent. Matt strummed songs on his guitar to the backdrop of laughter at Top Cat's amusingly unamusing one-liners. A different ranger, who had more chips on his shoulder than a chip shop could muster, silenced us just before dawn. Matt could not wait for dawn; and persuaded us to follow him through the rainforest in the pitch dark. He promised us 'a surprise.'

He did not disappoint. Dawn was truly spectacular. As the darkness of night withdrew, a deep-gold sun rose over the forested valley. Our vantage point atop a high cliff gave us a panoramic view as fluffy white clouds tinged with gold ascended from below. The exotic sounds of the forest fauna started up all around us. It was unforgettable. After that, everything else would be a bit of an anti-climax. We played at being Tarzan for the rest of the day—swinging on vines, climbing out onto branches, and falling into a stream. A couple of times, Amy called out, 'Is that a monkey?' when she spotted something rustling the vegetation. It only turned out to be shy local children collecting sticks.

'Proof you're from Alabama anyway,' I teased Amy.

Amy had heard of a place that she said would be worth a visit.

'It's not far from the rainforest,' she began. 'Apparently there is an odd looking thirty-foot high vertical cylinder of rock protruding from the ground with water gushing from a big boulder resting on top. It is known as the "crying stone," because in some ways it resembles tears seeping from the head of a person. They say it never stops weeping, even through droughts.'

Top Cat, who had actually seen it, interrupted.

'It looks more like a particular male body part!' he said, lowering the tone.

Amy ignored that one and enlightened me with a bit of background on the stone that she had heard from the local Africans.

'The Nandi tribe south of Kakamega even tried to knock it down when they ransacked the place during a raid a long time ago. They failed in their attempt. It's pseudo-sacred to the locals now. They revere it as a symbol of defiance against their enemies.'

I simply had to go and see it to satisfy my curiosity when I was this close. Bidding farewell to the Americans, I struck out on my own. Well, I thought I was close, but I ended up walking for two hours to get to it. Apparently, it only 'cries' in the wet season, or so a local informed me when I reached the spot at last. I ended up just staring at a tall grey column of rock. I suppose it was mildly impressive in a way.

Often in Kenya I was told, 'No, it is better in the dry season, come back then.'

Or else, as that local told me, 'No, no, no, you must see it in the rainy season. Fly back from your country then to see this rock.'

Worth seeing, yes. Worth going to see? No—as Dr. Johnson famously said about the Giant's Causeway.

After that episode, it was another few hours on the bus heading south through green hills and down a steep valley to be surprised by the sudden appearance of Kisumu City on the shores of Lake Victoria. Lake Victoria is bigger than Ireland. Since the lake's formation 400,000 years ago, it has dried up completely on three different occasions, the last time being around 15,000 years ago. Water levels have again been dropping over the last century. At first sight, the main occupation of people in Kisumu appeared to be backing their cars into the water for a wash . . . and their bicycles, and really just about anything else that needed washing.

I ordered food in a café near the Lake. After my earlier exertions, I was famished. It was going to take a while, though; once I made my choice from the limited menu, the waiter set off down the street to buy the ingredients for my meal at the outdoor market! The running joke among the Irish was, if you ordered chicken, you had to wait for an egg to hatch first. I was in no rush. After that, I bought some sizzling corn-on-the-cob from a woman along the roadside, and was all set to go again. I was not intending to stay overnight in Kisumu.

As I strolled down to the bus depot munching on my corn-on-the-cob, I spotted the ubiquitous crazy man dancing around.

No Hurry in Africa

He had bright eyes and a wide toothless grin, and was shouting a passage from the bible to me while he grasped my arm, smiled, and patted my shoulder. Then he jumped around dementedly. There was always one in every Kenyan community. So I was glad when, moments later, I encountered a group of a dozen or so Americans of mixed ages. They greeted me in a friendly manner, and offered to give me a lift in their own private bus onwards to Londiani, where I was heading. Some of them reminded me of the Peace Corps at first, so we began to chat. I should have known better. To my complete lack of surprise, within five minutes, one teenage lad piped up,

'We are members of the MCCB representing the CAAC, which is sponsored by ACBM,' as if I was supposed to know what any of that stood for, though by now I suspected some of the 'C's were for 'Christian.'

I did not really get a chance to ask, because they immediately launched into a tag-team monologue for my benefit.

'It is sooo great to be in Africa, helping people find God through the person of J.C.'

Jeez, I sighed to myself, irreverently, for I knew full well where this was leading. It had dawned on me that I still had to be 'saved'—in their eyes.

'And you know the really aaahsome part,' a young woman around my own age quickly swooped, 'is that it is also helping *me* to find God when I help *them* to find God. We are all Christ's children. It's truly aaahsome! God wants each of us to share his love with others.'

They were waiting in vain for me to engage with them on this. I was not about to.

CHAPTER 12 WAKING UP IN THE 'WHITE HIGHLANDS'

'Are you one of Christ's children?' a middle-aged man who was a dead-ringer for Senator Ted Kennedy chimed in.

'Yes,' was my one-syllable honest response, hoping that would placate them.

It did not. After several more minutes, by which time we had reached their bus, I piped up,

'No, I really think I might stay in Kisumu tonight. Change of plan. Thanks anyway for the offer of a lift.'

Just over an hour later, the service bus I was on painstakingly overtook them at just about the same pace as their own bus. The result was that all the Americans had a good long clear view of me sitting in a window seat heading for Londiani. They stared; one or two of them gave a nod and a wee wave of recognition—before the expression on their faces suddenly altered.

After travelling over 100km east of Kisumu, I reached the village of Londiani just as it was getting dark. Londiani is a former white settler village, sitting right on the equator line. No settlers live there now, and it is long past its heyday. The village has a distinctive look, consisting of clusters of wooden huts with rusty tin roofs, and a bumpy cobbled road that crosses some very suspect wooden bridges. The road itself was built by Italian PoWs during World War II, and is still in its original condition. I only intended to stay one night there with three Irish missionaries whom I had met some weeks earlier, when I was travelling up to Turkana with Fr. Tom. They were a good laugh, as we say, and I ended up staying several days.

Londiani is not far from Kericho, which is well known as the heart of the Kenyan 'tea country'; this is where a lot of our tea in Ireland comes from.

NO HURRY IN AFRICA

'Only the Irish drink more tea per person than the Kenyans,' a plantation guide informed me as the two of us strolled around.

However, Kenyans tend to make their tea in a flask of boiled milk with a few tea leaves and as much sugar as they have available thrown in. It occurred to me that Kericho, founded just after 1900 on the edge of the 'White Highlands,' resembled many of the plantation towns of Ulster; it has a central diamond and a large grey-stone Anglican church dominating the main street.

At the same tea plantation in Kericho, I was given samples of nearly a dozen different types of tea. The differences in how each type is grown, picked and processed were explained to me in intricate detail. There were teas of various colours, and teas with all manner of herbs, flowers, spices and fruits added. They all tasted much the same to my uneducated palate. Outside on the tea plantation, I was really struck by the dozens of women, visible from the waist up, working among the dense tea plants, like animated figures in a dark green carpet. They were busy picking leaves by hand and dropping them into creel-type baskets carried on their backs. Only months after my visit did they begin to automate the picking process; this was strongly opposed by the workers who feared losing their incomes. Fortunately, local people with small landholdings run many of the tea plantations around Kericho as co-operative ventures.

Even this area was not well-off, however. In the middle of this attractive tea country, amongst tidy uniform fields covering the gently rolling hillsides, children were on their knees, scooping water into their mouths a foot from where their cow was also drinking. I might have felt sorry, but Kenyans could sometimes bleed my goodwill dry when I was travelling around the country, unlike the Akamba people back at base.

'*Mzungu,* give me money because my wife has to go to hospital,' said one man.

I donated a few shillings. It was not much; I found it hard to turn people down outright.

'*Mzungu,* I need money for my wife's funeral,' he pleaded the next day.

The day after that, he needed money again.

'My wife, she has given birth to my son.'

I had no difficulty identifying him; he was wearing a Bellaghy GAA tracksuit-top! Second-hand clothes like that are sent over from charity shops in Ireland. A Kenyan buys them for a few shillings, and then sells them on again at a roadside stall for a few shillings extra.

I had long ago learned to be wise to some of their hard luck stories, but I still found them exasperating at times. Even if one does some Kenyans a favour, they *expect* another favour instead of seeing it as a once off. There is a great saying in East Africa that goes, 'Teach Ugandans Swahili, teach Tanzanians English, and teach Kenyans manners.' Kenyans are quick to forget a favour (but, to their credit, they are equally quick to forget an argument). I realised the Akamba are different in that way; tribal differences can be really pronounced. The Akamba are a proud people, nearly always smiling, really laid back, something rather Irish about them—and they would tend to conceal from me the fact they were starving. I was looking forward to living amongst them again in Kitui.

On the way to Kitui in the middle of February, I had to make another trip to the immigration office in Nairobi. After being in

Turkana and other remote places, entering Nairobi seemed like entering New York. The big city, as always, positively throbbed with life. Miraculously, I was informed that I actually had got one of the rare approvals the government gives for a work permit. The only problem was the permit would cost a small fortune, and I was not even receiving a stipend at Nyumbani. So I sat a while pondering my next move in the city's equivalent to London's Hyde Park, called Uhuru Park (which means 'Freedom Park'). It is the focal point of every demonstration or celebration in Kenya, and is a park of dusty paths bordered with barbed wire; and there are sizable gaps in the wooden footbridges over the streams.

Later on that afternoon, I got my hair cut at 'The Hure House' (not at all what it sounds), and stayed overnight at the 'Blessed Hotel & Butchery.' I was not butchered, but I was not sure what meat I was eating! The next morning, rather surreally, I walked by and said hello to a Maasai wearing a red blanket, herding his cattle under Nairobi's glass skyscrapers; like many others, he had come into the city to find water for his herd during the drought. Towards dusk, I was chased down Kenyatta Avenue, the main street of Nairobi, being loudly denounced as a devil worshipper—all because my t-shirt read 'Daredevil Show,' with an innocent picture of a cartoon dog wearing goggles flying a looping airplane. Where else would it happen but Nairobi? A big deal is made at any hint of devil worship in Kenya, as there have been incidents of children being sacrificed in caves just outside Nairobi—if the press were to be believed.

The same day I made a five-second appearance during the news on Kenyan television. I was a spectator observing a colour-ful political march on Kenyatta Avenue, a noisy protest over the government raiding the offices of the country's independent media. At the rallying point in Uhuru Park, the opposition politicians were throwing off their shirts on stage. Getting shirty, you could say.

Bright and early the following morning—it was Sunday—I boarded the ironically named 'Safety Bus' back to Kitui. Here and there along the way, giraffes and impala risked their lives by crossing the road. When I reached Kitui, I called in to see Fr. Paul and let him know how I was getting on. He was still working himself to the bone trying to resolve Kitui's longer-term difficulties, as well as fire-fighting the myriad requests for assistance that came his way on a daily basis. But he was in good spirits as always, and made time for everyone.

I cycled back to Nyumbani from Kitui village, stopping along the way at the mission house of Fr. Frank and Fr. Liam. I was looking forward to their company again. They were out. With no access to the house, I fell asleep under a purple-flowering jacaranda tree in the late afternoon sun, taking a siesta while waiting for them to return. By the time I woke up it was dark, and the two of them evidently would not be returning that night.

Darkness falls suddenly on the equator, like the dropping of a curtain; bright sunlight to darkness in about half an hour. When darkness falls in Kenya, sinister elements emerge from behind the curtain. One stays where one is for fear of snakes, hyenas, bandits and the like. I sought sanctuary in the nearby church as it had been left open, and slept the night in the back corner on the concrete floor.

After an uncomfortable sleep, I woke early and set off cycling while it was still dark, before the sun had a chance to wake up.

NO HURRY IN AFRICA

There were not even animals on the dirt tracks at that tranquil time of the morning. At first light, one young barefoot boy gazed at me as if I were a cycling ghost he had seen at this unholy hour. He accepted a lift. I propped him on the bar of the bicycle, told him to grip the handlebars tight and we proceeded down the dirt track towards Nyumbani. I was eager to return. Most of all, I was excited about meeting Nancy, Kiragu, Mwangangi, Nyambura, Kimanze, Nzoki, and all the others again. Nyumbani was my *raison d'être* in Kenya. I arrived before anyone had started work.

Anyone, that is, except Kiragu. Typically, he was already diligently planning the activities of the day ahead when I knocked on the door of his tin office. He jumped up enthusiastically from behind his wooden desk to embrace me.

'Brendan, it's very good to see you, *karibu sana!*' (you're very welcome).

I was to receive the same warm welcome from everyone else I encountered throughout the day. Kimanze saw me and saluted me with, 'You were lost, *bwana*,' as if I had taken a wrong turn on the bicycle weeks before and was only managing to find my way back now.

I was genuinely pleased to be back. It was only now, after being away from them, that I fully realised how I loved living in Kitui among the Akamba people. I quickly settled back into all the work that needed to be accomplished. Kiragu asked me to compile some progress reports on the computer, as well as to help with a proposal he was firming up. I was thrilled to see that Nancy and Nzoki had improved their computer capabilities even further during my absence. They were equally delighted to show me all that they were able to do, taking it all really seriously.

They were so keen to learn. I taught them some more advanced aspects. They picked them up fast.

I let it be known that I would be volunteering again at least until Easter, when Phase II of construction was due to be completed. I would want a short break for myself in-between. I would review my intentions again around Easter time. However, before the day was out, I sensed that things were still not as they should be. There were still covert power-struggles at play within the management and with the board of directors. I was also disappointed at another level. While the issue of fraud within Nyumbani was now being acknowledged openly, the politics of the ongoing situation allowed for the possibility of it being prolonged indefinitely. However, the central cast involved in the racket—whoever they were—were now clearly on the back-foot.

The American volunteer that Kiragu had told me about on the phone turned out to be a long-haired engineer named Aldo. He was another addition to the basic house where ten of us were living. An aging hippie, Aldo was a serial volunteer with a wealth of experience. On my first night back, we were having a deep conversation that was taking a philosophical turn—inspired, perhaps, by the infinite array of stars visible in the African sky— when he suddenly went off on a tangent.

'This sky reminds me of when I lived up in the Hindu Kush Mountains.'

'In Afghanistan? What were you up to there?' I asked, intrigued.

'I was building a water system for two years at a small village, straight after the fall of the Taliban.'

Immediately he was off on another tangent,

'Brendan, how is it that everyone seems to have a good word for you even with all these games being played out in the running of this place?'

This was the first inkling I had that the whole situation was causing him concern. He had been there such a short time. As for his question, however, I do not think he expected an answer.

A week later, the bombshell dropped. Kiragu was leaving. There was no question of him being involved in anything untoward, but perhaps he had not acted strongly enough to deal with the situation. I was still finding out things about him. Kiragu walked home one afternoon during his first year of school to find his father had been taken away. British soldiers countering the *Mau Mau* rebellion had burned down his thatched mud-hut. This was a dreadful period in Kenya's history, with estimates that up to fifty thousand people died in the insurgency, the vast majority of them Kikuyu. I could not help wonder whether this early experience had made him the driven character that he was. I was very sorry to see him depart.

I heard a number of reasons as to why Kiragu left; rumours that he was battling a drink problem; that he was being paid too much to be affordable; or that he did not see eye-to-eye on the way forward with Nyumbani's board of directors in Nairobi—which was headed by a Dublin-born Loreto nun named Sr. Mary, who, before she moved to Kenya, at one time lived in the convent-school where my mother taught in Letterkenny. Sr. Mary and Kiragu were two big personalities, and I think the project was just not big enough for both of them.

Progress had slowed dramatically since the New Year. The heady atmosphere of the ground-breaking development had vanished. I was hoping it would pick up again. Aldo was appointed to replace Kiragu. He was a very capable man, but I was not at all impressed by the idea of a *mzungu* being parachuted in to take charge of 500 Africans on-site. The principal directors in Nairobi were mainly white as well, missionaries who had been decades living in Kenya. There must have been, I felt, an Akamba or another Kenyan who was suitable for the role. The new appointment was utterly contrary to the spirit of the project as originally conceived. Nonetheless, there was no question but that I would give my all to Nyumbani and to Aldo.

The famine situation in Kitui District was still acute around this time, mid-to-late February. But the Akamba people, even after five years of failed rains, still possessed the positive attitude of 'sure they'll come sometime.' The build-up of heat was absolutely suffocating at times. The old people were saying they never witnessed it this hot in Kitui since the 1930s.

'A sure sign of rain,' one *mzee* told me—but sure was not everything in that parched land?

Anyway, sure enough and just as the elder had predicted, the heavens opened one day at the very end of February, and the place erupted in a carnival atmosphere of euphoric relief. Men were whooping and women, in their bare feet, were dancing joyously together in the mud. Children raced around excitedly, splashing in the speedily forming streams and puddles. I loitered around basking in their exuberance. I was in my bare feet as well; my sandals kept getting stuck in the muck.

But not everyone was rejoicing. The same old *mzee* warned me, and anyone else who would listen,

'The rains are too early. That's a sign of a short rainy season to come.'

The day the rains broke, I became stranded between two separate torrents that had been created with frightening suddenness. There was no way to cross either one of them safely until they subsided somewhat, perhaps hours later. Linking arms with other people who were caught out in a similar predicament, I waded to safety through water up to my waist.

Very early the morning after another night of heavy rain, with every last drop of moisture evaporated from the atmosphere, Mwangangi pointed over from the gate at Nyumbani to a most majestic sight in the far, crystal-clear distance. It was a rare glimpse of Mount Kilimanjaro, crowned in white, looming regally over the vast savannah beneath it.

Chapter 13
No Picnic on Mount Kilimanjaro

Very many Africans, including many who live within sight of the mighty Kilimanjaro, have never experienced snow close up. Mwangangi was one of them.

'Brendan, you know when your house is covered in snow in Ireland . . . well, how do you breathe?' he asked, when I told him that I would be climbing Mount Kilimanjaro soon.

I assured him it was not a problem. It might be more of a problem near the top of Kilimanjaro however, at nearly 20,000 feet.

In the ancient world, the Greek geographer Ptolemy included a mountain of snow in one of his maps roughly coinciding to Mount Kilimanjaro's location. The ancient Greeks were known to trade along the East African coast, and may have heard stories of its existence. The Romans even surmised a mountain such as Mount Kilimanjaro would have to exist as the source of the Nile, though of course this theory was proved to be inaccurate in the nineteenth century. It was not until the 1840s that a missionary named Johannes Rebmann was the first white person to set eyes on Mount Kilimanjaro, back in 1848. The Royal Geographical Society in London refused to believe his tale of snow so near the equator.

It was not until 1897 that Mount Kilimanjaro was finally conquered for the first time, by the German explorer, Hans Meyer, and his local Chagga tribe guide, John Lauwo. Germans played a large part in exploring this area. The map of Kenya had to be redrawn when the mountain was ceded to the then German colony of Tanganyika by the British at the behest of Queen Victoria; she had made a present of it to her grandson the *Kaiser*. With its permanent icing of snow, it did look a bit like a birthday cake, I suppose. A celebration was held in 1997 marking the centenary of the first ascent. The guest of honour was none other than John Lauwo, who was by then 118 years old.

Around the beginning of March, I joined a group of ten Irish people on a climb of Africa's highest mountain, hoping to emulate the feat of Meyer and Lauwo. I met up with the ten in Nairobi, a motley crew of all ages from north and south of the Border. An Irish Army officer named Dermot would be leading the group on the climb. He was a veteran of UN peacekeeping assignments. Among our group of ten was a gentleman named Pat Close, an engaging character in his sixtieth year who had been a teacher alongside an uncle of mine at a school in the Glens of Antrim before they both retired, yet another person whom I encountered in Africa that was known to a member of my family.

They were raising money on behalf of a Cork-based charity called Childaid, who were supporting a variety of health and education projects in Kenya and Tanzania. For the first couple of days, we were taken to see Childaid's activities on the ground. In the sub-dickensian smelly slum of Mukuru, they were amazed by the resilience and good humour of the children in school. As a teacher, Pat was greatly impressed by the children's willingness to learn and by the good discipline evident in classes of fifty or sixty pupils.

'These kids know the value of education. If only we could export these levels of motivation and discipline back to Ireland!' he said wistfully.

At a nearby school for the disabled we called into, Pat was even more impressed by the children. The disabled, both physical and mental, in many African communities are shunned by the able-bodied; the children often neglected by their parents. Dermot was reduced to tears at one point. A tiny girl in a wheelchair—she was about ten—suddenly burst into song. Little Catherine had a sweet voice and a huge personality to match it, expressing such joy through song despite her broken body.

We met up with Sr. Mary, the Dublin-born Mercy nun who had informed me before Christmas about the climb, at a street refuge for alcoholics and drug addicts that she runs. A remarkable octogenarian named Sr. Anne, who lives with Sr. Mary, was busy teaching recovering addicts to produce drawings and sculpted figures, which are later sold in their gallery. A teenager high on some exotic substance was roaming around, shouting and roaring. Sr. Anne carried on with her coaching, oblivious to any danger.

'She's retired, you know,' Sr. Mary reminded me.

Sr. Mary herself is a pretty gutsy character. She told us about a recent run-in she had with the authorities.

'It was the usual sort of thing,' she started casually. 'Last week, we were protesting against a government official who was trying to grab a piece of land unlawfully beside one of our training centres on the edge of Mukuru slum. They sent in the riot police who fired tear gas at us. I stood my ground, unlike the big burly guy from Northern Ireland beside me who bolted for cover. You'd have thought he would have been used to that sort of thing,' she said, taking a gentle dig at the six Ulstermen in the contingent, but even the three from west Belfast took it in good heart.

My anticipation was growing of the climb ahead of us during those couple of days. Being in Kenya at the time did not make for ideal preparation. For instance, I had trouble obtaining the necessary equipment. You have to allow for all conditions on the ascent—from the hot African sun to tropical rainforest to arctic blizzards. I had brought a small amount of gear with me from Ireland, I purchased whatever I could find in Nairobi, and I borrowed some things from Fr. Paul who had climbed Mount Kenya. I picked up a few items including a spare head-torch that some of the Childaid group had brought, and hired a couple of items at the base of the mountain. None of it was top of the range. I hoped it would prove to be adequate.

My fitness preparation was not ideal either. Unlike the others, I had no gym or swimming pool to train in. Though of course I cycled everywhere—this, I hoped, would stand me in good stead. I had talked to a few people who had scaled Mount Kenya, as well as a friend in Ireland who had attempted Mount Kilimanjaro itself. They were very helpful in giving advice on the preparations required, advising me to avoid common mistakes.

'The biggest mistake is to rush it,' Fr. Paul explained. 'Lack of oxygen is the greatest problem, no matter how fit you are. You have to try to avoid altitude sickness—nausea, extreme fatigue, nose-bleeds, physical collapse—so be sure to take it slowly, to keep the heart rate down.'

'Drink plenty of water. And keep a bit of chocolate for the

very top,' added Fr. Jimmy, helpfully. 'Remember, you need the energy to get back down again!'

He had successfully climbed Mount Kenya too. What they did not tell me, but what I found out from Dermot, was that, on average, 25 people each year die in attempting the slightly higher Kilimanjaro.

Mount Kilimanjaro is just over 200km southeast of Nairobi as the crow flies. It lies just across the border in Tanzania. On our journey out, the African wild animals were causing all sorts of excitement to the others in the group, as giraffes, baboons, zebras, elephants, and ostriches all made an appearance. Rather sadly, the carcasses of cattle, and in one instance a dead zebra close to the road, pointed to the effects of the drought and famine.

A short distance over the border inside Tanzania, our minibus became stranded in a muddy seasonal river that did not have a proper bridge (the rains, such as they were, had arrived in these parts the previous week). Our Kenyan driver called out for help to several Maasai herdsmen in their distinctive red blankets sitting along the bank. The Maasai are found in numbers along both sides of the border. After a short time pushing and heaving and revving, we were free. One of our number, a forty-something Belfast man named Dr. Shane, with his characteristic northern wit, shouted down to me,

'Who needs a tractor? After that feat, Brendan, those lads are better than tractors. Maasai Fergusons, that's what they are!'

Dr. Shane was proving to be our resident comedian on the trip. He roared a variety of funny remarks out the bus window all day at random passers-by. An odd one was not so clever.

He spotted monkeys at a village where we had stopped for a

break.

'Look boys. There's monkeys,' he pointed over. 'And there's some furry things climbing the trees.'

A little further on at a checkpoint, he shouted rather too loudly for comfort,

'*Vive la révolution,* down with the police!'

Thankfully, they gave the crazy *mzungu* the benefit of the doubt. He playfully tried to grab the rifle off a soldier at one point. A frown of concern appeared on Dermot's face. Pat and I were generally amused, though more by his wit than by his current antics. His doctorate, incidentally, was thought to be in veterinary science.

In Moshi, the nearest town to the base of the mountain, we met up with our guides, cooks, and porters—all seventeen of them. The Tanzanian authorities insist that climbers must be accompanied by official guides, to reduce the possibility of casualties on the climb, while simultaneously creating employment in the area. It is the porters' job to transport all the rucksacks, provisions, stretchers and other equipment up the mountain. These porters are young local Tanzanians, thin as whippets, who are acclimatised to mountaineering at altitude; they are indispensable. They carry up these huge loads on their backs and on top of their heads, racing past the gasping climbers at twice their speed. However, the porters do not climb right to the top.

We bonded with our porters and guides straight away. In Moshi, Dr. Shane and the other guys from west Belfast stocked up with a couple of crates of 'Kilimanjaro' beer, adding to their supplies of Tusker beer imported from Kenya. They insisted on sharing their drink with the porters on the bus. A couple of our porters were conked out asleep from the effects of alcohol by the time we reached the base of the mountain where the climb begins.

We planned to trek up the 'Marangu Route' on the south face of the mountain. The first day's climb was not too strenuous, on a fairly decent trail through the banana plantations and up into the rainforest. It took over six hours. We were deliberately taking our time right from the start.

'*Polé, polé*,' urged Frederick, the tall, lean Tanzanian in his forties who was our chief guide. 'Slowly, slowly. Take it easy. This has nothing to do with fitness. If you feel ill further up, we will take you back down. Don't be like the Japanese climbers either. They are all so determined to reach the peak that they crawl up on their hands and knees vomiting as they go. That's risking serious long-term damage to their lungs and brains from the effects of altitude.'

He made a crazy motion with his index finger.

'More than half of attempts fail to reach the summit anyway,' Frederick continued in his perfect English. 'Older people often do better than younger fitter climbers like yourself, Brendan. The key is to go slowly—right from the very bottom.'

He told us he was planning to retire soon; he had climbed the mountain over eighty times.

We had perfect weather to enjoy the lush vegetation, the many waterfalls, the soaring raptors overhead and the inquisitive monkeys. There were leopards around there, but they kept their distance. We sat down on rocks after our long walk just before night fell, and savoured the view of a volcanic crater and the flatlands below stretching out to the horizon. Everybody was in fine form when we checked into Mandara Hut, the rather basic A-frame wooden chalets where we would spend the first night.

'We've been lucky with the weather so far; a day in the rain-forest and no rain,' I said, as we tucked into a spaghetti dinner.

Pat, who proved to be a fount of knowledge on most things, agreed.

'February to early March is probably one of the best times of the year to climb Mount Kilimanjaro, if you want the most favourable weather conditions; the monsoon rains usually start later in March,' he informed us.

Another eight hours on day two took us up out of the forest into a terrain of giant heather, and then onto open undulating moorland as the vegetation petered out—except for some weird cactus-shaped plants and colourful alpine flowers.

'They are unique to this mountain,' claimed Frederick as he identified each type.

The last section of the day's climb was seriously steep. The only fauna at this altitude were a few large raven-like birds, and some multi-coloured rodents who joined us for dinner in Horombo Hut—even though they had not been invited. We were now at an altitude of about 12,000 feet and the air was very thin. The smokers in the group, like Dermot, were having great difficulty keeping their cigarettes alight because of the reduction in oxygen.

'The mountain is very shy,' he quipped, as he tried to light up.

This was a reference to the peak, which was still veiled in cloud; we had yet to set eyes on the top.

We spent the next day at Horombo Hut in order to acclimatise and help avoid altitude sickness, which is caused by a lack of oxygen to the body. This was a very necessary precaution. One or two in the group were already complaining of headaches, breathlessness, and dizziness. Having enjoyed perfect trekking weather up to now—dry and overcast—it poured on the third morning.

In the course of the afternoon, the cloud cleared for our first, fantastic, trembling glimpse of what lay ahead of us, and all that we were about to climb the following day. As it had stopped raining, we sat chatting on rocks outside, and we got to know a group of young English lads, as well as three attractive Iranian girls who were climbing Kilimanjaro with a middle-aged man whom they described as their 'trainer.' The Iranians had virtually no English; their trainer was fairly fluent. He asked where we were from.

'Ireland,' Dermot answered.

'Aah . . . Bobby Sands!' the trainer beamed radiantly.

Dr. Shane looked perplexed.

'That's right, sure Bobby Sands became a bit of a hero in Iran,' Pat piped up. 'And the Ayatollah named the street in Tehran where the British embassy was located "Bobby Sands Avenue," isn't that right?'

'The British, they were not amused,' the trainer laughed.

On the second night at Horombo Hut, I passed the time drinking beer with Dr. Shane and the others. We were marvelling at the spectacular lightning storm going on, not around us but *below* us. We were by now so high, we were actually above the storm. The other nationalities were aghast at our drinking and having a good time that high up the mountain. Some were radiating looks of disapproval.

'Nothing's going to stop *them* getting to the top,' Dr. Shane hollered, opening another bottle of 'Kilimanjaro' beer. 'Especially those Japanese climbers. *Attitude* sickness, that's what they have!'

I did not sleep that second night at Horombo Hut; it had more to do with the altitude than with the drink. Dermot and Pat were indicating they were suffering from insomnia as well.

Our first target on day four was Kibo Hut, which lies at over 16,000 feet. The weather began kindly enough. We put on extra layers of clothing and plodded onwards and upwards ever closer to the 'roof of Africa.' By now, the landscape had been drained of colour, was strewn with volcanic rubble and had become desolate, bare, barren tundra in appearance. The path was rougher and became even steeper than before, and as we passed a landmark called 'Last Water Point,' our guide, Frederick, reminded us that our bottled water supplies were likely to freeze from here on. The wind grew and sleet developed, crashing into our faces. After around eight hours trekking, we reached Kibo Hut in the late afternoon; it proved to be an austere T-shaped barn. This was base camp. There were two dorms full of double bunks and little else, and a 'long drop' toilet some distance away through the bitter cold. Here in Kibo, we would hope to recuperate for a few hours before beginning the assault on the summit at midnight.

At 16,000 feet, it was far too high up to allow us any decent sleep. Rather, we dozed fitfully and drank cups of soup and tea, and waited for the off. Everyone was still in the same high spirits that had prevailed throughout the week. But I found the prospect of the final push beginning to feel daunting. People were becoming more quiet and thoughtful—even Dr. Shane.

We set out for the summit in the pitch black at midnight.

CHAPTER 13 NO PICNIC ON MOUNT KILIMANJARO

'Make sure you apply plenty of sun cream,' was the last order Frederick gave to us.

Hearts sank when we emerged from the hut into a blizzard.

'We'll risk it,' Frederick declared.

The sight of a porter with a stretcher added to the chill.

'For God's sake, the man has done this eighty times; he knows what he's doing,' Dr. Shane remarked, encouragingly.

And so we set off, in a bizarre procession in single file, with each of us shining a head torch. I was looking down towards the ground lest my face got blasted with snow, literally following in the footsteps of the man in front. We were zigzagging up a viciously steep scree slope, made doubly slippery by a foot or more of fresh soft snow that came up to my knee. The ski poles that we had hired in Moshi were proving essential.

'It's a good thing we brought them,' Pat remarked. 'I nearly wasn't going to.'

Progress was painfully slow. Every step involved a huge effort. I put my boot down hoping to gain a couple of feet, only to slither backwards.

'*Polé, polé,*' said Frederick unnecessarily from time to time. How he knew where he was going in a blizzard on this dark featureless mountainside, I will never know.

The idea of a midnight start was, firstly, to arrive at the summit in time to experience a dramatic sunrise; and secondly, because in theory the snow is more likely to be frozen crisp at night, making progress easier. The fresh snowfall had put paid to the second reason. We trudged on, hour after hour, stopping eventually for a twenty-minute rest around 18,000 feet high at 'Hans Meyer Cave,' named after the explorer.

NO HURRY IN AFRICA

'This is the same altitude as Everest Base Camp,' Pat informed us, sipping warm water from his flask.

'No wonder we are wrecked,' Dr. Shane replied.

'The charge of the Night Brigade,' I suggested.

But nobody was in the mood for irony. Even Dr. Shane's wise cracks had dried up. Our luck with the weather had run out. I felt we were going over the top in a futile effort.

'Sometimes the mountain just beats you; it conquers you,' Dermot told us.

It was intensely cold. I had seven layers of clothes on, and I was still frozen to the bone. Actually, I was wearing my Dunnes Stores vest and whatever random clothes I could find in Kenya where there is, unsurprisingly, no such thing as thermals for sale. All the others in our group had really expensive professional thermal alpine mountain gear on, all Gore-Tex and Brasher boots— and they seemed as cold as I was.

After leaving the cave, the blizzard eased, but by now several people were beginning to feel sick or were falling in the snow, overcome with fatigue. Dermot and Frederick assessed their condition and urged them to resume after a short rest. As we neared the summit the slope became murderously steep, but no one wanted to give up now.

'Nearly there now, only a small bit left,' Frederick told us, though he had been telling us that the whole way through the night, to keep us going.

We believed him every time. And then, just as dawn was breaking at between six and seven in the morning, to our surprise and all of a sudden we arrived at the rim of the volcanic crater at the top of the mountain, a place called Gilman's Point. We had

CHAPTER 13 NO PICNIC ON MOUNT KILIMANJARO

officially climbed Mount Kilimanjaro. Most of the group was too exhausted to be elated.

Dr. Shane was even a touch disappointed.

'I had been looking forward to savouring a spectacular dawn and seeing right over the Serengeti as far the Congo from here,' he said.

But the blizzard had returned; visibility was about six feet. Pat showed me the muddy, snow-flaked snap he took.

'This could be anywhere. Nobody will believe I climbed it now!' he speculated.

After a fifteen-minute rest, my adrenalin started pumping again. Gilman's Point counts as having climbed Kilimanjaro, but a few kilometres around the rim of the volcano is Uhuru Peak, which is a few hundred feet higher, at 19,710 feet in altitude—literally the highest point on the African continent. With a fresh lease of energy and enthusiasm, I was up for it. My body was in good condition even then; most of the others were far from a hundred percent by now.

I'm probably only ever going to get this chance once, I thought, I'm going for it.

In the prevailing conditions Frederick was not keen on going any further; he rarely found the weather this bad. But four of us persuaded him to lead us forward, as Dermot, Pat, and the others gratefully set off back down the mountain to Base Camp.

So, with Frederick in the lead, the four of us, including Dr. Shane, set off along the narrow ridge that constitutes the rim of the crater. There were treacherously steep slippery slopes on either side. The crater still emits steam to this day, meaning that Mount Kilimanjaro is not yet an entirely extinct volcano; the beast is lying dormant. It may only be a couple of kilometres round to Uhuru Peak, but it takes a couple of hours to get there. It proved to be a slow testing trudge in icy winds through the mist. The cloud cleared a bit, falling below us as we progressed.

'Do you see the glacier?' Frederick pointed out to me with his glove.

I could just about make it out, camouflaged into the landscape.

Minutes later, Dr. Shane let out a yelp of disappointment behind me. I turned around rather concerned to see what could be wrong. For the last week, he had been carrying a bottle of Guinness in his rucksack the whole way up from Moshi. His ambition had been to share a sip with us on the summit, and he had taken it out in anticipation. Despite the alcoholic content, it had frozen solid. As we got ever closer to the top, he was really struggling, and kept needing to rest every few minutes.

Finally, we made it to the summit. I was euphoric! I found myself standing at the very apex of the highest freestanding mountain in the entire world. When I was about thirteen years old, I remember telling my father that I wanted to climb Mount Kilimanjaro. I was in the Scouts at the time, and loved climbing mountains. He smiled back, assuming I was dreaming. Now, my decade long dream had come true. I spent half an hour on the summit basking in the achievement of being the highest person in the whole of Africa, fully savouring the moment.

After taking the obligatory photos with the Irish flag, it was time to descend. In our ecstasy, we practically started running back down. I soon realised, however, that I had used up any surplus energy encouraging Dr. Shane in our ascent beyond Gilman's Point. I was totally exhausted. On the way down, I began suffering bad hallucinations, a symptom of altitude sickness. Protruding brown rocks turned into preying animals lurking in the snow. I was starting to get a touch of frostbite. I became so weary that I could not even take out the chocolate bar that I had been saving, as recommended by Fr. Jimmy, from my coat pocket. I could scarcely move with the fatigue, and seriously questioned whether I would get back down at all.

As we sat down in the snow to take a rest, three of us drifted off to sleep. It was about minus twenty degrees Celsius.

'Snow patrol!' barked Dr. Shane as he poked me with the end of his ski pole to wake me up. 'Move along, son, no loitering allowed.'

I looked up at him dazed. He certainly had made a good recovery. He cheered me up, and we kept going. You cannot understand how debilitating altitude fatigue is until you experience it. Frederick was a little concerned about us. Acute fatigue is yet another symptom of altitude sickness; hypothermia can follow quickly.

The sun came out as the morning progressed, making things slightly more pleasant, melting the snow a little, and at last revealing some spectacular views. It was over thirteen hours after setting out that I made it back to Base Camp at Kibo Hut, where the others were awaiting us. By this stage I was sunburned from sunlight reflected off the snow; I had not applied enough cream. It was over thirty hours since I had any sleep at all, and two days since I had a decent meal. However, we still had several more hours of walking ahead of us; Kibo Hut is a stopping-off point only on the way up. We would be spending the night back down at Horombo Hut.

I was simply too exhausted to fully realise what we had achieved by reaching the top. It was only over dinner at Horombo Hut, when we all gazed up and saw the peak emerging from cloud, lit up in ghostly moonlight, that we could finally appreciate what we had accomplished. The shy but unyielding mountain had defeated every nationality, including the Japanese, that had attempted the climb that night. Except the Irish, that is—and those amazing Iranian girls. We had our photographs taken with them, the three West Belfast men with their arms around them.

'Probably wouldn't be allowed in Tehran,' guessed Pat.

Next morning, as we walked with a lighter step down through the alpine terrain back into the humid rainforest, the rain started. It bucketed down all afternoon, accompanied by a dramatic equatorial thunderstorm. Perhaps the monsoons were arriving a little early.

'These ski poles will make excellent lightning conductors!' Pat unhelpfully pointed out.

By the time we got down to the bottom, where our certificates were issued and our bus was waiting, we were a sodden and rather low-spirited lot.

'The snows of Kilimanjaro are not nearly as romantic as Ernest Hemingway made them out to be,' I moaned.

'Brendan, you've just climbed the highest mountain in Africa and got back down safely. Cheer up lad,' urged Pat.

I decided to take him at his word, and smiled back in agreement.

Our hotel outside Moshi had lost its electricity because of the heavy rain that afternoon. We could not even take a shower after six sweaty days. Only in Africa, I found myself thinking once again. Another upshot of the rain was that for our fancy self-congratulatory dinner that evening, my dirty clothes were dry and my clean clothes were wet. After dinner, Dr. Shane, Dermot, the Belfast lads, and myself had recovered our energy, and we headed out to a disco in town. On the way back, in the early hours, the driver of our battered taxi drove us in the wrong direction and then ran out of petrol some way from the hotel. With much merriment, we pushed the car back into town.

The next morning, from the beautiful grounds of the hotel, I stared up to Mount Kilimanjaro; the ice-cap was gleaming, creating a truly wondrous sight. The highest freestanding mountain in the entire world was glistening white in the sun, resplendent before my eyes. Only then did I fully realise what we had accomplished.

CHAPTER 14
FLEEING TO UGANDA

ON MY WAY BACK from Mount Kilimanjaro to Kitui, on a crammed bus called 'Saddam Hussein,' we were not far out of Nairobi when the driver suddenly stopped. There was a tumultuous crowd milling around the scene of an accident. Our conductor invited us to get out of the bus so that we could take a good look at the bodies of the dead and injured on the roadside. A bus similar to ours had crashed a few minutes before we reached that spot. The Africans were morbidly fascinated by it all amongst the confusion. I kept thinking about poor Mutinda.

'*Twende*,' shouted the conductor after a short while, and we got back on.

A little further down the road, I spotted about twenty tall giraffes walking past a herd of grazing zebras. I seemed to be the only one who was engrossed by this sight.

The bus entered Machakos, the capital of Akambaland, for a pit-stop on the way to Kitui. A young boy frantically banged my bus window. I slid it open. These encounters often proved amusing. We had a chat; he established that I was Irish. His eyes lit up and he shouted excitedly in English,

'Gentleman, you are Irish, Westlife is Irish, you will buy a Westlife gospel music tape from me. Make it 4,000 shillings!'

NO HURRY IN AFRICA

Fifty euro for a Westlife gospel music tape, hmm, now if only I could bargain him down a small bit, I thought. But, as it did not seem to be the offer of the week, I gently shut the window on him.

I reached Nyumbani in the afternoon. Aldo was dying to hear how I got on. He had climbed a couple of high mountains in the Andes, and I had sparked the idea of climbing Mount Kilimanjaro in his head.

'If I could ever find the time,' he sighed, and then turned to more pressing business.

Some aspects of Phase II construction were well on the way to completion. A proper integrated water system worthy of Nyumbani was now virtually in place, boosted by water retained in the dams along the seasonal river. The dedication of Kimanze, Mwangangi, and others under Aldo's direction was finally producing results. Many of the community buildings including the hall and the school were being finished off. When I got back to work—which did not take long—I was able to assist Aldo and Nzoki in ensuring that each homestead would be stocked with the optimum amount of furniture and fittings that available resources permitted.

It was my responsibility to cost aspects of the Project regularly to make sure that we were staying within budget. I had to help ensure we had the right amount of raw materials to hand, and that there were no bottlenecks in the on-site manufacture of the different kinds of furniture. Other strands of the Nyumbani project had been shelved or postponed until Phase III. Consequently, it was quieter around the place as Phase II was winding down towards completion. There was still no sign of the children arriving

to take up residence—with all the work that that would entail—
so I found that my workload had decreased substantially.

When I returned to Nairobi a couple of weeks later to try to
get my rapidly expiring visa sorted out once again, I encountered
yet more bureaucracy at the immigration office. I was now informed that I was ineligible for the more affordable three-month
work visa that I wanted, because I had already been approved for
the expensive year-long work permit. The criteria for both were
identical of course. It was rather frustrating. After what seemed
like five hours being sent around a dozen different clerks, filling
in form after form, I was told,

'No, you were given the wrong forms. Start again please.'

Déjà vu, all over again! Eventually I gave up. In desperation,
I tried to find the Irish Consulate. That was difficult enough. It
proved to be a tiny anonymous prefab in the middle of an industrial estate on the outskirts of the city. They advised me to get out
of the country.

It was a pity my visa expired on Saint Patrick's Day. Later, I
heard that I had missed what was by all accounts a tremendous
Irish party in Fr. Paul's home. Instead, I marched in my own
one-man Saint Patrick's Day parade down Nairobi's Kenyatta
Avenue in the morning, and spent the rest of the day on the bus
fleeing the Kenyan immigration officials. But at least I had company. I had persuaded a twenty-two year old red-haired lad from
Armagh to come along with me for the adventure. Destination
Jinja, Uganda.

I had only met Damian a short while beforehand, when visiting the slum projects in Nairobi with the Childaid group. I
was amused to discover that it was he who was the 'big burly

volunteer' from Northern Ireland that broke ranks as the police launched tear-gas over the head of Sr. Mary in the slums. He was indeed big and burly in build, but also larger than life in character.

'This country isn't big enough for the two of you,' Sr. Mary ribbed us, when we were introduced.

Damian had been in Kenya only since the start of the year. He had flown in after he finished a music degree in college; he intended to stay in the country for six months. I was the first young (or for that matter lay) Irish person he had met since he arrived. Apart from Kevin, who had returned to Ireland by now, he was the first young Irish person I had encountered living there as well. We hit it off right away.

After the accident outside Nairobi a couple of weeks earlier, the journey up through the Rift Valley was uneventful—well, by Kenyan standards anyway. Damian was bemused at the sight of several extended families of baboons begging for food by the roadside. I suggested that, sadly, this particular monkey business was probably in imitation of some hungry humans they saw doing much the same thing.

As darkness fell, and we were approaching the border with Uganda, I was growing more and more nervous. By the time I joined the queue at the Kenyan passport control, I was so edgy I was actually shaking a bit, something I do not normally do. There were literally two hours left on my visa and the queue was moving infinitely slowly. Who knows what a gung-ho jobsworth of an official would do, even for a minor infringement of immigration law? The very least I could expect was to have to pay a bribe. And if I appeared nervous, they would suspect I was up to something.

The solemn Kenyan immigration officer silently perused the leaves of my passport for what seemed like ages, and duly stamped me out. As I began to walk away, he called me back.

'You will have to return to Ireland before you can re-enter Kenya,' he warned.

I nodded to him resignedly. We'll cross that bridge when we come to it, I thought.

We walked the short distance to the Ugandan border post. The official made Damian and me pay for a visa, even though it is free to Irish citizens. We were in no position to argue, not fancying being stranded indefinitely in no man's land. As we began to walk away hurriedly—we were by now the last two left to get back on the bus—he too called me back.

What now? I wondered anxiously.

'You have forgotten your bag, sir. *Karibu a Uganda.*'

Incidentally, these border formalities may not be necessary in the coming decades. There are moves to bring together Tanzania, Kenya, and Uganda in an East African federation, along the lines of the European Union. The sooner the better, perhaps.

Over the course of the week or so that I spent in Uganda, I experienced a series of mishaps in fairly quick succession. My camera broke, I broke my glasses, and African bureaucracy forced us to go three hours west of Jinja, our intended destination. We were required to go to the capital, Kampala, so that customs could check our backpacks. This could and should have been done at the border, of course. This enforced detour extended our travel time from Nairobi to over fifteen hours. When we got to Kampala, they did not even bother to check our bags, but it effectively lost us a day.

On the way back from the customs headquarters, which is several kilometres from the centre of Kampala, we had been kindly given a lift by a random Ugandan motorist. He was very smartly dressed, quite small, articulate, and extremely polite. He told us he was a Baluba. I suddenly remembered that in every class in school back home there was a big ignorant chap whom you would address as 'ya big Baluba ya' if he pushed someone around. It began as a racial slur after an Irish UN battalion had been ambushed by the Baluba tribe in the Congo in 1960. I was kind of disappointed. This quietly spoken gentleman did not fit the Baluba image I had in my head at all. He was an educated man, but his geography was a bit ropey. When telling us about Kampala, he said,

'It's the capital of Uganda, you know—the same way New York is the capital of America, Johannesburg is the capital of South Africa, and Sydney is the capital of Australia.'

Wrong, wrong, and wrong, I thought, but decided not to embarrass him when he was being so generous to us.

He kindly deposited us at the main bank in Kampala because Damian and I needed to obtain some Ugandan shillings. The bank appeared to have no security men, but instead there was a prominent sign, hand-written in marker on white paper, that was sellotaped to the front door.

'Please do not bring your gun inside the bank,' the sign pleaded.

Indeed Kampala, an impressive and vibrant city of a million people, has a much better reputation than Nairobi where crime is concerned. The Baluba gentleman had been telling us about this.

'Ugandans have an effective way of dealing with robbers and muggers when they are caught in the act. In Nairobi, they lynch them; in Kampala, we strip them naked and parade them up the street. It seems to work!'

'Mmm . . . we used to do something similar in the North,' Damian remembered aloud.

Having been to the bank, we proceeded across the road to a café for *chapatti* and *chai*. There were two big bibles sitting between the sauce bottles on every table, something you would not find in Nairobi. We fell into conversation with three other diners. Damian asked them about an animal whose head he thought he had glimpsed, in poor light, in the lake near Jinja.

'Could it have been a crocodile?' he wondered.

'It may have been a hippo you saw,' one of them answered.

'Any chance it was a dinosaur?' Damian joked.

'I don't think there are any dinosaurs in Uganda—only in South America,' we were told.

His colleague added, 'Yes, there are no dinosaurs in Uganda now,' before adding a caveat, 'there's not supposed to be, anyway; the government should tell us if there were. I'd say a hippopotamus, definitely a hippo.'

We caught a bus back to Jinja, planning to camp outside the town. Jinja is a fairly prosperous market town, dotted with many dilapidated colonial mansions now being used as tenement homes. The town's biggest claim to fame, of course, is that it is located overlooking the breathtaking gorge right at the source of the Nile where it emerges from Lake Victoria. It was on top of a cliff, with a commanding view of the spectacular Nile gorge, that we pitched our tent.

From childhood, I have been fascinated by stories of the great African explorers, and had been reading about them again recently in a book in Fr. Paul's house. While putting up our tent, I shared one such story with Damian. I told him how, while searching for the source of the Nile, Dr. David Livingstone became lost for so long that, in 1869, the *New York Herald* dispatched Henry Morton Stanley to find him. After two years searching for Livingstone, on finally catching up with him, Stanley allegedly could only utter the famous inanity, 'Dr. Livingstone, I presume?' Dr. Livingstone was the somewhat obsessive Scottish missionary and traveller who believed that his explorations in Africa would further his aims of 'Christianity, commerce, and civilisation.'

'Mmm, commerce and Christianity make dubious bed fellows,' was Damian's verdict, as he handed me a peg. 'Livingstone doesn't sound like a bundle of laughs.'

'But you would have enjoyed the company of Henry Stanley,' I suggested. 'Livingstone was a sober Scottish evangelist. Stanley was a bit of a Welsh boyo.'

I told him that Stanley was an adventurer who was born in rural Wales, who ran away to sea as a cabin boy, worked in New Orleans as a servant in a great mansion, fought for the Confederacy in the American Civil War before switching to the Union side on his capture, reported as a journalist in the Wild West, spent years exploring in Africa and was finally offered a seat in the British House of Commons before he died in 1904. On the darker side, it was he who was largely instrumental in grabbing the Congo for the odious King Leopold II of Belgium. The Congo suffered from being ruled in the most brutal manner of any

African colony. It was the size of Western Europe, and belonged to the King personally, and not to Belgium itself. Something of the horror of this period is captured in Joseph Conrad's great novel, *Heart of Darkness*.

'Yeah, Stanley wouldn't have been short of a story or two in the pub,' Damian agreed.

'Speaking of that, let's crack open a beer,' I suggested, and flipped the lids off a couple of bottles of the local brew.

Sitting down in the sunshine with our backs against a few rocks, while admiring the Nile gorge, we took a sip from our bottles, and I told him about another Victorian explorer named John Hanning Speke. He had served with the British army in the Himalayas and the Crimea War, and it was he who claimed to have discovered the source of the Nile at Jinja in 1862. While the Royal Geographical Society in London was still debating the merits of his argument a few years later, he shot himself—perhaps accidentally. Indeed, even today there is still debate about the true source of the Nile, as many argue that lesser rivers, which flow from the mountains of Burundi into Lake Victoria, are a continuation of the Nile. For the record, the detailed *Al-Adrisi* map made by Arab traders around 1160AD fairly accurately defines the outline of Lake Victoria, and identifies it as the source of the Nile.

On our third night in Jinja, after several hours of heavy rain, our tent became semi-submerged under a mini-landslide.

'Avalanche!' Damian screamed, before we knew exactly what was going on.

The tent had caved in on top of us. I crawled outside to assess the situation, but I forgot I was still nearly blind because my glasses were broken. It was too dark to see, and neither of us possessed a working torch. But we had the privilege of experiencing the steam rising from the misty waters of the mighty Nile as the sun broke. My pleasure was somewhat reduced, however, by the fact that while waiting for dawn, I had accidentally stepped on a line of flesh-eating *siafu* ants. They left many ferocious bite marks on my feet and legs before I could shake them off.

'Sure Livingstone and Speke had to put up with much, much worse to get here,' Damian piped up unsympathetically. 'Didn't you say they even encountered cannibals?'

The small backpacker campsite—incidentally, the first backpacker venue of any sort that I had found in Africa in over six months—was run by a few young Afrikaners. They had adopted a baby monkey as a pet. This monkey was very fond of going around drinking sips of beer out of people's glasses. I noticed the monkey was holding up better than we were most evenings. I noticed too that nearly every backpacker there was part of an organised tour package with an 'overland truck' company. Independent backpacking is East Africa is virtually unheard of.

On the bank of the Nile directly below the campsite was a signpost warning of crocodiles in the bathing area. Having found a natural pool, we decided to take a chance and jump in regardless. It proved to be safe enough and some very carefree hours were spent in the warm sunshine, immersed in the waters of the Nile. We were joined by a few Norwegian girls and two bearded brothers from Bavaria named Helmut and Jurgen. They were students doing post-graduate research for a semester at a university in Kampala.

Occasionally we spotted fish eagles chasing communes of bats over the river at dusk. Luckily, there were no big eyes peering menacingly at us over the water. I heard about an Irish missionary in Turkana once, who used to send all the children into Lake Turkana before him when he wanted a swim. They created so much noise it frightened away the humongous Turkana crocodiles, leaving the missionary free to swim in peace. I hoped the story was untrue, or at least exaggerated!

Ugandans are very proud of the Nile.

'It is responsible for providing water to Uganda, Sudan, as far as Egypt . . . and even the Mediterranean and Europe!' a man in Jinja told me.

Well, yes and no, I thought. I was beginning to think that the teaching of geography in Uganda left something to be desired.

Whether he learnt it in geography class or not, Damien was able to tell me,

'The rapids around here are considered to be among the finest in the world for white-water rafting.'

He was big into water-sports, like myself.

'And what's more,' he continued, 'in a year or two, rafting will be impossible because of the huge hydro-electric dam which they are planning to build. So it's now or never, Brendan!'

And that is how he and I decided to blow what money we had left, white-water rafting down the grade five rapids near Jinja.

Even getting to the rapids had its moments. At one point, we passed a couple of men in a large hollowed-out tree trunk traversing the mighty Nile with a cow on board. There were plenty of people bathing, naked, in the river. Others, equally naked, were washing their clothes and having a bath at the same time. And this being Africa, Rachel, our Afrikaner instructor, only warned us,

'There are crocodiles in the water very near the raft,' just as we were jumping out of the raft for another swim.

After a few tester rapids, we approached the first monster one. All of a sudden, our raft was swept swiftly into the mixer.

'Paddle! Paddle hard!' Rachel shouted her instructions to us. 'Get down! Get down! Paddle . . . '

We survived that one, just. Before being able to draw breath, we were frantically battling through the next funnel. In an instant, I was tossed over the side. My body was sucked under by the force of the water, and bounced off a few rocks, as I was rapidly pulled downstream by the currents, before my lifejacket finally pushed my head above the water for a split second to catch a gasp of air. It was really scary at times but totally exhilarating. After months in the parched deserts of Kenya, I was enjoying every minute in the water.

Damian had taken a fancy to a black-haired Norwegian student at the campsite. As he was not getting anywhere with her at all, he decided he wanted to stay in Jinja to continue the chase. I was most unenthusiastic about parting from a travelling companion, but as Damian was planning to remain in Uganda for up to another fortnight, and as I was keen to return to Kenya soon, I accepted that we had to go our separate ways. We parted on good terms, promising to meet up in Nairobi again.

With Helmut and Jurgen, I ventured about 150km northeast to Mount Elgon. A huge extinct volcano, Mount Elgon is Uganda's highest mountain and sits near the border with Kenya. Our destination was the spectacular and beautiful Sipi Falls near the village of the same name. It is in a fabulous setting of cliffs, gorges and caves. Here, three high iconic waterfalls tumble down to a peaceful unspoilt canyon below.

The brothers and I decided against staying at the 'Baghdad Hotel'; we were similarly disinclined to stay at the 'Downhill Quality Hotel' a few kilometres away, after we called in.

'Do you not think that the name "Downhill Quality" could be construed as meaning that your establishment is deteriorating?' I asked the owner, although not using those words specifically.

By the look of the place, he had the name spot on, or perhaps it was never up to much in the first place. The reality was that it was more a tiny B&B than a hotel. The owner still could not detect any irony in the name.

'The village is called Downhill, what's the problem?' he asked, not unreasonably, I suppose.

We settled in the end on a small Ugandan-run campsite in a banana grove. We were pretty much the only people staying there; certainly, we were the only foreigners staying in the village. Surrounded as we were on all sides by trees laden with ripe bananas, our campsite barman told us at breakfast,

'Sorry, no bananas at the market this morning.'

No explanation was offered. We found bananas a while later at the 'Jesus is Lord' shop. The whole country seemed so much greener and lusher than the arid lands of Kenya. It reminded me of the fertile lower slopes of Kilimanjaro just below the rainforest where banana trees are also found in abundance. When Winston Churchill visited Uganda as Minister for the Colonies in 1907, he observed how fertile it was and described the country as the 'Pearl of Africa.'

NO HURRY IN AFRICA

Uganda did not win independence from Britain until 1962. Since then, it has been relatively stable by African standards—that is, except for the 1970s. That terrible decade was dominated by the rule of one General Idi Amin. Despite being completely illiterate, the dictator considered himself well qualified for the job. On formal occasions he insisted on being introduced as 'His Excellency, Field Marshal Al-Haji, Doctor Idi Amin Dada, DSO, MC, VC, Life President of Uganda, King of Scotland, Lord of All the Beasts of the Earth and Fishes of the Sea, Professor of Geography, and Conqueror of the British Empire in Africa in General and Uganda in Particular.'

Sitting of an evening, lazily drinking sundowners with Helmut and Jurgen in the extremely pleasant surroundings of Sipi Falls, it was almost impossible to imagine the horror of those days. Amin was responsible for the massacre of an estimated 300,000 people—perhaps as many as half a million, according to some human rights groups. Perhaps his most brainless act was to expel the 50,000-strong Indian community, saying God had told him to transform Uganda into 'a black man's country.' This precipitated an overnight economic meltdown, because the Indians ran many of the shops and businesses of Uganda.

From 1971 until he was ousted in 1979 after a pointless war with Tanzania, he had banned hippies and miniskirts, attended a Saudi royal funeral wearing a Scottish kilt, forced four Englishmen to carry him around in a sedan chair at a summit of African leaders, and periodically jumped into swimming pools wearing full military uniform. I could not help wondering if the low standard of geographical knowledge I had encountered in the country was related to the fact that one of his many titles was Professor of Geography! He was known to Western reporters simply as 'Big Daddy' for his massive frame, and indeed, he was the heavyweight boxing champion of Uganda in pre-Independence days while he was serving in the British Army.

Given his bulk, he was also a useful prop-forward in rugby. As we climbed Kilimanjaro, Pat Close had told me that a retired Scottish meteorologist he knew propped against the future dictator, when Amin was playing for the East Africa Rifles. The Scot had found the young Amin to be physically formidable; but he was very polite and deferential, and was a great lover of everything British and in particular, Scottish.

'Had I known that he would later be rather partial to human liver lightly grilled, I would have been a bit more concerned when our scrums collapsed!' said the Scot.

Amin was, by his own account, quite partial to live women also. He was believed to have sired over fifty children.

'In communist countries, you do not feel free to talk; there is one spy for every three people. Not here. No one is afraid here,' he told foreign journalists in the 1970s. 'It's like Ugandan girls. I tell them to be proud, not shy. It's no good taking a girl to bed if she is shy. Do you get my point?'

After several extremely pleasant days at Sipi Falls, I was running out of money. I was planning to return to the bank in Kampala, the one with the request to leave your gun at the door; it was the only place in Uganda I knew of where my ATM card could take out Ugandan shillings. It was then I discovered that due to bureaucratic restrictions, my American dollars could not be exchanged because the notes were over five years old; in short, they were worthless.

NO HURRY IN AFRICA

I had to get back into Kenya as soon as possible. In my attempt to reach the border crossing, south of Sipi Falls, I had to resort to haggling and barter with the conductor of the bus.

'The best price is 2,000 shillings,' the conductor insisted after I haggled him down a bit.

That was equal to about a euro. I looked in every pocket and every envelope I had, and amassed just over 1,000 Ugandan shillings. I had a moment of inspiration. I pulled out a packet of spare AA batteries I kept for my hand-held radio. Reliable batteries are a precious commodity in East Africa, as most of their battery-operated imports run out of energy faster than a paper airplane. His face lit up. He knew the batteries were worth far more than the original asking fare.

'If you give me a black pen and some paper as well,' the conductor advised, 'then we have a deal.'

'No bother,' I agreed, and hopped on the bus.

At the bus terminal in the decent sized settlement that is Tororo, I needed another bus onwards to the border crossing. A Ugandan man noticed my desperation as I was going round in circles, vainly trying to find someone that might exchange my small amount of Kenyan shillings or my six-year-old American dollars to pay for the fare. He was a big man, yet another hawker trying to offload some of his merchandise on me, I surmised. In fact, he was selling strips of rubber. I was not in the mood to entertain more endless banter over their hard sell.

'Look, at the moment I have no use for a strip of rubber, thanks, and nothing to pay for it anyway.'

'OK, *bwana*. I am not trying to sell you anything. I am a member of the Pentecostal Church.'

CHAPTER 14 FLEEING TO UGANDA

Oh God, I sighed not exactly prayerfully to myself, I'm not in the form for this right now either.

'There is only a single *mzungu* like you in this town,' he continued, 'I will bring you to her. She will help you with your problem.'

He guided me down some dirty backstreets, around the back of a building, and up a dark flight of stairs. There was a young English lady from the Home Counties working as a nurse. They knew each other from the church. After exchanging stories of what each of us was doing in Africa, I explained my predicament to her. She immediately handed over much more than the anticipated fare, but it was still only about three euros worth. I thanked her profusely, and the big African guided me back along a few streets to the correct bus for the border. Tactfully, I tried to hand him the amount above what I needed for the fare. He refused point blank. They were the two Good Samaritans of Tororo. Most of the Ugandans I had met were decent, friendly people.

I might make an exception of some of the hawkers an odd time, though. It was along those roads to the Kenyan border that locals were offering hot cooked chickens for sale; indeed, they were thrusting them through the open bus windows on the end of poles. At another village, every single person was intent on selling coat hangers to passengers. It is always the same in East Africa; in one village it is all carrots; in the next village it is all four-foot hat stands; in the next, only signposts are for sale; in the next, it is newspapers, and so on. Nobody ever thinks to sell something different from the rest. And why they would ever think I needed to buy a wicker chair or a big woolly sheepskin through a bus window, I simply do not know.

I was aiming for the smallest border crossing I could find on the map south of Sipi Falls because I always found smaller border posts less officious. Areas north of Mount Elgon might have been susceptible to danger from the notorious rebel Lord's Resistance Army, crazed rebels who have been known to commit acts of cannibalism. I had other worries. While walking up to the border post, I was still debating in my head whether I would be prepared to pay a bribe if it became necessary to be allowed back into Kenya. It might cause trouble further down the line if I was found out, but I knew people who had done it before.

In the end, at the border post in a no-horse town, after my several misadventures in Uganda, I managed to charm my way back into Kenya. After a bit of smiling and joking, the official handed back my passport, and with a handshake I was through . . . I did not have to return to Ireland, as I had been told I must a week earlier.

CHAPTER 15
RETURN TO NYUMBANI

A SINGLE MONGOOSE ended my extensive hen empire. At least that was the story I was told towards the end of March on my return to Nyumbani from Uganda. In other versions, a large hawk had swooped on the hens one by one; sometimes I heard that an unidentified human had snatched some, apparently with my permission. Now hen-less, I decided to give away my goats too. This entailed cycling with one goat at a time tied to the back of the boneshaker. They were gifts for some of my Akamba friends— so that they could take advantage of some of the rather illogical economics of Kitui. Goat prices skyrocketed once the rains came; with all the new vegetation to munch on, the goats fattened up. Of course, everyone knows this is going to happen at the exact same time every year.

In the days after my return to Nyumbani, when I was not preoccupied with hen thieves and goat prices, I was worried about Damian. I had tried to ring him a good few times whenever or wherever my phone picked up a signal again. There was no answer. With increasing concern, I contacted Sr. Mary in Nairobi, hoping that she could update me on his whereabouts. She became fretful as well, for she had been assuming that we were still together in Uganda.

It was a few days later that I got a message on my phone from

Sr. Mary. Damian had finally made contact with her. He was still in Uganda. It was about a week later that he crossed back into Kenya, and we were able to speak. He told me he had ventured deep into the rebel territory of the Lord's Resistance Army after he gave up chasing his Norwegian girl. He had encountered an African man in Kampala who drove him to Gulu refugee camp in the far north. I knew how dangerous that could have been. I nearly felt like telling him off.

'There is taking a risk,' I said, 'and there is asking for trouble!'

But I was pleased and relieved that he was back safe and well nonetheless.

Back in the office, I sometimes felt I was nearly becoming redundant. I had trained up Nancy and Nzoki so well in the use of the computer, especially in the use of Excel, Word and basic management accounting functions, that by this stage they were doing a lot of the work that I had been doing initially. They were enjoying the challenge, preferring to do the work themselves. Also, because extra funding from abroad would not be released until the land deeds were officially handed over, Phase II was being further curtailed, at least for the time being. Things at this point were just ticking over. I was beginning to feel that there was a certain lack of continuity to the planning and running of Nyumbani since Kiragu vacated his position. Certainly, there was not the same urgency.

I wanted to find a new role for myself, and I did not have far to look. The impressive water system of pipes, dams, tanks, and boreholes that had been installed allowed, for the first time, fruit trees and a variety of crops to be grown on Nyumbani's farm. So

CHAPTER 15 RETURN TO NYUMBANI

instead of managing the finances, I decided to become an organic farmer. Regardless of other developments on the site, there would be a need for continuity on the farm. Nature abhors a vacuum; it was important that something was happening. Nyumbani was experimenting by trying to create a microclimate on its desert farm—for example, by creating layers of vegetation of differing heights, and trapping moisture by different methods. A lot of scientific analysis had been devoted to this possibility since well before Christmas.

I was learning new skills. I spent a couple of days ploughing cleared bush with two powerful oxen in the hope of planting a fruit orchard in the expectation of more rains coming. The immediate result was blisters and aching arms. This is really how the early white settlers lived, I was thinking. I was reminded of Elspeth Huxley's beautifully written memoir, *The Flame Trees of Thika*. I too was furrowing virgin bush by steering these great patient, stubborn beasts, with a gang of Africans around me busily planting the fruit bushes and trees. I was gratified to learn later that the orchard is still flourishing.

It takes a team of four people to whip, shout, whistle and swear in order to plough with oxen and prepare for planting. One of the 'planter' team was known to one and all as 'Mama Mbolea,' meaning 'Mammy Manure.' This was not meant to be an insult, merely a factual description of her main function in the operation. A fine sturdy woman, she was the most important community worker in Nyumbani.

Whenever the oxen went out of control, another one of the four, a tall slender fellow named Kaveti, came to the rescue. He always took the opportunity to ask me questions.

NO HURRY IN AFRICA

'*Mzee* Brendan, do you keep camels on your farm in your country?' he wondered.

I had to explain that camels would find the Donegal climate very unpleasant. The day Kaveti was being married in church, his fiancée began her contractions in the middle of the ceremony, and she had to be rushed away to give birth. Kaveti and those like him are often intelligent, but many are sent out to herd goats by their parents instead of being sent to primary school. In fact, herding is the most common male occupation in Akambaland.

Perhaps because of the impression given by these herdsmen, Africans have an undeserved reputation for laziness among some Europeans in Kenya. Rather, it is usually idleness—having nothing to do—rather than laziness, in my view. It was my experience that many, if not most, Africans are excellent workers. For instance, one time I hired two men to dig a hole. I came back some hours later with food for them. I could not see them anywhere and presumed they had absconded—only to find them below ground level at the bottom of a seven-foot hole. The Africans on the other hand, used to hand me a broken spade and then say,

'Oh, that *mzungu* cannot do hard work.'

That was their expectation. When I took to the ploughing, they were as surprised as they were impressed.

While many white people have a distorted impression of Africans, the Africans also have a particularly distorted view of white people from what they have seen of us. Many Kenyans, for example, believe everyone in Europe has a hired cook in their home. The settlers all have at least one. The Irish missionaries have cooks as well; this is often not just to save time and effort, but also to provide much needed employment.

CHAPTER 15 RETURN TO NYUMBANI

A lot of Kenyans believe nobody in Europe knows how to ride a bicycle, simply because they never see a white person riding one. They were astonished at first to see me on the boneshaker. Many Akamba exhausted themselves trying to overtake me at this novel activity—the *mzungu* on the bicycle—just for the thrill of it.

'Your bicycle, it is too old. You are rich, buy a car, *mzungu!*' one man jokingly shouted when he finally got past me.

This was greeted by roars of laughter from bystanders. If I managed to beat them at draughts, playing on the dust using discarded bottle-tops, they were all genuinely shocked at the outcome.

'This game is only played in Kenya,' I was told on numerous occasions by the disbelieving.

There was almost universal curiosity about Europe. Kimanze, like Nzoki and nearly every other Akamba adult, used to ask me regularly about Europe with the innocent wonder of a child. They had an image of Utopia in their heads. They invariably told me they hoped to visit Europe sometime. I could tell them nearly anything and they would believe it, and I sometimes did. Ireland was rarely mentioned in Kenyan newspapers. One story I remember reading in the *Daily Nation* was about a lorry spilling a cargo of hens that ran loose in Cavan; I also read about someone caught crossing the border at Newry with crocodiles in the car boot. The only other stories from Ireland reported in Kenya in my time were about the Rev. Ian Paisley.

'Why are you always fighting with only two tribes when Kenya has forty-two tribes and we live in peace?' Mutinda not unreasonably once inquired before he died, and of course before the outbreak of violence in 2008.

Kenyans think *we* are strange. Mwangangi, Nzoki, Kimanze, the lot of them had worked it out too that I was a son of Sr. MM, Sr. MM was a sister of Fr. Liam, Fr. Liam was the father of Fr. Paul, and Fr. Paul was somehow also the son of Fr. Frank—or variations on that theme. They had it figured out in such a way that all the dozen or so Irish around Kitui were from the one family.

'All you white people look the same,' Mwangangi told me.

Even though I knew that many did not get the chance of an education, and may not have been that much exposed to the media or visited other regions, I was still taken aback by the limitations of their knowledge. I remember around this time showing our cook, Nyambura, a photo of me nearing the top of Mount Kilimanjaro.

'And what is this?' she asked me with childlike curiosity, pointing to the snow I was standing on.

On an exceptionally clear morning, one could just about see Mount Kilimanjaro from Nyumbani. In the far distance, in the opposite direction, Mount Kenya was also sometimes visible. Of these twin peaks, my sights were now set on the latter—but that would have to wait for another day. Incidentally, it was from a high point not far from Nyumbani that the missionary Johann Ludwig Krapf became the first European to set eyes on Mount Kenya, in 1849. A Swahili slave trader, whose descendants still live in Kitui village, escorted him inland from the coast to confirm the hitherto legendary tales of snow on the equator.

At Nyumbani, I was living at an altitude higher than the highest point in Ireland (Carrantuohill being 3,409 feet above sea level). Before Mount Kilimanjaro, the highest I had ever climbed was Mount Washington in the Appalachians at over 6,000 feet—the site of the fastest ever-recorded wind speed on earth. I recall that, after clambering for hours and hours over rocks and boulders through thick cloud, the curtain of rain briefly parted to reveal a tarmac car park, a steam-train chugging along, and a restaurant at the very top. Such memories used to stir me amid the aridity of Kitui. Climbing Kilimanjaro had not entirely assuaged the urge to climb. I was conscious I might never again be as close to another world-renowned mountain as I was to Mount Kenya. I resolved to attempt an ascent in the coming months.

Phase II of Nyumbani was now rescheduled to finish at Easter. It had been a lot of hard work, and for the most part, I had enjoyed it. Now that I was back, I had considered volunteering for an extended period. But as I had largely worked myself out of the job to which I was best suited, I looked into the possibility of volunteering at one or two other places in Kitui instead. I also contemplated working in the slums of Nairobi. I had been informally offered a position as a volunteer with one organisation in the slums, either in an accounting role assisting people trying to start simple businesses, or possibly working with the slum children.

The slums very rarely attract any white people. Only a limited number of missionaries or aid workers venture in. The inhabitants of the slums are more hardened by their harsh living-conditions, and do not treat a white person with the same sense of celebrity as the Akamba do around Kitui. Nevertheless, the slums are amazing places, and I felt I might have something to offer.

An accidental fire had swept through Nairobi's Mukuru slum

one night at the start of April, leaving 30,000 people homeless. Within days, the shacks had been rebuilt, after a fashion, with the charred leftovers of the fire. During a one-day visit to Mukuru shortly afterwards, when I was making further enquiries about volunteering, I saw open filthy sewers flooding through the front doors of the wretched hovels. The second coming of the rainy season had reached as far as Nairobi by then, and that was the immediate cause of the problem.

The rains that had petered out so early in Kitui, on the other hand, had still not returned—to everyone's great disappointment. It was now officially the worst drought in the region since 1964. The donkeys, which people used to help carry water several kilometres home, were dying from starvation and drought. Their demise would mean it would be impossible for some families to collect enough water to survive. It could mean people, weakened by hunger, having to walk up to a fifteen-kilometre round-trip carrying heavy jerry-cans filled with water.

In times like these, Fr. Frank's skills as a gifted water-diviner were much in demand. He could unerringly pinpoint nearer sources of water that could be developed by the locals. Some Akamba had trouble coming to terms with his uncanny accuracy for water-divining; it verged on something they viewed to be within the realm of witchcraft.

'I have seen years when there have been longer spells without rain, but I have never seen it affect the entirety of Akambaland as disastrously as this year,' Fr. Frank worriedly remarked. 'I don't think I have ever seen the people as demoralised as they are now.'

Government relief measures required thousands of people to

walk anything up to fifteen kilometres to the home of the local chief to collect the single kilogram of food. This was the ration allocated to a whole family. There was a terrible uncertainty about when, or if, another delivery would arrive. Hunger and frustration were testing the resilience and patience for which the Akamba were renowned. Desperation, inevitably, led to an increase of crime. A gang of over thirty hungry people took to raiding homes around Kitui during this time. The mission station—or, for that matter, a white man alone on a bicycle—would make a tempting target for attack. Apprehension filled the air, especially when darkness fell.

At Nyumbani, I had often taken out a blanket and slept on the back of an ox-cart under the breathtaking galaxies of stars. I was having second thoughts about it now. I started doing it initially because, apart from the heat, any beds that there were in Akambaland were all too small for me; the Akamba people, from my lanky perspective, were only slightly taller than Pygmies. Western beds have never been part of life in Akambaland. Even if *I* was having second thoughts, I still sometimes saw mothers and children sleeping on the ground at night outside their huts. They had no choice. This left them vulnerable to poisonous snakes.

Kimanze kept a cat around our house to keep such snakes at a safe distance. I once made the mistake of asking him what his pet cat was called.

'Cat,' was the bemused response. 'What else would I call it? It's just to keep the snakes away.'

It was a very unsentimental, indeed African, attitude to animals. In Kenya, I discovered, the dogs choose their owners; the owners do not usually choose their dog. The only nexus between them is food. All the 'pets' are scrawny as cardboard, rib cages showing on nearly every one of them. Kimanze laughed incredulously when I told him people in Ireland buy specially made pet food from a shop. I discovered too that a lot of these dogs have rabies around this time of year.

'If they are tame and seem friendly, it's a fairly sure sign they have rabies,' Kimanze warned me, ominously.

That lethargy could be a stage of rabies was another thing of which I was blissfully ignorant.

Nonetheless, during daylight hours it was still a joy to live in Kitui. Most people kept smiling despite their tribulations. I was still the Pied Piper. Noisy children encircled me and ran after me when I mounted the bicycle. I still had to cycle for hours when I wanted to get to a landline to ring home. I often carried a young passenger perched on the handlebars as I wove my way around colobus monkeys and greeted happy barefoot women slapping their can-carrying donkeys out of my way—happy because they had found some distant source of precious water. I waved to the women; they danced and made shapes in response to my tooting the bicycle horn or ringing the bell.

In early April, Mwangangi and Kimanze installed an ordinary outside tap, drawing water from Nyumbani's largest tank. This enabled me to strip off and have a proper wash. It was so pleasurable with the cold running water that, on one occasion, I did not notice six or seven women steal up behind me. I was the talk of the place for days afterward.

' . . . and he is all white below his neck too!' they giggled.

The Akamba were often telling me I was dirty, meaning I was usually covered in a filament of dust.

CHAPTER 15 RETURN TO NYUMBANI

'A *mzungu* is always clean,' Nancy, Nyambura, and Nzoki would insist, implying that I was letting the side down. In truth, I found it impossible to keep clean with the plumes of fine red dust billowing up every time I put my foot to ground. The Akamba, the women in particular, are meticulous about washing when they find water. Often, they are immaculately turned out in the African fashion, radiant in their clothes of primary colours.

I, on the other hand, tended to dress more pragmatically than fashionably: broad-brimmed hat, brown-chequered long-sleeve cotton shirt and long khaki-coloured cotton slacks. The full-length trousers and the long sleeves were to prevent sunburn during the day and to stop the mosquitoes biting me in the evening. Just as important, long trousers helped me blend in among the local adults who would never dream of wearing shorts. They also offered protection against the multitudes of thorns around Kitui and Nyumbani. As well as being supposedly insect-repellent, the khaki colour has a distinct advantage in a dusty region like Kitui: one's clothes appear cleaner than they may be in reality even if, in my case, they sometimes failed to meet the high standard of cleanliness that eagle-eyed Nancy and her friends expected of a *mzungu*.

Cotton had the practical purpose of keeping me cooler during the daytime. I could usually avoid over-heating too, if I took a siesta in the middle of the day and stayed in the shade during much of the rest of the day. The latter was impossible, of course, when I was working on the farm. But, with the passing months, I gradually became more accustomed to the energy-sapping and sometimes-tortuous heat.

No Hurry in Africa

Around this time, the heat had been turned up, metaphorically, on the people involved in the fraud. I had suspected something was going on since before Christmas, but it was finally dealt with by the removal of a financial accountant and a secretary. I was extremely disillusioned by this fraudulence, given the amount of hard hours and money I, and so many others, had put into Nyumbani. Many Kenyans do not set out to be dishonest; but if in gainful employment at all, they come under intense family pressure, even from second cousins, to cream off a bit to help make ends meet for the extended family or to help pay school fees. Far too many succumb in the end, at all levels. In some cases, of course, the motivation is just greed—as apparently it was here.

The Nyumbani workers were to be paid late again in April; it was taking time to work the fraud out of the system. This always spelt danger. Discretion being the better part of valour, I cycled off on the boneshaker to the mission house several hours away, just as a riot looked as if it was about to break out. I was half expecting to be hijacked along the way; but there was an even better chance I would be lynched if I stayed put.

CHAPTER 16
CELEBRATIONS AND A MARRIAGE PROPOSAL

PHASE II OF THE NYUMBANI Village Project was officially opened at the start of Easter week. There were great celebrations from early in the morning: hours of jubilant music and colourful tribal dancing by the five hundred or so Akamba workers, as well as a joyfully riotous gala performance by the schoolchildren from the vicinity. The two fattest bulls had been slaughtered especially for the occasion. Rice was simmering in an enormous iron cooking pot outside, on top of a large fire. The feast was shared by all, and hugely appreciated given the famine conditions that prevailed. Under a sunny blue sky, several dignitaries addressed the large and not very attentive crowd from on top of a soapbox. I was so pleased to be a part of this festivity that all the ups and downs of the past months were forgotten. Even Kiragu returned to witness the moment.

Everyone was glowing with satisfaction, radiant in his or her Sunday best, and revelling in a sense of accomplishment. I had bought a dark beige suit especially for the event. I was looking like a real colonial, a white gentleman settler in Africa. The suit cost me 200 shillings (two euro) at the outdoor second-hand clothes market in Kitui village—but who would have guessed! For a good part of the day I was pleasantly tormented by a crowd of local children; they scrummaged around me, jockeying for position to ask questions of the exotic *mzungu*. Some of them claimed to know me from my visits to Nancy's and other outings. I even remembered several of them. As usual, the more audacious ones were pinching the hairs on my skin.

'You are a monkey with your hairy arms!' one boy exclaimed in Kikamba, to general fits of giggling.

A flash of irony crossed my mind; the crude slur of Dr. Shane's a couple of months earlier had unwittingly been turned on me.

The few children who spoke English well were being urged to ask me the questions that were troubling the others.

'Gentleman, is your blood red?'

'Aye. Why, what colour did you imagine it to be?'

'I thought your blood was white. I thought that is why your skin is white. Tell us, what are your glasses for?' (No Akamba around Nyumbani wore glasses.)

'So I can see in the dark,' I revealed.

'Well, why have you them on now?'

Children can be relentlessly logical.

'So I can see far away,' I answered.

'Can you see my mother on that hill?'

A cheeky boy was pointing to a group of huts on a hill a few kilometres away.

'Yes, she is outside scrubbing your clothes in a basin right now,' I replied.

A collective murmur of amazement rippled through the audience. I had their full attention and was enjoying it.

'I want to see her. Can I try them on?'

'No,' I refused, for I knew I would never get them back in one piece.

CHAPTER 16 CELEBRATIONS AND A MARRIAGE PROPOSAL

'They look ugly. They don't go with your suit, gentleman.'

This was very observant; since I had broken them in Uganda, they were being temporarily held together by tape. The cross-examination continued.

'Tell us, have you elephants in your country?'

'No.'

'What!'

There were gasps of incredulity as the word went round.

'You mean you have no elephants in your country—and what about giraffes?'

'Just a few, they don't like the cold. We use them to pull our carts,' I explained.

Very impressed at this novel use of giraffes, they grilled me further.

'Do you get rain?'

'Every day. We have as many rainy days as you have sunny days.'

'Do you grow bananas on your farm with the rain, and what about your snakes?'

'We grow bananas under water so the snakes can't eat them.'

My tall tales thereafter became more and more far-fetched, though I tried to make them credible with authentic details.

In the middle of it all, I was taken aback when one young boy suddenly piped up,

'Most thankful we are for the blessings of God.'

He must have been echoing what he had heard at home or in church. He probably did not know the meaning of the words. And yet it was true; on the face of it, so little had been bestowed on these children, who many days went hungry, yet they were so appreciative of what little they had, the very simplest of things.

They were hanging on my every word for well over an hour, until I was innocently asked,

'And who is your president?'

'Mary McAleese,' I answered, correctly this time.

There was the usual simultaneous translation, then a momentary silence. They turned to each other with looks of disbelief on their faces. I thought they did not like the sound of a female president. It turned out they did not like the thought that they had all of a sudden been lied to.

'No! A woman president! You are cheating us,' one older boy brazenly complained.

If I lied about that, from their perspective, had I been lying all along? I sensed their suspicions.

Soon after, Mwangangi and Kimanze trotted over to rescue me, and we divided ourselves into two sides for a mammoth game of football. My 'cheating' story was soon forgotten in the shrill excitement of the game.

In the afternoon, I got to talk with several of the dignitaries present. For them the celebrations were somewhat dampened by a plane crash the night before, in which several ministers and MPs from Eastern Province (of which Kitui is a part) had been killed. Among the dead were also several district commissioners and a bishop. Our local district commissioner and several chiefs were present, however. I noticed that district commissioners tended to dress in khaki uniforms, the ensemble topped off with a bowl-shaped colonial-style hat. Evidently they were following the fashion set by white British colonial administrators a century before, when shorts were worn with socks pulled up to the knees.

CHAPTER 16 CELEBRATIONS AND A MARRIAGE PROPOSAL

I marvelled that no one had thought to change the uniform after Independence.

An English MP named Jeremy Hunt was present as the representative of significant fundraisers in the UK. It was he who officially opened Nyumbani school, though of course there were no children in Nyumbani to be educated as yet. He and I discussed how the education system of Kenya seems to have inherited many traits of the Victorian school system introduced when the British first arrived. Schools are mostly single sex, while all secondary schools and some primary schools have boarding facilities. Uniforms are considered very important; they are often a child's only decent clothes, so they are commonly worn at weekends too. Pupils seem to be overloaded with homework. Beatings are not unknown, despite corporal punishment being banned in 2003.

Jeremy, an up-and-coming member of the Tory front bench at the time, was curious to discover how I had ended up in Kitui, what I was doing there, and how I fitted into the local community. He came across as deeply interested in Africa and its people. He explained to me how he had come to be involved in the fundraising for Nyumbani. I was impressed by the fact that his commitment to Africa was practical, not just theoretical, which I suspect may be the case with some politicians. He was acquiring first-hand experience of Africa's needs, and he appreciated that education is the key.

In rural regions and in the slums, many children go to school just to be fed. Most pupils take education very seriously though, and many are highly intelligent. Even as children, they realise it is their only way to a better future. Sr. Nora, an Irish Mercy nun who taught near the mission house of Fr. Frank and Fr. Liam, had a classroom with over seventy pupils. There was never a peep out of them. The students also realise the sacrifice their parents make to pay their school fees, even to the point of selling off their cattle.

Free primary education was only introduced in 2002, the first major reform by the new Kibaki government. Up to then, huge swathes of the population received no education at all. One ninety-seven year old Kenyan man got himself photographed in the papers for being the oldest primary school pupil in the entire world when free education came in. The schools are desperately under-resourced, but their aspirations are high. Each school has its own motto, some of which can be unintentionally amusing. One of my favourites was the Kitui school whose motto was 'Educating next generation.' The absence of the definite article made it sound as if the present generation was being neglected, which was far from the case.

Even the names given to schools in Kenya sometimes can have amusing consequences. For instance, an order of nuns outside Nairobi runs the 'Precious Blood Secondary School.' An enterprising man beside the school opened a shop called the 'Precious Blood Butcher.' He had no idea at all what it meant, nor did he understand why the nuns would become very angry over the perceived blasphemy!

Towards the end of Nyumbani's great day of celebrations, the rain began to pour like in the time of the Ark, turning the fine dust to cloying mud in minutes. I was trudging home bare-foot when I found myself having to wade through a torrent that came up to my waist, which had suddenly materialised from nowhere. I had experienced this before with dried-up riverbeds, but the suddenness of it always frightened me. Once I was across, I shook my head when I realised how my new suit was ruined from the muddy water. But a second later, I turned and spotted some of the children I had been joking with earlier in the day stranded on the other bank. I shouted at them to stay where they were and not to attempt to wade through the rushing torrent. Children often panic and drown in these situations. They would have no choice but to spend the night on the other side of the river from where their homes were. Eventually I reached my own house and alerted Mwangangi, Kimanze, and the others to the children's predicament.

Later on, when the monsoon subsided a bit, Mwangangi and I arranged for the stranded children and some adults to be transported in the back of a lorry to Kwa Vonza where they would stay the night with any relatives they had in the area. People were very accommodating and we found each of them a home. News of our rescue operation spread rapidly via the ever-reliable bush telegraph.

When things were sorted out, Mwangangi suggested we retire to a café in Kwa Vonza village for some *chapatti* and *chai*. It was a tiny room built with unplastered concrete blocks and dimly lit with a paraffin hurricane lamp. The inevitable scrawny dog was reclining on the café's only bench. The sole item on the menu was fried dough. Outside, the rain was becoming torrential again after a brief respite. There was the rather odd sensation of bolts of lightning seemingly striking the exact same spot, over and over and over again, but without any sound of thunder accompanying them. Presently, the café started to flood. It had been an eventful day.

NO HURRY IN AFRICA

The following night, our Kikuyu cook, Nyambura, and I were sitting in silence next to a hurricane lamp. My time at Nyumbani was coming to an end. The radio had run out of batteries and we had run out of conversation. A solitary mouse scuttled past. A good few times in that house, I had awoken in the middle of the night to the unmistakable sound of a mouse rummaging, or one scurrying past my bed. We spent the next hour chasing down all the mice in the house; it was pure *Tom and Jerry*. Nyambura was convulsed with laughter.

Having banished the mice, we continued our vermin hunt by tackling the bats resident under the high tin roof. The scorpions were a tougher proposition. Hidden deep in crevices, we only knew of their presence when they fell out, dead, after we had sprayed poison in their general direction. Ants were a perennial problem; they mounted frequent invasions of the house. The Akamba have a novel solution to this problem; they get everyone to urinate on the ant mounds in order to poison the ants inside. Curiously, the local monkeys tended to bury their dead in the anthills.

A couple of days later, I moved out of our house and took up residence in Kitui. There was no longer any need for me to stay at Nyumbani. The day I was leaving, I found myself reminiscing over my time there. It was the place where I had come closest to living the authentic African life. Some Africans used to joke to me that I was living more Kenyan than some Kenyans (such as the ones in Nairobi who tried too hard to act European). Most of the time, I loved the fact that Nyumbani was so remote and without any modern comfort. Above all, I got to love the Akamba people, their outgoingness and their spontaneity. Their dancing, whether impromptu or on special occasions, was always a pure celebration of the joy of living.

Nyumbani had been the place where the local Akamba workers loved to welcome me to their humble homes and to entertain me, with the whole neighbourhood invited to join in. It had been a pleasure working amongst these people who are generally regarded as the friendliest tribe in Kenya. I had experienced the seasonal rhythms of life among them in the long dry seasons and the short rainy seasons. I had really enjoyed living in our house in Nyumbani—most of the time anyway. Just as important, I had found most of the work fulfilling. I nearly always felt it was exactly where I should be at that point in my life.

Easter week was a big deal in Kitui. There were crowded religious processions outside the church on Palm Sunday; people were waving large palm leaves and carrying crosses woven from palm reeds. On Good Friday, even larger crowds processed through Kitui village bearing giant crucifixes and holding up umbrellas to shade them from the sun. Rather incongruously for Good Friday, people turned the evangelical churches into something resembling a disco, and worshippers danced merrily around the street preachers. On the other hand, the Catholic ceremony in the Cathedral was solemn and atmospheric. It was celebrated by Fr. Paul, in Swahili.

I bumped into Leo ('Jesus Hitler') by chance on the night of Good Friday in Kwa Vonza village. We exchanged news and views. He was planning to begin a roundabout overland journey back to Germany the next day. He wrote to me later. He had made it as far as Shashemene, the Vatican of the Rastafarians near Addis Abiba in Ethiopia. There he was refused an onward visa for Sudan, so he flew back out of Nairobi to Germany a couple of months later. Well, the best laid plans of mice, of men, of Rastas . . .

Another highlight of Easter week, for me, was the wedding of Cecil, the Nyumbani driver, on Easter Saturday. He was getting married to an evangelical Christian woman in Nairobi. As usual, getting there by bus was half the entertainment. At Kitui's chaotic bus station, the drivers, touting for business, were sitting in the back of the buses and paying a bunch of hawkers to sit there too. This was to make the bus look nearly full, and so fool people into thinking it was about to leave shortly—as buses in Kenya generally do not run on timetables, but rather they leave only when full. While the bus was waiting to fill up, the hawkers tried every trick in the book to make me buy a sharp dagger, then a lampshade, and ultimately a picture-frame. I did not really require any of these things on my way to a wedding.

Having off-loaded the hawkers, we finally started moving about an hour later, after a ten-minute prayer for a safe journey. I had the honour of leading the prayer!

'Father British will give the blessing,' the driver announced confidently in front of everyone.

'Sure why not?' I replied rhetorically.

I stood up and as reverently as I could, started the prayer off; to my great relief, it was taken up by other passengers. The conductor, while hanging precariously out the door, banged the side of the bus noisily as we did three laps of the village. Then, with several extended blasts from the driver of the eight-note melody on the horn, we were off.

The wedding started off fairly sedately by Kenyan standards.

CHAPTER 16 CELEBRATIONS AND A MARRIAGE PROPOSAL

As the ceremony progressed, however, the congregation's excitement mounted. Soon everybody started jumping up and down, and waving their wooden stools above their heads. Some were scampering and dancing around the church. One reverend, among the several in attendance, appeared to be a few psalms short of a psalter. He was fervently casting out demons from the bride's womb while bent down shouting at her midriff. It was so surreal that I was falling off my stool with suppressed laughter. What was abundantly clear, though, was that Cecil and his bride were truly head-over-heels in love. Though both were Akamba, they had grown up together in Nairobi.

It was straight after the wedding ceremony that Nyambura proposed to me, while we sat eating a bowl of rice and black beans together on the steps of the church. She was a bright attractive young woman, with high cheeks bones and the round darker-coloured face so characteristic of the Kikuyu. I turned her down. She was not the first woman who had made me a similar proposition since I arrived in Kitui, but no other proposal was as genuine as this one.

'I am sorry, but I am not allowed to marry outside my tribe,' I told Nyambura, just as I had told the others in order not to hurt their feelings.

Endogamy was something most of them could understand. They would then carry on with the normal activities of the day as if they had never asked. I think Nyambura was quite disappointed, though. I knew her so well, and sensed that she was good at hiding her feelings.

A few hours later Nyambura told me a story.

'Gikuyu and Mumbi—they are the Adam and Eve of the Kikuyu tribe, Brendan—lived next to a *mugumo* fig tree at the foot of Mount Kenya. They had nine beautiful daughters. One afternoon, when the daughters were nearly adults, they walked to a lake to fetch water. There they found nine handsome men swimming at the lakeshore. That's how the nine clans of the Kikuyu tribe began.'

She paused to see if I wished her to continue. I certainly did, as myths of origin I always found interesting. I was reminded of the old Celtic myths.

'Women ruled the Kikuyu tribe for generations and generations. One night, the men secretly decided to rise up against the women. So they formed a plan. They got all the women pregnant at the same time the next night.'

She hesitated at this revelation, turned away shyly, and then resumed her story.

'After waiting for eight months, the men seized control, taking advantage of the women's condition. Ever since that moment among the Kikuyu tribe, two people of the same clan are forbidden to marry each other. It is taboo.'

How this story might apply to our situation was a bit of a puzzle. More than once, I had been asked by Kenyan women to give them a *mzungu* baby. I was just required to do the deed; plant the seed, so to speak. No beating around the bush with them. One particular Akamba woman, as she requested this service, said rather poignantly,

'I want lots of babies, because I am afraid they will not all survive infancy.'

Around Nairobi, Western influence can be detected in the classifieds of the *Daily Nation,* in the section of the newspaper where people look for love. This was one I spotted (as I searched for a wife!):

I am a 33 year old unattached devout Catholic woman, who would like to meet a devout Catholic man. Should be unattached, never married, passed 'O level' exams or above, must be from Nyanza Province, to share love and life with. Should be 32–37 years old and business minded, financially stable, well groomed and good looking, ready for a HIV test, friendship, settle down in marriage soon and have children.

I'm probably too young to apply for an interview, I thought, and I could hardly pretend to be financially stable.

One day when I was drinking at a bar in Nairobi, a red-faced middle-aged man walked in, looking for all the world like a small farmer in rural Ireland. He was wearing a brown flat cap and sported a prominent moustache. Soon he was propping up the bar and being chatted up by the beautiful 'Nairobi girls'—or prostitutes, as some might call them. Anyway, I had to satisfy my curiosity and walked over to talk to him. Within a few sentences, I was piecing together a picture in my mind.

'Oh, you were once a priest?' I speculated.

By way of reply, he mumbled something vaguely negative.

'You must know Fr. Frank and Fr. Liam in Kitui then.'

It was a long shot, but the few hundred Irish people living in Kenya all seemed to know one another.

'How do you know them? Sure I used to live with them,' he responded.

Suddenly he was more forthcoming. It turned out that he had indeed been a priest, and was stationed in Kitui Diocese. He eloped with an Akamba woman, quit the priesthood, and married her. I did not want to pry further.

When I later told Fr. Liam about my encounter with him, Fr. Liam commented,

'It happens, Brendan. There was another Irish priest in Kitui once, but he stuck it for only a couple of years. He ran off and married a nun.'

There are many pitfalls and hazards for the novice missionary. When I gave Fr. Frank my account of Cecil's wedding, he told me,

'One of the Irish missionaries in Kitui, a number of years ago, was not familiar with all the checks needed in Kenya to approve a couple for marriage in the Catholic Church. He had just arrived from Ireland a short time before. The morning after one particular wedding that he performed, an angry Akamba man, a brother of the bride, stormed up to the mission house.

"You have just married a man who already has two wives," he reprimanded the priest. "This is his third."'

Easter Sunday was another opportunity for a missionary dinner; the jokes and tales came thick and fast, with punch-lines delivered in Swahili and Kikamba and even in Irish. There was much uncontrollable laughter at the exploits of our Kenyan friends. Yet, we gave our full attention when one of us recounted experiencing an Akamba custom for the first time, for even after over forty years living among them, the missionaries were still discovering new aspects to the people every week. The stories told at these missionary get-togethers were as unbelievable as they were true. Fr. Frank started the ball rolling that evening.

'I buried a man yesterday. Half-way through the Mass, they were still busy banging away, nailing the wood together for the coffin.'

CHAPTER 16 CELEBRATIONS AND A MARRIAGE PROPOSAL

'I can top that,' Fr. Liam boasted. 'Yesterday I was called out to banish a "genie" from a parishioner's home. As I was blessing the home, sprinkling holy water on it, I became aware of a witch-doctor—I know the man to see—watching me. He disappeared, then returned a minute later and splashed a bucket of water over me! In retaliation, I suppose.'

As the stories multiplied, a large orange full moon rose dramatically from beneath the horizon, almost as if it were a second sunrise. Just then, the electricity went off at the mission house, immediately followed by the usual loud cheer from the nearby boarding schools. We lit the candles, and pondered once again in the darkness whether it was rain or bandits that had cut the electricity to the whole village. Ah well, I thought as I drifted off to sleep, at least it will stop the fundamentalist preachers roaring their heads off, keeping people awake offering their cures for cancer over their loud-speakers.

Shortly after midnight, I was awakened by blood-chilling screams coming from a home nearby. In all probability, a robbery was in progress. Were we going to be hit next? I lay awake half the night, with mounting fear. Eventually I fell into a fitful sleep; in my troubled dreams, the *panga*—the machete—figured prominently.

CHAPTER 17
TO HELL'S GATE AND BACK

AFTER EASTER, I RESOLVED to seize the opportunity to explore more of Kenya before returning to voluntary work. So I headed off by myself with the intention of spending around a fortnight camping in a number of places in the Great Rift Valley. Camping would be the best option, I imagined; all the cheaper hotels in Kenya seemed to double up as brothels. I always discovered evidence of this dual function throughout the night, when I could clearly hear business being conducted on the other side of the thin walls.

The Rift Valley is the geological fault line that runs from Lebanon, down the Dead Sea, the Red Sea, Ethiopia, Kenya, Tanzania, and as far as Lake Malawi in the southern end of Africa. In millions of years' time, East Africa will become separated from the rest of the continent, geologists claim. However, when anyone speaks of the Great Rift Valley, the classic image in people's minds is that part of it that stretches for the 250km or so north of Nairobi.

My first destination was Lake Naivasha, over fifty kilometres to the north of the capital. Lake Naivasha used to be the heart of the 'Happy Valley' hedonism, where predominantly upper-class English settlers regularly engaged in interminable drink and drug fuelled, partner-sharing orgies. These decadent colonials launched the reputation of Kenya as being a playground for the privileged, especially in the years between the two world wars. This abruptly ended when Lord Errol was mysteriously gunned down in his Buick late one night in 1941, generating much unwelcome publicity and a medley of conspiracy theories. Lord Errol was the most alluring of them all, a prolific philanderer who happened to be the premier peer of the British Empire at the time.

A sensational court case ended without a conviction. Theories abounded about who could have done it, from any number of jealous husbands, to British agents sent to assassinate the alleged fascist sympathiser. Whoever was responsible, it meant the Rift Valley orgies of self-indulgence were over. Tales of aristocratic debauchery did not go down well in the England of ration books; this was the time when England was at the lowest ebb in World War II. The life and times of the cast of 'Happy Valley' are well depicted in the book *White Mischief* by James Fox.

My own interest in this part of the Rift Valley and in its recent high-living history was sparked by a remarkable old boy who had visited Nyumbani one afternoon. A bald, sprightly octogenarian white man introduced himself to me. He told me his name was Rudolf, and was the owner of a company selling medicinal plants to Nyumbani. I suggested that he wait in the shade with me until someone came to look after him. He had eccentric written all over him—and all the more interesting for that. He told me that he grew up at Lake Naivasha during the 1920s and 30s, in the 'Happy Valley' period, and had lived his whole life in Kenya. He was softly spoken, with traces of a Germanic accent.

'My parents, they were descended from Italian and Austrian

nobility,' he asserted with pride. 'They sailed to Kenya to shoot game on safari and ended up staying for good. Back then, the waters of Lake Naivasha were Kenya's main airport, for all the hydroplanes on the Imperial Airways route between Southampton and South Africa.'

Once Rudolf had started reminiscing, there was no stopping him. As a young man, he was a witness to the rampant shenanigans among the aristocrats and adventurers of his parents' generation; the drinking, the drugs, the wife swapping. He had seen it all. I was pretty sure he was not making it up. When I implied that he might have joined in, he denied it—but I was not entirely convinced. Later, when I read Fox's book on Lord Errol, I became certain he knew what he was talking about.

It was after this encounter that I made up my mind to spend some time in the Rift Valley. Rudolf had persuaded me that there was a lot more to it than the wife swapping of bygone days. Today, Lake Naivasha is one of only a handful of enclaves left in Kenya with a sizable white farming community. Rudolf informed me that the second biggest foreign currency earning industry in Kenya is (would you believe?) flowers. These are all grown on the white-owned farms on the lake's southern shores, and exported fresh overnight to Europe.

On arrival at the lake in the late afternoon, the bus dropped me off near a campsite on the southern lakeshore. At a checkpoint along the way, the bus conductor had told us in Swahili,

'I will give a few shillings to the policeman *for tea.*'

We all laughed knowingly. It took only a few minutes to pitch my tent beneath a sturdy tree on the smoothest part of ground away from the water's edge. There were small wavelets soothingly lapping up over the pebbles.

I recalled Yeats' line about '*lake water lapping with low sounds by the shore.*'

It was an inspiring scene. As evening evaporated into night over the vast lake, enclosed by the two imposing escarpments of the Rift Valley on either side, I could hear the call of exotic birds in the growing darkness and the sound of other unidentified creatures all around. I had heard there was a good chance of hippopotamuses wandering around the outside of the campsite at night. At least, I hoped they would remain on the outside. Hippos live under water during the day, and graze on land at night.

I woke before dawn the next morning, looking forward to an adventurous day ahead. For breakfast, I rustled up a bit of fruit and bread I had bought in the nearby village the day before. I was biting hungrily into a sandwich in the half-light when a monkey bounded past, apparently intent on stealing my belongings. As I jumped up to chase him away, his friend grabbed the sandwich straight out of my hand. Those creatures were proving very cute at creating distractions. As I peeled a banana, another monkey suddenly swiped it from behind, leapt up the tree, and threw the peel back down onto my head. I was being bullied by monkeys of all things!

I had risen before dawn in order to cycle through the long red canyon known as Hell's Gate, beside Lake Naivasha. I was going to test the theory that the best chance to see game animals is in very early morning and towards dusk. I entered Hell's Gate to find myself alone; it was still too early for any other visitors, who might arrive later. I found myself in a dramatic landscape of hot steaming springs amid towering columns of red volcanic rock, with vultures circling overhead. It was even more dramatic later in the day, when the searing daytime heat was ripped apart by a thunder and lightning spectacular. Few places on earth more deserve the name 'Hell's Gate,' I thought. Back in 1883, a pioneering German explorer called Gustav Fischer had his entire party of porters massacred by Maasai warriors in this place. Fischer himself survived, however, and later returned to Germany with his tale. His name is commemorated in Fischer's Tower, a red volcanic column about a hundred feet high.

The very name of the place was the main reason that attracted me to explore Hell's Gate. It lived up to its other reputation, too; a great place to see a wide variety of African wildlife. The canyon was filled with animals. I dismounted from my hired bicycle from time to time to watch the eland leaping, zebras grazing, ostriches cantering—and the inevitable bickering baboons. The playful warthogs were my favourite; they are very comical in their ugliness. I did not spot a cheetah or a leopard; maybe they spotted me first, and I was happy enough about that because I was the only human around. I sat on the grass, alone amidst near perfect silence, inhaling the beauty of the scene.

At the far end of the canyon, several Maasai men were busy taking a shower underneath a warm waterfall that seemed to spring from the earth on top of one of the cliffs. The hot springs and waterfalls are heated by the Rift Valley volcanic activity. Four months earlier, an earthquake measuring 6.8 on the Richter scale hit the Rift Valley, causing even more chaos than usual in Nairobi. I asked the Maasai about the cheetahs and leopards. One of them spoke Swahili and quite good English.

'A couple of weeks ago,' he told me, as he boiled an egg using water from a hot spring, 'a shepherd near Naivasha stepped into the darkness with only a wooden spear to fight off a leopard that was hunting his goats. The man was very nearly eaten himself when the leopard attacked him—but he is still alive today.'

For the next fortnight—it was now the second half of April—wherever I visited in the Rift Valley I practically had it to myself. There is hardly a tourist in all of Kenya around that time of year, apart from a slow trade at the Mombasa beaches. After a couple of days spent relaxing around Lake Naivasha, I journeyed by bus on to Lake Nakuru National Park, over fifty kilometres further north of Naivasha and one of the best game reserves in the country. The park officials would not accept my genuine Kenyan resident's card, but took my slightly doctored student's card instead for discounted admission.

Darkness was approaching as I searched for a suitably flat and secluded position to erect my tent at the designated camping spot within the Park. Waterbucks were obliviously munching nearby. I could just about make out Lake Nakuru itself, the soda lake world famous for its flamingo population. I convinced myself I could detect in the fading light a streak of pink on the distant shoreline. That would be tomorrow's excitement. Before that, however, a more familiar drama was unfolding, the performers a troupe of baboons.

I had bought enough fruit and bread in Nakuru town to satisfy me while I would be in the Park. As I made preliminary inroads into my rations, I became aware of what I imagined to be an extended family of baboons edging closer all the while. I did not feel in any way threatened; the young and the females were grooming each other and seemed to be in a playful mood. It is fascinating to observe how a clan of baboons has a sentry system with males encircling the females and their young.

All at once, I came under co-ordinated attack from four or five males, a classic smash-and-grab raid on my sandwiches. I had taken trouble to conceal them, but these baboons were more up-front and aggressive than the monkeys of Naivasha. Their tactic was intimidation, hence the numbers. They took every morsel of food I possessed. My token resistance proved as futile as a sand-castle resisting the incoming tide. These were real vandals. They entered the tent and strewed my clothes all over the place. Nancy had been right to warn me about them.

Still reeling from their shock tactics, I was left standing clutching my one solitary sandwich in my hand. The largest ba-boon advanced on me, snarling. I threw it to him in fright. This seemed to signal a general retreat, mission accomplished. To an observer, the whole scenario might have looked quite funny. For me it was beyond a joke! I was going to have to go hungry for maybe twenty-four hours. Save for a rumbling tummy, it did not bother me at all. I had become kind of used to going hungry in Kenya from time to time.

In the middle of the night, I was startled out of my slumber by loud rustling sounds very near the tent, far too close for comfort. I was picturing a lion about to pounce on the tent and devour me, or envisaging a rhino charging with its horn and trampling the tent while I lay inside. I stayed on my back, perfectly motion-less, too terrified to make a move or create a sound. I did not want to excite its attention, whatever *it* might be.

Minutes passed, time stretched out interminably, and my nerves grew taut. Eventually I peeped out with one eye though a gap that I noiselessly established in the front of the tent. Through the veil of darkness, I could just make out a hyena and, worse still, at least three buffalo only yards away. I knew the latter could be among the most dangerous animals in the bush; and I recalled Akamba stories about the viciousness of the trap-jawed hyenas. After an eternity, they moved away. I could breathe again.

Early next morning, the orange sun was setting aglow the eerie mist that was levitating off the soda lake. Nobody else was about, except for a Peace Corp volunteer who had arrived before dawn in his jeep. I had met twenty-six year old Glenn the day before in Nakuru town, and we arranged to go together to view the flamingos. For hours, we were rewarded with an unforgettable spectacle; a vast bright pink carpet of maybe two million long-legged flamingos spread around the edge of the lake. We tried to think of a collective term for the birds; we settled in the end for a 'blush' of flamingos.

These birds, the so-called 'lesser' flamingos of East Africa, were mainly breakfasting on the algae soup that forms on the surface of the lake. Nakuru's soda lake is an alkaline brew with a high volcanic ash content. These soda lake waters are poisonous to virtually all other creatures, thus protecting the birds from predators like the hyena. I was most surprised by the din that they created, a loud ceaseless nattering as they conducted their noisy early morning business. We watched with pleasure their characteristic running take-offs, and gradual descents as they came in to land. It resembled a vast flamingo airport. It was a truly wonderful sight.

After three hours or so, we dragged ourselves away from one of Nature's most colourful spectacles. Our departure was delayed by Glenn's jeep becoming entrenched in the soft silt at the lake-shore, but we had the rest of the day to revel in the wildlife of the Park. We were mentally ticking off the species: the rare black rhinoceros, the Thompson's gazelles, the giraffes towering above the acacia trees, the herds of buffaloes and zebras, the comedy of warthogs mating . . . and wildlife I never even knew existed before. It was absolutely exhilarating to observe such diversity. Sometimes, it resembled an untouched Garden of Eden, or maybe the concentration of animals being rounded up for Noah's Ark. They were nearly a bit too easy to find at times. Sometimes, I was conscious that the animals of Lake Nakuru Park are enclosed, like a humongous outdoor zoo.

It was onwards for me after that. Glenn dropped me off at the bustling bus station in Nakuru town (the fourth-largest urban centre in Kenya), where one of the many conductors loudly pounding the side of the buses persuaded me to travel to Lake Baringo on the other side of the equator. I had not really been planning on going there, but, on impulse, I decided that I might as well explore further.

On the bus, I found myself wedged between two drunken old women, wizened with age, who were sharing a bottle of something potent. They motioned the bottle to me a good few times to take a swig. I gestured back: not a chance! By now, the fertile farmlands were gradually giving way to a Turkana-type desert landscape. Nearer Lake Baringo—which is about 100km north of Nakuru—the bridges were long washed away, necessitating a hazardous crawl through the rock-strewn riverbeds. Men were hanging off the sides of the bus hollering and gesticulating at the people on bicycles who were holding on to the rear of moving lorries. The lorries themselves were crammed with people standing on the back, and were puffing out monstrous clouds of black exhaust just like every other vehicle on Kenya's roads. During one of the many breakdowns on the journey, fruit sellers stormed the bus pounding loudly at the sides trying to sell melons and peanuts through the open windows. Every journey in Africa is an adventure; passenger boredom is unknown.

Lake Baringo turned out to be one of my favourite places in the whole of Kenya. The freshwater lake, which is picturesquely encircled by cliffs and dotted with islands, appeared to have taken on an unusual red-purple hue from the silt on the bed of the lake. The campsite, right on the water's edge, was really just the grassy lawn of a modest colonial-era house. It belonged to an old-stager, an upper-class white-Kenyan lady named Betty. The afternoon I arrived, a party of white-Kenyan visitors came to stay for a few days. We met up at the lakeshore shortly afterwards and bonded almost immediately. Having been virtually alone in the previous campsites, I was glad of their company and the laugh we were having together.

This is hippopotamus country. My very first night there, I was woken up in my tent by really loud chomping coming from literally feet away. Here we go again, was my first fearful thought. But I soon relaxed because I had been forewarned that the hippos would graze close to the tents at night. They are unlikely to attack unless scared by bright lights or loud noises. I was more excited than scared this time, though still not entirely at ease. I knew that hippos are vegetarians, but I could imagine that a mutant carnivore might want me for dessert. It is *not knowing* what is out there in the darkness that is really scary.

CHAPTER 17 TO HELL'S GATE AND BACK

Lake Baringo is also ornithological heaven. The stillness of dawn is delightfully disturbed by the singing, sweet as harp music, of hundreds upon hundreds of birds, most of them spectacularly painted species of every size and shape.

'There are nearly five hundred different species here,' old Betty told me as we breakfasted at first light.

She herself was an avid 'twitcher.'

While I was keeping a beady eye on the crocodiles, sunbathing on the grass at the lakeshore beside my tent—I was pretty sure they were keeping several beady eyes on me—I encountered Ruarí. At 6"9' tall, it would have been hard to miss this outgoing Scot who was doing voluntary service in Kenya. He had grown up on the Isle of Skye, and had just completed training in Edinburgh to be a teacher. For the last six months, he had been working in a school a few kilometres outside Nairobi. We traded stories about our respective adventures and experiences.

On the second afternoon, Ruarí and I climbed up the near vertical cliffs set about two kilometres back from the lake, clambering up the scree with great difficulty. At the top we were rewarded by spectacular views of the lake beneath, with its many picturesque islands, some of them inhabited, to judge from the tell-tale trickles of smoke.

We encountered a barefoot herdsman tending his goats, the only human being around on the high plateau. He was carrying a bow and arrow. He could speak English surprisingly well, and seemed glad to have someone to talk to.

'Do you see that island there?' he asked us, as he pointed with his arm to one of the islands with a line of smoke rising from it. 'It's called Devil's Island. That one is uninhabited, but there has always been a fire on the island. It never goes out.'

I could not quite follow his explanation.

Ruarí and I had difficulty finding a safe way back down the cliff again. After some time, our friendly herdsman, who was watching our predicament from above, came to our rescue and, with his nimble-footed flock in tow, benevolently guided us part of the way down.

'It will rain later on today,' he predicted.

As it was about forty-degrees Celsius at the time and there were unblemished blue skies to the far horizon, Ruarí and I exchanged glances of disbelief.

'I have already lost fifty-four goats in the drought out of my total herd of sixty-eight,' he lamented.

We could only sympathise. His fourteen remaining goats were making music, the bells around their necks clinking merrily. When we stopped to take our bearings, I pointed to a pristinely tarred stretch of wide road below, apparently coming from nowhere and leading nowhere.

'Aye, probably the best road in all of Kenya,' Ruarí agreed in his Highlands burr.

During an entire hour of our descent, there were at most only a dozen people walking on it, and one cyclist—not a solitary vehicle.

'That stretch of road leads to former President Moi's home village,' Betty explained, back at the campsite. 'Moi was a typical "Big Man" of Africa; a virtual dictator with a fondness for his own name. In the Rift Valley, for example, he changed "Hoyes Bridge" to "Moi's Bridge." That took great imagination, boys!'

He commemorated himself all over the place, like Moi Avenue in Nairobi and many other examples I was forever coming across on my travels.

Moi treated his own Kalenjin tribes very preferentially, and is still revered around Lake Baringo. However, he is also rumoured to be the richest man in the whole of Africa—not bad for someone who started off as a schoolteacher. In saying that, he is one of only a handful of African leaders to have retired—as opposed to dying in office or being ousted militarily. He is still highly respected, if not exactly liked, by many sections of Kenyan society today.

A short while later, the herdsman was proved right, of course. A deluge started in the evening, as we were enjoying dinner and a few drinks with Betty and the other white-Kenyans on the verandah of the colonial house. On the positive side, the sheet lightning clearly illuminated the wildlife all around the campsite, especially the hippos at their nightly graze. On the way back to my tent in the darkness I had to be extra careful, as I slithered through the mud, not to disturb the mighty beasts, especially the mothers with their young.

Nearly everybody assumes that lions are the most dangerous animals in Africa. (Some nominate the tiger, unaware that tigers are only found in Asia). In fact, hippos are responsible for killing more humans than any other animal in Africa, followed by buffaloes. What is common to both hippos and buffaloes, apparently, is their lack of intelligence. They will certainly charge if one comes too close, or if the mother feels her young are under threat. Some male hippos also kill their own male offspring in response to some primitive territorial instinct.

On my third day at Lake Baringo, Ruarí, two white-Kenyans

NO HURRY IN AFRICA

and I hired a boat for a day and rowed out on the lake. We marvelled at the local Kalenjin tribesmen who were wading out with nets to catch fish in the crocodile and hippopotamus populated waters, walking out a kilometre or more in the shallow waters. On an island in the middle of the lake, we bought fish from one of the Njemp tribesmen who inhabit those islands—they are related to the Maasai tribe. His only clothing was a loose loincloth. The Njemps row with their cupped hands, sitting on a simple two-foot long one-man wooden raft. Betty had earlier told us if they ever drop their guard, they occasionally fall victim to both hippos and crocodiles. Living this close to nature, though, their survival instincts are sharply honed.

While I was travelling in the Rift Valley, a row erupted in Donegal when a well-known guidebook rubbished the county. A Donegal councillor went on the local radio station, *Highland Radio,* and countered that the guidebook on Kenya in the same series had claimed that a lake in Kenya had been safe to swim in. However, after reading the guidebook, an English student went swimming in the lake and was killed by a crocodile. This was his proof that the guidebook often got it wrong, and that Donegal was indeed a tourist paradise.

In no time at all, I got a phone call from my mother warning me not to swim in the lakes, not to go here or there, not to do this or that. I am afraid the story had meant more sleepless nights for her. If there were riots as far away as Zimbabwe, I might get a phone call to check was I alright. Bird flu broke out in Nigeria, and she was urging me to stay away from my chickens. When bird flu broke out in southern France a few days later, I rang her to make sure she was safe in Ireland. I think she got the message after that.

My mother's concern made me appreciate that the strong maternal instinct to protect the young is not restricted to hippos! At this point, she had children living in four different countries on three continents, but an awful lot of her sleepless nights seemed to centre on me. My father, on the other hand, only lost sleep to answer my occasional phone call home early on a Saturday morning.

Even though I did not really want to leave Lake Baringo, I decided I should move on and explore some more of the Rift Valley. It was a perfect sunny morning when I set out on the fifty kilometres journey south to Lake Bogoria, where I intended spending a day. At the very moment I reached Lake Bogoria, a sudden tempest whipped up an impenetrable fog of dust, followed by torrential rain. I watched most of the campsite becoming flooded before my eyes, but I risked pitching the tent anyway on the only island of dry land.

'You are the first person in well over a month to camp at Lake Bogoria,' the ranger informed me.

After the good craic with Ruarí, Betty, and the white-Kenyans, I would have to get used to my own company again.

Once again, I woke before dawn, haggled over the price of hiring a rusty boneshaker for the day, and cycled into Bogoria National Reserve. I seemed to have Lake Bogoria entirely to myself that day. Hauntingly beautiful, it resembled Donegal's Glenveagh in the summer, or a Scottish Highland glen under a tropical sun. A few kilometres further on along the lakeshore, I reached the impressive hot volcanic geysers. I had not appreciated how hot these could be until I hopped among them; maybe there could have been some warning signs to alert the unwary, but I was not in the least surprised at their absence. Further on down the soda lake were thousands upon thousands of pink and white flamingos chattering away. I sat on the rocks there for ages, amazed that I had such a magnificent scene of perfection to myself. Eventually I resumed cycling, gently puffing and sweating my way to the far end of the lake. Here I relaxed beside a babbling stream, under shady trees at the tip of the soda lake, watching a herd of kudu deer with long spiral horns. They were watching me too.

Suddenly, from out of the forest there appeared a ranger in a state of panic. He stopped, shocked at the very sight of me.

'Run, run *bwana,* there are dangerous buffalo approaching!' he shouted with urgency.

Apparently, if you venture beyond the hot springs, you are supposed to be accompanied by an armed ranger. I had not seen any signs warning of the danger—I doubt there were any. I mounted the bicycle and raced back as fast as I could manage under the sizzling sun.

There is no regular bus service from Lake Bogoria. I waited around for hours in vain, hoping to thumb a lift from passing tourists. But, of course, there were not any. Just as it fell dark, I finally succeeded in hitching a lift in the direction of Nakuru town in the one and only vehicle that left Lake Bogoria the entire day. It was an old Volkswagen hippie van. Inside, to my great surprise, were several councillors and a Kenyan MP. The politicians were touring this part of Kenya looking at 'models' of development in the Rift Valley that they hoped to apply to their own constituencies. They seemed to be up for a bit of fun along the way. They were having great craic, and had Dolly Parton playing on a tape. A typical politicians' junket, I decided.

The MP was in expansive mood. Maybe he had enjoyed a liquid lunch!

'Will you not come and tour with us for the next couple of days?' he cajoled.

'Thanks a lot,' I replied. 'But you can drop me here in Nakuru, please.'

Still, the old hippie van proved a better way to travel than some vehicles I had experienced—like the forty year old *Flintstones* taxis with no floor, where you can see the road uncoiling beneath you. These were the ones I would invariably end up pushing back to a petrol station halfway to town.

I always got a thrill from crossing the equator, even though I had lost count of the amount of times I had passed over it by now. My excitement on this occasion was curtailed somewhat when I spotted three different 'You Are Now On The Equator' signs a few hundred yards apart on the one road going north to Nyahururu town. Souvenirs were available at each point. Someone was milking it.

'They are all the real one,' the bus conductor insisted.

Theoretically, I suppose, they might all have been on the line of the equator, but somehow I doubt it.

Nyahururu is about fifty kilometres north-east of Nakuru, up twisty mountain roads, and is reputed to be the highest and coldest town in Kenya at nearly 8,000 feet in altitude. It was founded as a white-settler town on the terminus of a railway line, and lies in the Highlands east of the Rift Valley. I stayed in a freezing wooden lodge built in 1930 that had never been revamped since, but was oozing character in its own down-at-heel way. I was the only overnight guest. There was a log fire in the bedroom overlooking the impressive Thompson's Falls, a waterfall plummeting 240 feet into a narrow, misty ravine. It was named after the Scottish explorer and scientist, Joseph Thompson.

The doorman informed me that circumcision ceremonies of Kikuyu teenage boys were to take place under the Falls a couple of days later.

'The freezing water numbs the pain,' he casually remarked.

I certainly was not about to hang around to test his assertion and witness their pain! So I boarded the 'Stalingrad Shuttle' bus for the 200km ride south to Nairobi. The bus was emblazoned with glittering decorative lights, a loud horn that played a tune, and bright artistic graffiti, like so many of these quaintly named vehicles.

Only hours before we came down the same road, bandits had hijacked an earlier bus. The police shot them dead. Bystanders looted the bodies of the bandits, and burned to death one of their number who tried to escape. Somehow, a news camera was on the scene, tipped off by the police perhaps, and relayed the story in all its gruesome detail on the television news that night. *Pour décourager les autres!*

I was looking fairly rough that afternoon. I badly needed a shave and my clothes were layered in dust. A passenger on the Stalingrad Shuttle managed to get sick over my only set of clean clothes. In spite of this, I headed for the grand luxurious Norfolk Hotel in Nairobi for dinner. I decided I deserved to treat myself to a decent meal. In colonial days, it had been at the very hub of business and social life in the Kenyan capital. It still is, though to a much lesser degree than in the days of the Happy Valley set.

The early colonial settlers used to ride horses through the hotel lobby, firing pistols aimed at the chandeliers or ornaments on the grand piano. The original Lord Delamere, dressed in finest evening wear, used to attempt to leap his horse over the large dining room table without disturbing the delicate crockery. He would then blast the whiskey bottles off the bar with his gun.

'Gentleman, I see you have been on a long safari. Let me take your bags, sir,' the waiter welcomed me, as he pulled my chair out and carefully placed a white napkin on my lap.

I could get used to this, I was thinking. The meal proved to be the best I had all year.

CHAPTER 18
A VOYAGE TO LAMU

IT WAS A QUICK DASH in the back of an old London black taxi from the Norfolk Hotel to Nairobi railway station; I wanted to catch the night-train for Mombasa. Nairobi owes its very existence to the East Africa Railway and to this station. The city started as a rail depot in a swamp in the 1890s, and quickly developed as the new centre of the colonial government. It was conveniently, though not intentionally, located at the meeting point of the Kikuyu, Maasai, and Akamba tribal lands. During Nairobi's formative years in the early 1900s, inquisitive lions and other game could be seen roaming the dusty streets, having wandered in from the nearby bush.

My intention for the coming fortnight was to make my way to Lamu Island, near the border with Somalia. The train journey to Mombasa has been described as 'one of the great rail journeys in Africa.' The train has also been nicknamed 'The Lunatic Express.' There is truth in both descriptions, though the word 'express' is an optimistic misnomer. Admittedly, first-class travel cost hardly anything. And the journey had a certain, if faded, charm. The dinner service and carriages remain largely unchanged since colonial times. Even the station timetable, I noticed, was dated 1971. It was located beside a wooden notice board on which wooden letters and numbers were manually inserted into the slots.

As we pulled out of Nairobi station, young Africans ran alongside the tracks, jumping on and off at will; or they clung perilously to the sides, as the train leisurely snaked its way out through the acacia trees of the savannah. I stuck my head out the carriage window, basking in a cool evening breeze. I spotted giraffes, ostriches, and elephants, and waved back to Maasai families who were waving at the train from outside their mud-huts and compounds.

Not long after departure, a conductor playing the xylophone walked up and down the carriages, signalling the commencement of the silver service dinner. The waiters, immaculately dressed in starched white uniforms and white gloves, busily laid the five-course meal on the crisp linen tablecloths in the wood-panelled restaurant car. That the waiters steadily slipped into drunkenness as the meal progressed, contributed to the novelty and charm of the experience.

I shared the compartment with a middle-aged Kenyan teacher and a slender youth, a rather timid and apparently deaf and dumb Indian boy who looked about twelve years old. The teacher and I kept fussing over the boy, who reacted in a somewhat bemused fashion.

'Isn't he so brave to be travelling all alone,' the teacher remarked to me as he helped him into his bunk.

The next morning, the boy handed me a page on which was written,

'Hello, my name is Josh. I am an American Peace Corps volunteer in Kenya. I am thirty-one years old. I have also served with the Peace Corps in Indonesia and Peru for six years. What

CHAPTER 18 A VOYAGE TO LAMU

is your name?'

In amazement, I handed the note to the teacher.

'Sure, who was to know?' he shrugged jovially.

To while away the hours, I read an account of the tribulations of the pioneers who built the railway in these inhospitable parts at the end of the nineteenth century. The British imported thousands of Indian labourers to lay the tracks. It is estimated that around ninety percent of them died from disease and other hazards, including lions. In the Tsavo region, the lions are large and maneless, and have a fearsome reputation. It is a matter of record that two lions killed and ate 140 of those Indian workers over a period of months in 1898. This occurred at the construction of a bridge across the Tsavo River, about halfway between Nairobi and Mombasa.

The lions became known as 'The Man-Eaters of Tsavo' and were the subject of a book written by Colonel J.H. Patterson, the chief engineer on the project. The tale was later turned into a movie starring Michael Douglas. The two lions possessed an uncanny knack of avoiding every ingenious trap laid for them. It was Patterson who finally shot them. Eventually their pelts were acquired by the Chicago Field Museum where, by some coincidence, I happened to view them in 2004. Little did I realise then that I would, within a couple of years, pass through Tsavo.

The ten percent of Indians who survived the construction of the East Africa Railway were allowed to remain in Kenya after its completion. They flourished economically, being very enterprising, and still today control the retail trade of much of Kenya. From time to time, an African would complain bitterly to me that the Indian shopkeepers never gave discounts, or that they would not bargain with them, like the Africans do.

The railways played an important part in opening up East Africa in the colonial period. They also featured in tribal mythology. The Maasai and Kikuyu tribes each had separate legends of 'a snake' (i.e. train) heralding the end of the power of their tribe. (Similarly, some people in Donegal thought the first journey of the train through Barnesmore Gap, in 1882, was the coming of the 'Black Pig,' that Saint Colmcille prophesised would mean that the end of the world was imminent). Masaku, the father figure of the Akamba tribe—after whom the Akamba capital Machakos is named—also prophesised the coming of 'a long snake.' The Kikuyu legend foretold that this event would be linked with the coming of a white tribe. The white tribe quickly made themselves at home. Back when Kenya was an infant colony, there were special cages with chairs on the front of the train engines where adventurers, who had landed off the boat at Mombasa, could fire at game animals on their way inland to Nairobi.

We were only an hour late arriving in Mombasa in the morning, though of course I did not mind in the least; seasoned travellers might allow a window of three hours for delays on the line. I was reminded of Percy French's song, *Are you right there, Michael, are you right?* The West Clare and East Africa railways had much in common, mainly uncertainty. But, at least, it is relatively safer than travelling to Mombasa by road. And I had managed a few hours of restful sleep.

I caught the 'Hitler' bus (you could not make it up!) heading north along the coast. There was a 'relief' stop after a while, involving mass urination by the roadside. I alighted at Gede, near Malindi, about 100km north of Mombasa.

CHAPTER 18 A VOYAGE TO LAMU

Gede, which today consists of extensive ruins in a good state of preservation, was an important Swahili city-state six hundred years ago. Mystery surrounds this historic city. There is no written record of its existence; yet archaeologists have discovered elaborate tombs, mosques, and an impressive palace. It was inexplicably abandoned in the 1700s, and swallowed by the forest; it was re-discovered less than ninety years ago.

I explored the ruins with an English girl I had met on the 'Hitler' bus. Among the ruins, Amanda's eagle eye lit on a fine fragment of what was surely an ancient Chinese glazed bowl. It is known that the coastal Swahili people traded with the Chinese as well as the Arabs, the Persians, the Indians and, later, the Portuguese. The reason Gede was left untouched and reasonably intact, apparently, was because the local Swahili population feared the ghosts that are reputed to haunt the ruins.

Standing in the annex of the ancient palace, I had a sense of the diversity of cultures in East Africa. The coastal Swahili people are undoubtedly African (one of the Bantu peoples), but their blood and culture is heavily infused with influences from the Arab and Eastern civilisations they traded with over the centuries. The Sultan of Oman ruled the Kenyan coast for a long time. Swahili music around Malindi and Mombasa (known as *Taarab*) sounded very Indian to my admittedly untrained ear.

Giant baobab trees dominated the forest around Gede. The monumental trunk of the baobab is sometimes so thick that it takes more than half a dozen people with arms fully extended to stretch around the circumference. These 'upside-down' trees interested me, not just because of their outlandish appearance but also because of the legends attached to them.

'The baobab was very late for a meeting of all the trees in the world,' my friend Mutinda, the medicine man, once told me. 'He kept them all waiting. The other trees were so annoyed with him that they uprooted him and stuck him in the ground upside down. That is why it has no leaves and its branches look like roots.'

In another version, Nzoki claimed,

'The baobab became too big and greedy, blocking God's view of his other trees. God was furious. He ripped up the baobab and planted him upside down to punish him.'

In yet another version, God permitted the devil to choose and plant a tree. Being the perverse type, Lucifer planted a tree with its roots in the air—the baobab.

In the nearby coastal town of Malindi, I found lodgings in a cheap hotel. In the bedroom stood a wonderful, ornately carved, four-poster bed in dark wood that would not have looked out of place in the Norfolk Hotel in Nairobi. It was one of those pleasant surprises one finds from time to time when travelling in Africa. Despite the fact that the lock on the door was broken and the tap lifted off the dirty sink, I was looking forward to a good night's sleep. But, as so often with the cheapest accommodation, I soon discovered that the establishment doubled as a doss-house. I fell asleep to the sounds of the prostitutes at work next door. This hotel had signs for 'badrooms' instead of 'bedrooms.' It definitely was not an intentional joke on the part of the owners, anymore so than the sign that insisted, 'No *miraa* (a popular drug) and no unmarried women allowed.'

The following day, I was part of a convoy of buses protected by the Kenyan army as we passed through Somali tribal bandit country. This part of the coast is close to the Somali border and has a reputation for lawlessness, and not just on land. In recent times, Somali pirates have ambushed cruise ships and freight vessels out to sea. Any confidence I had in the protection of the Kenyan soldiers was somewhat weakened by the observation that the broken door on my bus had been repaired with cardboard!

The Swahili passenger sitting next to me did nothing to increase my confidence.

'Somali bandits came inside Kenya and snatched two lion cubs off their mother,' he told me in slow English. 'The lioness went on the rampage to recover them. She killed three innocent humans before being captured by rangers.'

The 200km journey north from Malindi along untarred gravel roads was slow and challenging. It meant that it was dark by the time I boarded the over-crowded wooden Arab dhow bound for the fabled Swahili island of Lamu.

Lamu town sits on an island that is part of an archipelago, several kilometres from the Kenyan coast near Somalia. We sailed out in the dark without lifejackets or lights, guided to port by the glistening lanterns of Lamu's seafront. I knew I had arrived somewhere different when, upon stepping off the pier, I read the sign, 'No parking of donkeys here.' My first impressions were of a town caught in a time warp. It was dirty, smelly, medieval and vibrant, and untainted by tourism and modernity. It was like what Marrakech must have been long ago, or an Arab version of the old-towns of the cities of Europe hundreds of years ago.

I had been told that the pace of life among the narrow alleyways of Lamu was slow. That was very true for most of the day. Lethargic is too animated an adjective to describe it. But I had arrived, purely by chance, right in the middle of the exciting annual *Maulidi* festival—hence the over-crowded dhow—and the place was buzzing. The festival takes place every year towards the end of April to celebrate the birth of the prophet Mohammed. The people are overwhelmingly Muslim, and Lamu society deeply traditional.

The festival was in full swing for several days after I arrived. The narrow streets were jammed with men dressed neck-to-toe in pristine white *khanzu* robes and the occasional green turban. The women were a lot less flamboyant in their black *bui-bui* robes, with only their faces on show. Some were in full *purdah*. But enjoyment was the order of the day. Colourful parades snaked through the tight alleys, with drumming, dancing, singing, pushing and shoving. I pushed and shoved with the rest to get a better view. Flags and swords were being waved in the air. It reminded me of a frenetic disorganised version of a large Orange Order parade I had witnessed in east Donegal, just before I arrived in Kenya.

On the morning of my second day there, I was reminded more of the Galway Races than Raphoe. There was a donkey race that generated impassioned shouting and cheering which echoed through the lanes and alleyways. The balconies along the seafront were thronged with people watching one of the last great dhow sailing races anywhere in the world. From upstairs windows with shutters thrown back, spectators were waving bright scarves, and giddy crowds on the ground below were cheering on their favourite competitors. One of the dhows was manned by a Rasta wearing only Y-fronts. Another one was captained by a huge overweight Swahili man who was wearing only what looked like a sarong around his lower half. No, definitely not something you would witness at an Orange parade.

Life around the archipelago, and indeed along the coast, revolves around these wooden sailing dhows; they are used for fishing, ferrying, and transporting freight. The dhows are still used for trading to as far away as Zanzibar, and even Arabia on rare occasions. Lamu is one of the very few places remaining where dhows are built. They were still being constructed by hand using age-old methods and skills; indeed, as I saw myself, even the nails that hold them together are crafted locally in simple forges.

Life in Lamu, inevitably, is beholden to the timing of the tides; the keening from the many mosques also gives structure to the day. There are no vehicles or proper roads on the island (only sandy paths), and no 'new-town' district has developed. No roads, no cars—no hurry. Men ride on donkeys, steering them through clusters of children who are playing marbles in the six-foot wide passageways between the ornate three-story stone tenement buildings. Many of the latter have elaborately carved and decorated doorways. Amongst the maze of unpaved alleyways other men sit, totally absorbed in African board games (mainly *bao*). There are animated exchanges with the passers-by on donkeys over the next move. It is medieval, but the place throbs with life. The markets are particularly noisy. I passed one man as he placed the decapitated head of a cow on the ground beside the antique weighing scales he had just lifted it from. He wanted to sell me the head; it was an offer I could easily refuse!

One late afternoon, I spotted small boys trapping a rat near the pier. They tried to drown it in the sea by throwing the cage they had captured it in into the water. The rat escaped and started swimming. The boys, all six of them, jumped in and swam after it. They were having great craic. It was an unusual little drama and I found it amusing. It was high tide, and the water was overflowing onto the promenade. Men were urging their donkeys through the deepening water.

The women may be largely hidden under their black *bui-bui*, but if you look closer, you will see young smiling faces giggling as they size up and comment on the men passing by. If you look closer still, you will sometimes see fleeting evidence of brightly coloured lingerie underneath the dark robes. Many girls have intricate *henna* tattoos painted on their feet and on their hands. They are out to make an impression, to the extent that they are allowed. The *Maulidi* is not just a religious occasion; it doubles as a matchmaking festival among the islanders of the Lamu archipelago. A majority of Swahili marriages are arranged by the families, in accordance with Muslim practice. Interestingly, in these parts, the would-be wife can refuse to marry, but the would-be husband cannot. It seems a little unfair to me!

Near Lamu, a 15km-long white sandy beach stretches out invitingly. Hardly anybody was there in late April, except for a number of women covered in full *purdah*. I introduced myself to the only Westerners present, two blond English girls taking a break after volunteer work in South Africa, and a young Frenchman who was on time-out from teaching in Ethiopia. Much as I enjoyed mixing with local people on my travels, it was always good to meet fellow Europeans from time to time.

Together we headed for the 'Seafood Restaurant' beside Lamu pier. The waiter presented us with a menu of twenty different kinds of fish. Having studied the menu, we ordered our food. The waiter returned much later.

CHAPTER 18 A VOYAGE TO LAMU

'Sorry, we don't have any fish today,' he apologised.

He did, however, create a pint of fresh fruit juice for each of us before our eyes from a choice of any tropical fruit imaginable; and it only cost forty shillings (roughly forty cent). For that taste and those prices, we had more than one.

There is only one ATM on the island, which of course was broken when I arrived. The bank was closed; no reason was given, but perhaps it was because of the *Maulidi* festival. The ATM remained broken for several more days, and I promptly ran out of money. On my travels in remote places, I sometimes got caught out for money. I was mightily relieved when the bank finally opened its doors again.

After I withdrew some shillings, I visited a cinema that was showing a pirate copy of the latest *King Kong* movie. The audience kept shouting and gesticulating through every scene, until the film broke down. There was a crescendo of booing and tut-tutting until it started up again. This audience participation was like the time I went to see the *Da Vinci Code* in Nairobi. Noisy exception was taken to the idea of Jesus's bloodline. Near the cinema, a Rasta hawker was offering a seven-films-in-one pirate DVD for only 300 shillings (three euro).

'Would you like to see the special price DVDs?' he then asked me.

'And what are the special price DVDs?' I responded, in my innocence.

I was thinking he meant regular pirated DVDs at reduced rates. He promptly cascaded me with movies of a distinctly adult nature.

Most of those who were hawking trinkets to the very occasional *mzungu* in Lamu were Rastas. The island is popular with the Rastas because of the ready availability of marijuana. I enjoyed talking to these drop-outs; they could be very entertaining characters. I discovered that one of them was from Kitui. In truth, he was more of a capitalist tycoon with business interests as far away as Akambaland, but he was masquerading as a real Rasta. Some Rastas I found to be the most money-grabbing people in Kenya.

I became friendly with one young local Rasta man of stocky build named Abdullah. He was the real deal. His well-trimmed black dreadlocks hung around his pleasant light-chestnut face. He had pensive eyes and could simultaneously give the impression of being both engrossed and detached in conversation. It was uncanny. But everything about him oozed a carefree, sunny disposition.

At first sight, he came across as a bit of a smooth operator, but once I made it clear I was uninterested in purchasing his merchandise, his real personality emerged. True Rastas believe that Emperor Haile Selassie of Ethiopia was the reincarnation of Jesus Christ. With a name like Abdullah, I assumed he was more interested in the Rastafarian lifestyle rather than in any religious aspect.

In his unique accent, he invited me to his home place, another island in the archipelago named Paté Island, a few lazy hours from Lamu aboard a slow dhow.

'Brendan, I'm going home to my mother for the village festival on Paté. She would love to meet you. Paté is far superior to Lamu, Heaven's over there!'

Who could refuse an invitation like that?

CHAPTER 18 A VOYAGE TO LAMU

A journey by Arab dhow is always exciting, but there are always health and safety issues. The voyage to Paté in a heavy swell was no exception. The craft was impossibly overcrowded and in the course of the journey, the captain invited the male passengers to help bail out the in-coming water. Of course, there was no such thing as safety rails around the perimeter, or any sign of life-rings on board. The dhow was strictly segregated too, with all the women and children at one end, and all the men at the other.

When we reached Abdullah's island, the next leg of the journey was up a shallow inlet in a dodgy wooden dug-out canoe. Then I had to wade ashore carrying my bag over my head. Finally, after riding on the back of a donkey, along a one-foot wide dirt track, through thick bush and forest, we were there.

Paté is indeed an island paradise, but is remote far beyond remoteness. The only Western visitors it attracts, according to Abdullah, are anthropologists—once in a blue moon. The islanders are supposedly quite distinct in dress, culture, dialect, and even ethnicity. The village dwellings are fairly simple—made with coral stone as well as daub and wattle, with thatched roofs. As a friend of Abdullah's, I was warmly welcomed by the villagers.

There was yet another Muslim festival on Paté Island while I was there; each island celebrates the prophet's birthday on separate dates. I was invited to attend the celebration by an elder of the village (one of the few villagers who could speak English). I was declared to be the only outsider on the entire island. The elder made one condition, though.

'You will have to wear our gowns. Abdullah, find some spare robes for him, won't you.'

And that is how I became 'Omar Al-Jazzera,' dressed in a

purple single-piece Muslim robe and a white *kofia* hat provided
by Abdullah. I thought it ironic that I, a Christian, was allowed
to attend their *Maulidi* celebrations, while the Muslim women of
Paté were excluded.

The form of Islam observed along the Kenyan coast is, by and
large, tolerant and inclusive. Their acceptance of the Rastas was
evidence of that. Shortly after my visit to the Lamu archipelago,
on the fifth of June 2006, Islamic extremists stormed Mogadishu
and seized control of Somalia. The puritanical Taliban style of
Islam imposed on Somalia is completely at odds with that practiced across the border in Kenya. Paté's religious festival was both
solemn in parts, but joyous too—albeit in the absence of alcohol
and women. After the tuneful chanting, and the rising and falling of the assembled on their mats to the rhythms of prayer, it
erupted into a climax of genuine celebration. The faithful seemed
to get the same buzz from it as Westerners might from a boozy
weekend disco. Abdullah gladly partook of the ceremonies with
all his friends and relations, even though he could best be described as a lapsed Muslim.

After the religious celebrations, we all sat on the ground in
the middle of the sandy unpaved laneway, and ate rice and coconut beans with our bare hands out of the same wide communal
dish.

'It saves on the washing up afterwards at any rate,' I joked
with Abdullah.

At a hint from him earlier, I had bought several lobsters for
the crowd. I had paid the full asking price of forty shillings for
each lobster off a fisherman who had just landed his catch. That
equated to less than fifty cent for a full adult lobster, and the

naïve *mzungu* may well have paid over the odds.

It was all washed down with delicious, spicy, Swahili-style tea with a hint of sugar. Gradually as the evening wore on, the numbers dispersed. I stared up at a perfect star-filled night sky as a few stray children played in the alleys lit by paraffin-lanterns, before their parents rounded them up for bed. I lay down to sleep on a bed of reeds upon the uneven stony floor of Abdullah's home, having been fussed over by his mother—as he had predicted. I drifted off to sleep thinking of the many diverse things that make humans happy.

The following day, Abdullah and some of his friends escorted me through the bush to the even smaller and more remote villages of Paté. We travelled on the back of donkeys. The scene was almost biblical. It seemed to me as if the whole island had gone for a day-long siesta—it was the same every day. Languid does not begin to describe the lifestyle. The only movement was of children playing football with a hollow coconut, or youngsters raiding the mango and coconut orchards before being chased away by Abdullah and his comrades. Just as in Kitui, children would run away from me, scared, and hide from the *mzungu*. I thought about getting back to Lamu.

'No hurry,' said Abdullah.

We called on 'the mayor' for a couple of hours on our way back. A reclusive old *mzee,* his three-sided home of coconut-leaf walls was surely unique: one side was entirely open to the elements. He quizzed Abdullah about his life in Lamu. As darkness approached, we rode back through the coconut trees, being tortured by mosquitoes along the way. Back at Abdullah's place, I showered from a bucket at an ancient stone well.

NO HURRY IN AFRICA

A fisherman friend of Abdullah offered to take me out on his sailing dhow. He even suggested that I spend several days fishing with him, using methods that had remained unchanged for centuries. No wonder the anthropologists love this place, I thought. I was forced to decline, though. Time was pressing for me even if the locals were in no hurry. But truthfully, I was also a bit concerned. I could not be sure the dhow would be safe in a storm. Also, few enough people even knew my current whereabouts to chance venturing onwards. All in all, as much as I would have loved to, I could not take the time or the risk.

I ended up on Paté Island a day more than I had intended. I was stranded because the dhows are not allowed to sail on Muslim holy days. When I eventually got around to leaving, several of us set out in a dug-out canoe to make contact at sea with a dhow crossing back over to Lamu. When a large rotund man tried to climb aboard the dhow, the canoe tipped over and sent Abdullah and another man flying into the water. Luckily, I had just clambered out of the canoe onto the dhow seconds before.

'There are many sharks around here,' Abdullah commented, still breathless as he dried himself.

Fortunately, he saw the humour in the situation. The passengers on the dhow were in stitches.

The dhow was overcrowded as usual. For the next few hours, Abdullah and I had to perch on top of a pyramidal mountain of luggage, the only space available.

'Here, look, do you see the dolphins, Brendan?' Abdullah pointed excitedly.

As he gestured, he lost his balance on the pile of luggage and ended up smothered in bags and cases. Everybody was in stitches again. I made my way to the side of the dhow, and sat down with my legs dangling over the water. A large school of cartwheeling dolphins escorted us the whole way back to Lamu.

The Lamu archipelago did hold one last surprise. On what I assumed to be my last day in Lamu, I was having a drink at one of only two bars in the whole archipelago. There I met Stephen, an unshaven Englishman in his late thirties. A small ring dangled from his pierced ear. He was drowning his sorrows.

'Mate, my girlfriend's just left me. She's been paired off at the *Maulidi* matchmaking festival.'

He went on to tell me that he would be sailing out to his home at a seasonal hippie commune on one of the islands. He had been living there for ten years, on and off.

'You should see it mate, you'd love it there,' he assured me.

How could I turn down an invitation like that? I spent a day and night there.

It was nearly straight out of Alex Garland's novel *The Beach*. Young people were skinny-dipping on the paradise beach, playing volleyball, and smoking dope around a campfire on the sand at night. The commune declines to be in any of the guidebooks, and they just bribe the authorities to turn a blind eye to their activities. I wanted to stay longer. Maybe forever!

But I had to leave.

Chapter 19
The Assault on Mount Kenya

The muezzin in the mosque roaring over a loudspeaker at 5am outside my bedroom window (I just could not seem to escape these religious loudspeakers anywhere in Kenya) woke me just in time to catch the dhow from Lamu back to the mainland. I had to catch the only bus going south to Mombasa that day. If I am ever lucky enough to return, Lamu may be irrevocably altered in its way of life. I noted, somewhat regretfully, that building is due to begin soon on a new super-port that will rival the port of Mombasa. I know progress should be welcomed, but it is a pity that such a unique place has to change, especially as it has avoided modern ways until now.

My bus south was having a race with three other buses for the first part of the journey. The crammed passengers, caught up in the excitement of the race, were speculating communally and noisily in Swahili on the likely outcome. As we attempted to overtake on a hill, I had a feeling that one of the juggernauts thundering towards us might well determine the outcome for us. It was almost a relief when, after an adrenalin-fuelled hour, our bus broke down. Further on, it broke down again, and again. I was wondering now about whether I would arrive in time to catch the night-train to Nairobi. The communal conversation had turned to the possibility of pushing the bus to Mombasa. When we finally neared the city and the police checkpoints on the outskirts, the passengers standing in the aisles dived for the floor in unison.

After a good night's sleep on the train, it was Nairobi again, and *ugali* for breakfast. On my way back to Kitui later that day, it was *déjà vu,* as they say, all over again. This time I did have to get out with the other male passengers and push our minibus; it too kept breaking down. Finally, away out in the open countryside, it spluttered to what sounded like a terminal standstill. In quite a stroke of luck, the Nyumbani truck approached. Cecil recognised me, stopped, and gave me a lift. After a bit of banter about married life, he filled me in on developments in the Village project. Phase III of construction was still on hold.

'In fact,' he said, 'there is not even a sign of a firm starting-date. The organic farm is the only part of the project that is continuing. Now, Brendan, tell me all about Lamu, please. I have never been there.'

In due course, I reached the mission station of Fr. Frank and Fr. Liam, exhausted after all the delays and an eight-hour journey from Nairobi. It had taken me thirty-six hours in total to get back from Lamu. I found Kitui refreshingly green after the recent rains there.

Fr. Liam up-dated me.

'You remember the first crops failed when the early rains petered out? Well, when the rains returned, there was a great crop growing until a plague of caterpillars came and ate most of the young tender maize plants. The people were philosophical, as only the Akamba can be—"sure it happens"—and those who could find seed planted yet again. For the third time this rainy season!'

I spent a couple of days resting at the mission house. While I was there, the electricity supply failed yet again. It was back to living with candles, and playing chess, chatting or reading by the gas lamp in the evenings.

The reason I had left Lamu was because Mount Kenya was still calling me. It was partly the Kilimanjaro bug, and partly the fact that I had just finished reading *No Picnic on Mount Kenya* by Felice Benuzzi. The book tells the true story of an Italian PoW in Kenya during World War II. He could see the mountain from his prison camp and was determined to escape captivity by the British, specifically in order to climb to the top. He became one of the first men ever to reach the summit. Then, as was always his intention, he returned to the PoW camp in Nanyuki. It is a gripping read.

I reached the town of Nanyuki one rainy day in early May, a bustling white settler town lying right on the equator line. About 200km north of Nairobi, it is situated below the western face of Mount Kenya. The cafés and shops were all abuzz with gossip that afternoon. One of the white settlers in the town informed me that Tom Cholmondeley, who is the heir to Baron Delamere, allegedly knocked off his second native within a year that very morning. He claimed the victim was a poacher. This news was huge. Just before my arrival in Kenya, Cholmondeley had had murder charges dropped after admitting to having killed a Maasai game warden in self-defence on his estate in 2005. In the days that followed, the Kenyan people cried foul, alleging a conspiracy, and that hidden powers were secretly influencing the prosecution service behind the scenes.

NO HURRY IN AFRICA

This time, Tom Cholmondeley claimed he was carrying his Winchester hunting rifle only because a white friend had been gored to death by a buffalo the previous year; and that he only shot at the dogs of the poachers. The latter had emerged from a thicket brandishing spears. He claimed they had killed and skinned an antelope. He argued that he was being targeted by the authorities because he is the only heir to the Rift Valley estate of 100,000 acres. He had tried to save his victim by treating him with first aid and bringing him to hospital.

The victim's wife, however, maintained her husband only hunted antelope very rarely to source food for their four hungry children. There was a groundswell of anger among Kenyans over the incident. It developed into the most talked-about and controversial trial in Kenya since the murder of Lord Errol in 1941. Coincidentally, Baron Delamere's stepmother had been the central female figure in the Lord Errol scandal.

The original Lord Delamere was a charismatic character who first arrived in Kenya in 1897, having crossed the northern deserts from Somalia with a caravan of 200 camels. He was a gambler, who bankrupted his estate in Cheshire for what ultimately turned out to be successful experiments at mixed agriculture in the Rift Valley. He managed to breed cattle in Kenya that were better at withstanding disease and drought. His family dominated the social scene, arguably until the present. The news bulletin on the small television in the café that evening showed the 6"6' heir, wearing a trilby-shaped straw hat and beige coloured suit, being escorted away by police through a scrum of photographers.

In the café, I had been conversing with a middle-aged white lady named Victoria. She later generously provided me with a lift in her rattling old Land Rover.

'Tom is the godfather to my best friend's child, you know . . . The unfortunate family of the deceased man . . . it is such a tragedy,' she told me. 'It is such a terrible pity for Tom, of course.'

She paused to reflect and then said, rather enigmatically,

'But I am not at all surprised in a way that it has happened to him.'

Victoria was third-generation Kenyan herself. Her only period away from Africa was attending secondary school and university in England.

'My parents' generation, and their parents—they were absolutely mad! We are more sensible these days. We have to be.'

The white settlers who were born and reared in Kenya are easy to spot from a distance. They tend to drive huge jeeps that are often as old as themselves; they still dress like English country gentry of the 1950s, in browns or khaki with the obligatory hunter's hat (though no longer sporting two wide-brimmed hats as the colonials did, in case the sun could penetrate the first one). The settlers talk with posh Eton accents, and refer to 'Keeenya.' They frequent their own shops, hotels and bars, and play upper middle-class sports at their country clubs. They look thoroughly out of place in today's Kenya, yet at the same time are a quintessential part of it. It struck me as I was talking to Victoria that they must be one of the most misplaced peoples in the entire world. Just for the record, the Highlands west of Mount Kenya were mooted as a Jewish homeland long before Israel was founded. A tiny community of Jews lives in Nairobi to this day.

My curiosity about the white-Kenyans led me once to visit Baroness Blixen's former home outside Nairobi. She was the Dan-

NO HURRY IN AFRICA

ish aristocrat and coffee planter who immortalised colonial life in her classic book *Out of Africa*. The Nairobi suburb of Karen is named after her. Her house and gardens can now be visited. I had been expecting something like Stormont, but it is a lot smaller, though still preserved inside exactly as it was in the 1920s.

The settlement around Karen is one of a handful of well-heeled white communities left in Kenya. Karen's inhabitants are the diplomats, rich expatriates, and white-Kenyan professionals who work in Nairobi. These people live in gated mansions. Karen is only a few kilometres from the slums of Nairobi; economically and socially, it is a world away from the rest of Kenya.

Not all of the white-Kenyans lived in luxury, however. A lot of the early colonists, even some titled gentry, actually lived initially in mud-huts—rectangular ones where the native huts were round. Many lived isolated lives in remote places; life was a physical and emotional struggle in a harsh environment; some faced financial ruin as well. Good times followed for others, to be sure, as the country's natural resources were exploited. But with Independence, life has become a struggle again for a lot of those who remain. Victoria admitted as much.

'I love Keeenya to bits, but I am just about making ends meet each week,' she told me, dropping me off at the end of 'Go-Down Road,' near where my cheap hotel was located.

Early the following morning, I hired a Kikuyu guide, named Alfred, in Nanyuki. Alfred was about thirty years old, had a lean and hungry look, but was very experienced. I also hired a porter who would carry all the food and the cooking equipment for the climb. Compared to the organised assault on Kilimanjaro in early March, this would be a solo run, as it were. I could call upon the experience gained on the earlier climb, so I was fairly confident I could reach the summit which, that morning, was wearing its grey hat of clouds. It is Africa's second highest mountain at 17,058 feet, with the peak only a few kilometres from the equator.

The three of us boarded the 'CanniBus' out of Nanyuki to the base of Mount Kenya, below its northern face. Our conductor was an African albino whom I first mistook for a *mzungu*. He was hanging out the door of the bus taunting the driver of the 'Princess Diana' as we flew past it.

As the two bus drivers raced each other, and the passengers egged them on to greater speeds, the bus was transformed into a mobile disco, with people dancing in the aisles to the catchy Kikuyu tunes on the radio.

When viewed from a distance, the dark rocks and gleaming glaciers on the peaks of Mount Kenya can resemble the black and white plumage of a male ostrich. From this, the Kikuyu people named the mountain *'Kirinyaga,'* meaning 'the area of the ostrich.' Their God, whom they believed lived on the top of Mount Kenya, was called *'Mwene Nyaga,'* or 'the owner of the ostrich.' He was also known as *'Ngai,'* and Mount Kenya was and is sacred land. The missionaries, incidentally, exploited the fact that the Kikuyu had one supreme Deity; they simply told them he was actually their God from the Bible.

The Akamba people, who speak a language related to the Kikuyu language, pronounce *'Kirinyaga'* as *'Kinyaa.'* So, when the first European explorers like Johann Ludwig Krapf were shown Mount Kenya from Kitui, they heard it pronounced *'Kinyaa'* (as in 'Keenya'). The whole colony was later named after the mountain.

It was actually Kenya's first president, *Mzee* Jomo Kenyatta, who was responsible for the modern pronunciation. He ruled from 1963 until his death in 1978. In a clever piece of spin doctoring, he exploited the likeness of his own name to that of his country. Thus, people gradually began pronouncing the country as Kenya (i.e. ken, not keen), which is closer to the pronunciation of his name.

The Kikuyu God, *Ngai,* who lives on the peaks of Mount Kenya, must have arranged favourable weather for us that week. We enjoyed perfect clear skies for practically the entire climb over the next five days. The exception was an hour or so of a deluge just as we were trekking across the equator to the southern hemisphere. Luckily, I was prepared for all conditions, having retained all-weather gear from my ascent of Kilimanjaro. Normally, a lot of rain can be expected in these parts during early May. August and September are really the ideal months to climb Mount Kenya from the north side. In May, we had the mountain virtually to ourselves.

I ventured up the harder, less used, but more scenic Sirimon route.

'The trek passes through Kikuyu farms up into the rainforest, then through a bamboo zone, before we reach bog and alpine terrain,' Alfred told me in his husky voice. 'After that, you face the higher snow-covered reaches of the mountain. All in all, we will walk eighty kilometres.'

In reality, there was hardly even a trail to speak of for a lot of the way; I was very dependent on Alfred's familiarity with the climb.

CHAPTER 19 THE ASSAULT ON MOUNT KENYA

We got off to an inauspicious start. After eight months of re-fusing to countenance it (except for a policeman near Kwa Vonza the first week), I was finally forced to pay a bribe. As we entered Mount Kenya National Park, the female park ranger saw that my Kenya resident's card was out of date. She demanded 500 shillings (five euro) from me to ignore the date. For her, that could amount to two days' wages. Even so, paying the resident's fee rather than the tourist charge ended up saving me a small fortune.

Alfred sympathised with me for having to bribe the ranger. There followed a slight tirade against non-Kikuyu tribes. It was the sort of anti-immigrant rant you could hear anywhere.

'The white farmers around Mount Kenya employ people from the fringe tribes, uneducated people like the Turkana. They end up working mostly for food only,' he complained.

That first crisp, starry, moonlit night, a hyena was laughing outside my tent at Old Moses Camp. I did not find it at all funny! I lay very still for an age, recalling all the Akamba stories about the viciousness of the hyena. Back in 2003, a plane crashed near the summit of Mount Kenya. Hyenas took the bodies. This, it is said, is why the beasts can now be seen patrolling up to a height of 14,000 feet. When I peeped out to see if the hyena had gone, I caught a breath-taking glimpse of Mount Kenya's distinctive white peaks, gloriously reflected in the light of a full moon. I fell asleep eventually, and woke to a chilly sunrise and the sight of buffaloes and zebras grazing a few hundred yards away.

The second day involved ten hours trekking through moor-lands, climbing over rocks, sliding down mucky slopes, and jumping across mountain streams. Now and again, I began to feel some of the effects of altitude and had to stop for a breather. '*Polé, polé,*' urged Alfred.

After several tiring hours, I experienced a truly revelatory moment. Puffing, panting and sweating, I climbed over a steep rocky ridge and there before me, all of a sudden, lay Makinder's Valley. This long high-sided valley, bathed in brilliant sunshine, swept spectacularly upwards, framing exquisitely the mountain's distinctively jagged and snowy peaks in all their grandeur. Truly, a home fit for a god! Makinder's Valley is named after Sir Halford Makinder, the first successful climber of Mount Kenya. That feat was first achieved just over one hundred years ago, in 1899.

On the second night, when I popped the tent up in exposed terrain at 14,000 feet high, I watched it simply blow away like a balloon. My heart leapt. Fortunately, the tent lodged in rocks some distance away and I was able to retrieve it. The strong winds abated, thankfully, and an eerily calm night ensued at Shipton's Camp. I had a slight headache and got no sleep due to the altitude. But, in all other respects, I felt good. Rock hyraxes invaded my tent searching for food. They look like a cross between a rabbit and a small tailless beaver. They were easily frightened off. Despite the difference in size, they are the closest living relative to the elephant, according to Alfred, though I would often be sceptical about such stories.

We were forced to change completely our planned route for the summit.

'There is not enough snow on the glaciers,' Alfred informed me. 'There would be insufficient grip on the surface for climbing.'

I saw a certain irony in this situation. I could not help contrasting this dearth of snow with the blizzard conditions on Kilimanjaro, where it was the fresh snow that was treacherously slippy. The change of plan meant I had to abandon a day meant for acclimatisation at Shipton's Camp. I had been looking forward to having the time to explore the tarns and glacial valleys beneath the summit; and having time just to admire the fabulous views of much of Kenya from this high altitude.

Alfred and I set off for the summit at 3am. The thinness of the air and steepness of the ascent were now severely testing my energy reserves. But, unlike the final assault on Kilimanjaro, visibility on this cold starry night was excellent. The white jagged summit towered over us in the moonlight; a full moon sat wedged between the two main peaks.

At such high altitudes, weather conditions can change with frightening rapidity. It started snowing on us at about 15,500 feet. The fresh snow was making it dangerous and slippery in many places, especially clambering over the loose scree. Most serious climbers use ski poles as walking aids in the mountains; I was using a cheap umbrella that I had bought off a hawker in Nanyuki. It did the job for me just as well as a ski pole, though.

We finally reached the summit just as a hazy orange dawn was breaking. The snow had stopped, revealing a stunning panorama of luminous peaks, dark tarns, glinting glaciers, and valleys quilted in snow. Looking around, the rest of Kenya stretched away to distant hazy horizons, and far to the south in Tanzania, I could make out the distinctive outline of Mount Kilimanjaro. I was overjoyed with a sense of achievement.

I discovered later that Alfred and I were the only people who attempted the summit that day by any route. Almost half of those who set out to climb Mount Kenya fail in their attempt. Some do not even get beyond the rainforest, driven off by elephants or buffalo. So, there was considerable satisfaction in realising, that for a brief while, Alfred and I were the highest two people in Kenya, on the second highest mountain in Africa. The batteries in my camera froze after I had taken a few photos to record the moment. As it was bitterly cold, and Alfred was keen to begin the descent, we did not linger too long at the top.

Re-united with our porter, we set off on our way down from Shipton's Camp in the blazing mid-morning sun. After my Kilimanjaro experience, I had applied lots of protective sun cream. Then it was down through a thick mist that had entrenched itself in Makinder's Valley in the afternoon. Something near total exhaustion meant that I slept very soundly indeed at Old Moses Camp that night. Early next morning, it was back down to the road for Nanyuki.

'I have now retired from climbing African mountains,' I announced to Alfred, as I slipped him a tip.' . . . for the time being anyway!'

Back in Nanyuki, I wanted to catch a bus to Nyeri. I asked one local Kikuyu man for directions to the bus depot. He started a loud communal debate in the Kikuyu language with half the street, which lasted for five minutes. After much arguing among themselves, I was provided with an answer.

'Just turn right here,' he told me.

The journey got off to a slow start. Several passengers, including a Kikuyu proudly sporting a leprechaun hat, helped me to push the 'Maggie Thatcher' a few hundred feet in order to start the engine. We made it in the end however. Nyeri is the capital of Kikuyu country, a lively town about fifty kilometres south of Nanyuki. It nestles among the picturesque valleys in the Central Highlands, south-west of Mount Kenya, in the very heartland of the coffee farms. Nyeri, it is claimed, is at the optimum altitude for growing coffee.

In Nyeri, like every other sizable town in Kenya, I fell in with a gang of Akambas making bicycle brakes from worn-out sandals, and making sandals from worn-out lorry tyres. Other Akambas specialise in woodcarving or basket work, and are renowned for their artistic inclination and skill; they too are to be found in towns throughout the country. I always greeted the Akamba people wherever I went, and they were always thrilled to meet a *mzungu* with a few phrases of their language. One Akamba man insisted on me visiting his home for tea when he heard about my months in Kitui. He was from a village near Kwa Vonza and, inevitably perhaps, he turned out to be related to Mwangangi. But then who wasn't, I was thinking!

Before I left the Nyeri region a couple of days later, I had to make a pilgrimage to Lord Baden-Powell's final home, a modest cottage on the outskirts of the town. He died here in Kenya, having lived in the colony for some years, and is buried in the local Anglican cemetery. His cottage is now an interesting little museum. It was Baden-Powell, after all, who founded the Scout movement, and it was in the scouts that my interest in mountaineering was born. Having just climbed Mount Kenya, there was a certain appropriateness in paying my own tribute by visiting his cottage.

After the short stay in Nyeri, I returned by bus to Kitui village to spend a few days there in mid-May. I was staying in a cottage next to Fr. Paul's home. On the second evening, it flooded. 'There has never been as much rain in Kitui since the *El-Niño* rains of 1998,' Fr. Paul remarked as we watched the water levels rise and rise around us.

I woke up the next morning to find that a huge tree had fallen straight through the roof of a neighbouring cottage, a matter of yards from where I was in bed. I had not even heard a thing; I was still recovering from the exertions of the climb.

I was more concerned that morning about a mosquito infection that was spreading up my left leg. I visited Kitui hospital to have it treated. From the outside, the hospital resembled nothing more than a couple of old farm outhouses in Ireland. When I called into the compound, there was a hundred-strong queue of patients standing outside, all patiently waiting to have their eyes scientifically checked—by calling out letters on a sheet that was pinned to a tree. Some seemed to think it was like a school test; they were memorising what the people in front of them were calling out.

I eventually lost patience and ended up cycling to the Irish Mercy nun, Sr. Helen, who treated my leg at her new dispensary near the mission station. On my way back from there to Kitui village, I was forced off the road by the approaching 'Monica Lewinsky' bus, its horn blaring. It was a hairy moment. There was a sheer drop on one side and a giant crater on the other side that could have sent me over the handlebars. Luckily, it did not. To add insult to potential injury, some joker on board threw his banana peel at me. It crossed my mind that I might be safer climbing high mountains.

CHAPTER 20
'HONEYMOON' IN ZANZIBAR

IN THE SECOND HALF of May, my girlfriend, Bríd, flew over from Ireland to spend a few weeks with me. I had already organised my time in Africa before we started going out together in college. She had been my perfect match; her beauty and charming persona had left me smitten. That was then. Now my mind was a whirlpool of thoughts and emotions. Would she still feel the same about me, and did I really feel the same even though I thought I did? Had her first year of work changed her? Had I changed? Could we simply pick up where we had left off nine months before, as easily as all that? So many questions.

I tingled with nervous apprehension while waiting at the arrivals gate of Nairobi Airport; but mostly it was an eager feeling, an impatience to embrace her. People continued to straggle out past me as I searched for someone with jet-black hair. Finally, after an eternity, we set eyes on one another. The months simply evaporated as we raced ecstatically towards each other. Bríd and I hugged warmly; it felt wonderful, magical.

We chatted and laughed so naturally on the back seat of the bus into the centre of Nairobi, it seemed like it was only the evening before that had been our last moment together. Over dinner at our hotel, she handed me a few special items she had brought from Ireland. I was so elated to be once again in her presence, to be able to admire her winsome features, and be beguiled by her gentle heartening smile.

We soon established that our loving feelings for each other had not diminished. Absence does indeed make the heart grow fonder, as the saying goes.

'Brendan, you haven't changed a bit!' Bríd assured me.

This was confirmation I needed. Though my outlook on life had changed in subtle ways, I was hoping that my experiences in Africa had not changed me as a person.

Bríd was only in Nairobi a few hours when she was greeted by the sound of gunshots in the street below the bedroom window during the night. Welcome to Nairobi, I thought.

'It's probably criminals, or maybe police in a shoot-out. It's not exactly unheard of in any big city nowadays,' I suggested.

She was alarmed, understandably, but I was able to calm her fears.

We were up early to catch the Kitui bus, which we ended up sharing with three smelly goats. Bríd was experiencing culture shock. She was wide-eyed with excitement when we had to stop to let a herd of giraffes cross the road.

'Welcome to Kwa Vonza,' I said as I helped her alight from the bus. 'It's a long way from Tipperary.'

The reply stuck in her throat, as she suddenly realised that all the eyes of the village were focused on her. The villagers always met the bus and greeted the passengers, out of idleness as much as curiosity.

I had not even noticed anything unusual; I knew all the people of Kwa Vonza by this stage. I had to tell the villagers that Bríd was my wife. They would not grasp the concept of a girlfriend. One of the ladies whom I had turned down in marriage ('because I cannot marry outside my tribe'), grumbled to me in English,

'But you are light brown (my tan), and she is white. You are from two different tribes.'

Then it was on to Nyumbani, bouncing on the back of a pick-up. I introduced Bríd to all my friends. They welcomed her warmly, and with varying degrees of shyness and curiosity. Just as I imagined, there was not much Village activity going on, only a few workers keeping the organic farm running, and Nancy and Nzoki keeping the offices ticking over. I was not required in Nyumbani any more, because there was not enough work to be done.

'It may be months yet before Phase III commences, Brendan,' Kimanze speculated. 'But at least the deeds have finally been signed over.'

This was a positive development. I was delighted, too, that Mama Mbolea and Kaviti were busy harvesting ripe vegetables to sell to the market in Kitui village.

Kimanze located a motorbike for us. Bríd sat on the back holding onto me grimly as we careered through the bush. I painfully stubbed my toe at twenty kilometres an hour as we bumped our way to Nancy's most African of African homes. We found Nancy's children sleeping in the dome granary. I explained to Bríd that sleeping in the thatched granary on wooden stilts gave the children some protection from the baboons and other nuisances.

Bríd was fascinated by Nancy's home in its compound of round thatched mud-huts.

'It looks as if nothing has changed since neolithic times,' she observed.

Inside the compound, we were treated like royalty. We received the usual honour of being invited to pick out which chicken Nancy would slaughter for us. I suggested a medium sized one. Bríd winced at the idea.

'No Bradan, it must be the biggest hen! Choose the big black hen,' Nancy demanded generously.

By this stage, the food shortage in the region had eased, which made me feel less uncomfortable about accepting Nancy's generosity. I knew from experience that the Akamba would go hungry themselves in order to feed a guest. They have a term for any visitor that translates as 'a blessing,' no matter what time of day or night the visitor calls. Food is always on offer. Nancy had been in the process of wafting smoke through her harvested maize to protect it from pests and, hopefully, disease. Other members of her family were harvesting the rest of their maize crop nearby.

Nancy's neighbours quickly assembled when the bush telegraph announced our arrival. The adults had great fun fitting together the jigsaw puzzle that Bríd had brought with her—even though it had been meant as a gift for the children. The younger ones were as timid with Bríd as they had been with me months before, but she soon won their confidence. There was some disappointment when her arms proved not to be hairy like mine!

Bríd and I were planning to spend the next three weeks touring in Tanzania. Our send off from Kitui was another excuse for Sr. MM to host a colonial-style party for the Irish in the area. Fr. Paul was anxious to thank Bríd, who had worked tirelessly with our college friends to raise funds for Kitui. And so, as another big red sun was consumed by the horizon behind us that evening, we found ourselves devouring a sweet trifle fortified with some of the altar wine meant for the week's Masses—Sr. MM had run out of anything else to flavour it with!

The next morning, Bríd and I set off on our 900km journey to Dar es Salaam in Tanzania. These distances always appeared much smaller on a map. The standard world maps tended to portray countries that are closer to the Polar Regions as relatively larger in comparison to the countries close to the equator. This, apparently, is because the European colonial nations pressured early cartographers to distort the reality so that African colonies would not look multiple times bigger than the size of the 'mother' country. So, when taking this into account, coupled with the fact that many main thoroughfares are not even tarred, journeys in Africa inevitably take much longer than anticipated.

We crossed the Kenyan border at Namanga, directly south of Nairobi. Just as I was handing my passport over, I suddenly spotted for the first time that when I entered from Uganda in March, the Kenyan official stamped it 23/06/03, instead of 23/03/06. Unfortunately, the immigration officer at Namanga spotted the date too.

'Mr. Brendan, I see you have been in Kenya for a long time without a valid visa,' he said menacingly, and threatened to have me thrown in jail!

'Look, no need for that. I will just leave the country,' I pleaded.

Luckily, his superior officer believed my story, but made clear in his gruff voice,

'You should not have been allowed to get that visa in the first place—if you leave now, you will not be allowed back into Kenya again.'

Déjà vu, not again, I thought. This would be very problematic because my flight home would be from Nairobi; not only that, I had to leave Bríd back to Nairobi Airport in three weeks' time. By this stage, she was in tears over the whole business. I would have to take my chances.

'I've been through worse before,' I tried to reassure her, 'and it always turned out alright.'

A few kilometres inside Tanzania, our bus was found to be slightly overweight at a weighbridge. Weighing vehicles is a necessary precaution because of the weak structures that pass for bridges. The bus conductor looked around and up and down, then forced the two fattest women off the bus. The bus circled back onto the weighbridge and passed muster the second time around. The two women walked ten yards on up the road, and we picked them up again. Negotiating bridges after that, Bríd and I crossed our toes as well as our fingers!

When we finally reached Dar es Salaam, weary from the epic journey, we hired what may have been the only stretch-Lada taxi in all of Africa. I never knew such a thing existed. Our driver demanded the equivalent of sixty euro for a five-minute drive. I handed him about two euros worth and he was delighted. Dar es Salaam proved to be a large city; it is the largest in Tanzania, with a population of over two million people. It is a thriving port on the Indian Ocean, and is the economic capital of the country, as well as being home to most of the government departments. Dodoma, in the centre of the country, houses the parliament and is officially the capital, contrary to what most people would answer in a pub quiz. Tanzania itself is a vast country, nearly twelve times the size of Ireland; it is home to more than 120 indigenous ethnic groups.

'How much is the pineapple?' I enquired in Swahili from a fruit seller sitting on the footpath the following morning. I was given an answer that converted to about sixty euro. He settled for a lot less. I could see a pattern emerging.

Exotic Zanzibar Island lies around fifty kilometres from Dar es Salaam, in the Indian Ocean. Our boat to the island resembled nothing more than a refugee ship; noisy multitudes, mostly in Muslim dress, were jammed on deck and in every available corner, some being seasick because of the choppy seas. We only realised, after some time, that Bríd was on the male-only end of the segregated boat. We pleaded ignorance and laughed it off in the Irish language to ourselves, knowing we would not be understood by anyone—unless that amazing *Gaeilgeoir* shopkeeper in Mombasa was on board!

The slow boat to Zanzibar town was supposed to take three hours from the time we boarded at midday. In the end, the engine broke down, and we limped into port in the dark, a full nine boring hours later.

'Slow boat to China more like,' I quipped to Bríd.

She was still coming to terms with the strangeness of it all.

At passport controls, we declared our intention of staying for over a week on the island. For historical reasons, Zanzibar maintains its own immigration controls. It gained its independence from Britain in 1963; a year later it voluntarily united with mainland Tanganyika to form Tanzania, and it maintains a very strong degree of political autonomy to this day. After stamping us in and inquiring about our accommodation, the immigration officer immediately morphed into a tout for a particular guesthouse—his wife's!

'I will show you very good guesthouse. That one you want to stay in is no good. You will find my wife's guesthouse much superior!'

Zanzibar town and, in particular, the old Stone Town quarter resembles Lamu in many ways: in its narrow winding alleyways, raised terraces, shady squares, bazaars, and mosques. Unlike Lamu however, Zanzibar has a new town attached, a few souvenir shops for tourists and, more significantly, has cars. We were only just off the boat when we saw a car crash into the back of another. The lights were smashed on both cars, but both just drove away without even an exchange of abuse.

Another big difference is that Zanzibar has pet monkeys that attempt to pull the skirts off women walking down the narrow lanes. Had they been trained to do so, we wondered. We heard quite a few high shrieks of annoyance from the women. Being from Mars, I subtly chuckled to myself in amusement; being from Venus, Bríd told me off.

'Whist, Brendan, you shouldn't laugh at that!' she scolded, while laughing herself.

It was a pure delight for us to wander together through the maze of alleyways in the old town, exploring the spice markets with their exotic array of cloves, cinnamon, lemongrass, and vanilla. How could you resist the invitations to taste? Occasionally, we got lost in the labyrinth of laneways, distracted by the brightly painted signs. Some of those in English were more noteworthy for their colourful artistry than their grammar; one read:

CHAPTER 20 'HONEYMOON' IN ZANZIBAR

The main man in town for motorbikes is a colou—
rful caracter called Ally Keys. He not as disrepta—
ble as he looks and her bikes is safe [sic]

On one lane, real daggers and children's toys were being sold together on the same stand. Beside the market, a crop of maize was growing in the courtyard of the Old Fort in the middle of town. Along the seafront, we discovered one of the highlights of the town; a lively open-air market, lit up from evening by paraffin lamps, that was offering delicious fresh seafood. We regularly re-fuelled there with octopus, squid, shark and such like, that the talkative proprietors barbecued on the spot—all for next to nothing. We savoured eating our feasts as we sat on the seawall, while the pleasant aroma of smoke from the barbeque fires fused with the warm sea-air.

We were the only people in the previous fortnight to stay in our large ornate guesthouse. The most distinguishing feature of Zanzibar town is the exquisitely carved, large wooden doors on the front of the tenement buildings, formerly mansions, dating back to the more prosperous era when the Sultan of Oman ran all the ivory, spice, and human slave trades of East Africa from his palace in the town. Zanzibar fell under the control of the Sultan of Oman in 1698 when he routed the Portuguese rulers. The island boomed as the coastal epicentre for trade with Africa's interior. The Sultan's territory in Africa at one time stretched from Mozambique to Somalia, and the island became the ninety-nine percent Muslim it is today.

Trading in slaves and spices became so lucrative that the Sultan had moved his capital from Muscat to Zanzibar in 1840. Then, in a succession struggle between his two sons in 1856, the sultanate was split into the separate sultanates of Oman and Zanzibar. Britain seized control of Zanzibar in 1890 in a dispute over human slavery, but the Sultan was retained as a figurehead. The Sultan took over once again on independence in 1963. However, a mere 32 days later, he was forced to flee on being ousted by a popular uprising of the indigenous Swahili Africans.

Bríd found our visit to the underground slave chambers very moving. The conditions the slaves were forced to endure, before being sold at the slave market, were indescribably callous. It is estimated that over half a million of these unfortunate Africans were sold here in the forty years prior to 1870.

It was in Zanzibar that the pioneering missionary, Dr. Livingstone, first landed in Africa, stayed a few years and invited the British to intervene in order to abolish the slave trade. The British dutifully—some might say opportunistically—accepted the invitation, then won the shortest-ever war in history. It took only forty-five minutes for Zanzibar to surrender. Dr. Livingstone then built an impressive Anglican Cathedral, right on top of the underground slave chambers on the site of the slave market.

I was intrigued and somewhat amused at the end of our guided tour of the holding cells when, without knowing I was living in Kitui, the English-speaking guide explained,

'There is a tribe somewhere in Kenya, I think they are called Akamba or something like that, who, when every other tribe would be fighting off the Arab slave traders, the Akamba would tell them, "Pssst, I'll sell you my neighbour here. I'll go catch him. How much will I get for him?"'

The Akamba indeed had, and have, a reputation as traders. They were always well known to the Arabs, and to the British later on, as the middle-men between the coastal Swahili traders and all the tribes of the interior with whom they wanted to trade beer, ivory, medicinal plants, tools, weapons, ornaments, food, and cattle. Such was the tide of corruption spread by slavery that many African tribes engaged in capturing and selling their tribal neighbours. However, I could not verify the guide's claim that the Akamba were so willing to trade their own people.

For the next week or so, Bríd and I headed to the near-deserted picture-postcard tropical beaches and coral reefs further up the island towards its northern tip. When we arrived in Nungwi village at 11am, a staggering drunk showed us to nice chalets overlooking the fabulous palm-fringed beach. Then he proudly boasted in almost his only words of English,

'I am the watchman. I protect the chalets.'

I pointed him out to Bríd later that evening. He was lying asleep on the beach, an AK-47 on his lap.

The security guards at these places, including the upmarket hotels that charge guests hundreds of dollars a night, are paid about one euro for an entire nightshift lasting from 6pm to 6am. Before coming to Africa, I used to hear this tired old 'dollar a day' cliché so often from Bono and Geldof that it did not really register. Only now could I fully comprehend it. I was not entirely surprised when our bag was stolen on the second afternoon, while we were swimming at a secluded beach. Luckily, we did not lose anything important.

We found the long white sandy beaches of our tropical paradise largely deserted. Nungwi, and nearby Kendwa, seemed like some of the private islands of the Caribbean; it was so relaxed and tranquil and laid-back under the palm trees. Bríd and I were co-

cooned in our own state of bliss, waltzing on the sand as the sun set, to the sound of the waves breaking lazily on the seashore.

We fell in with the same English lads I had met while climbing Mount Kilimanjaro in March. Small world, we agreed. They were now in their last days in Africa, having spent a year teaching in Tanzania. They had attended some of the more famous English public schools, but were far from the posh-school stereotypes. We played pool one night with the resident sharks at an outdoor bar next to the beach. Unfortunately, the Africans were much more familiar with the contours of the dodgy table, and we lost a few Tanzanian shillings. Part of the appeal of beautiful Nungwi is that it caters for a variety of people in season. It is one of a tiny handful of backpacker hideouts in East Africa. As such, it can be relatively cheap, provided you stay away from the expensive hotels catering mostly for Western newlyweds.

Bríd and I went snorkelling at the nearby coral reef. In the warm tropical waters, we were treated to a spectacular display of colourful fishes and other exotic marine life, including turtles. It was hugely enjoyable, but I felt slightly seasick coming back on the sailing dhow. On our last evening on Zanzibar, I held Bríd in my arms as we drifted with the tide in a warm turquoise sandy bay. The setting sun produced a magnificent array of colours, from bright orange to deepest purple. It was one of those perfect moments in life, with everything in harmony and the two of us deeply in love.

CHAPTER 21
SAFARI IN THE SERENGETI

AFTER A FEW HOURS' SLEEP on the overnight boat from Zanzibar to Dar es Salaam, Bríd and I went looking for a bus to the inland city of Arusha next morning. A tout tried to drag us onto the 'Pope Benedict XVI' bus.

'How much is it for the popemobile?' I asked the driver in Swahili.

About fifty euro was his asking price. No big changes in Dar es Salaam in the meantime, I thought.

Near one small village on the way to Arusha, where we stopped for a break, a complete brass band, instruments gleaming in the sun, was practicing on the roadside. Were they expecting a celebrity? Had they been misled about the popemobile? It was one of those bizarre random sights frequently witnessed in the African bush.

Stepping off the bus in the dark, when it finally reached Arusha, we were immediately accosted by Robert Mugabe's double. He offered us a good deal on a safari. In fact, we decided it was good enough for us not to shop around, and we were to set off early the next morning.

Arusha lies 650km to the north-west of Dar es Salaam, along the main road to Nairobi. The clock tower in the centre of the

NO HURRY IN AFRICA

town is supposedly the exact midway point between Cairo and Cape Town, the two termini of the British Empire in Africa. Its importance in modern times is for being East Africa's 'safari capital.' Practically every safari in northern Tanzania starts and ends in Arusha. The 14,980 feet high Mount Meru, towering over Arusha, was clearly visible from the hotel rooftop where we had breakfast—as was every male using the urinals along the sidewall of the corridor leading to the rooftop buffet. The staff took away the breakfast buffet long before it was due to end.

'That's because you've gone up to help yourself too many times,' Bríd suggested.

I had been looking forward to our classic four-day safari on the vast Serengeti plains since before I left Ireland. I really wanted to complete my sightings of the 'Big Five' trophy animals in the wild: lion, rhinoceros, buffalo, leopard, and elephant. I termed this particular trip the 'soup, dinner, and dessert safari,' as we were starting with Lake Manyara, followed by two days in the Serengeti proper, and finishing with a day in the wildlife bowl that is the Ngorongoro Crater. They are all located in a corner of Tanzania to the west of Arusha, between the city and Lake Victoria.

Bríd and I were joined in Robert's jeep by an East Belfast man named Brian, who bore some resemblance to Peter Fonda in *Easy Rider,* and by his New Zealand-born wife, Leonie. Brian and Leonie were travelling overland together from Copenhagen to Cape Town via the Middle East. They were typical of the intrepid adventurers you meet in Africa.

'We're going the whole way by using only public transport,' Leonie explained. 'The Middle East proved much safer than we anticipated, certainly better than Sudan. Northern Kenya was another story again. Tell them about the dust, Brian, and about those Africans in the back of the lorry with us . . . '

Brian and Leonie were an outgoing couple in their mid-forties. As a group, we hit it off straight away. Less than an hour after meeting them, I looked through my binoculars straight at Leonie, and joked,

'Look, look, there's a kiwi!'

She turned around instantly.

'Where, where?' she exclaimed, before twigging.

There followed four days of never-ending bad jokes that often had us all in stitches. Robert eventually stopped trying to teach us about the animals because we only ended up laughing at some surreal gag we made up about them.

The Serengeti plains provided us with one fantastic surprise after another. We watched a pride of female lions sitting in a tree, watching, waiting, then jumping down to hunt down gazelles crossing a nearby river. The gazelles just made it to safety on this occasion. Later on, we were enthralled by the sight of a lone male lion suddenly standing up from his camouflaged position in the tall dry grass, then licking his front paws, before mounting a small rocky hillock and roaring at full volume only a matter of yards from our jeep. Then he turned his back on us and walked casually away. King of the Plains.

Shortly after this, we saw a leopard lunching on an impala that it had hauled up onto the branches of a tree. That first day in the Serengeti, we also spotted white rhinos, zebras, ostriches, elephants, giraffe herds, and a cheetah with her playful cubs. Bríd was beside herself with excitement. There were lots of baby animals about at that time of year, and many mothers nurturing their young. Then there were the countless animals, both big and small, that I had not heard of before: topis, hartebeests, klipspringers . . . Robert identified them for us as we drove across the plain.

On Bríd's birthday in the first week of June, we were up and going before dawn. This was a great time for spotting hippopotamuses, elephants, and zebras crossing the tracks, lit up by the headlights of Robert's jeep. A rosy dawn in the Serengeti is pretty spectacular too. This particular morning we happened upon a feeding frenzy. Several wildebeest had drowned while crossing a river during the night, so it was breakfast time for any number of hyenas, crocodiles, vultures, and jackals. There was fierce and noisy competition among these predators and scavengers as they attempted to drive each other off.

Hovering serenely above the savannah that morning was a solitary hot-air balloon. Leonie was in a bantering mood.

'How come you didn't organise a flight in that for Bríd on her birthday, Brendan?' she teased.

'One hour in that balloon with a champagne breakfast to follow,' Robert interjected, 'would cost you over four hundred dollars!'

'Is that all?' I remarked. 'Sure let's book it for the whole day tomorrow.'

We had timed our safari extremely well. In the vastness of the Serengeti, we appeared to be the only jeep observing the huge annual wildebeest migration.

'This is something special, Bríd—even for Africa,' I explained, as she stared in amazement through binoculars. 'This is one of

CHAPTER 21 SAFARI IN THE SERENGETI

Nature's greatest spectaculars. At the end of the rainy season over a million wildebeest and around 200,000 zebra and various types of deer migrate north to Kenya's Masai Mara. It happens every year at this time. They are endlessly on the move in search of water and grazing.'

'But what are the zebras doing in the middle of the wildebeest? Bríd asked, reasonably enough.

Robert took up the story as he drove the jeep right into the middle of them.

'The zebras actually marshal the wildebeest herds, because the wildebeest forget the migration route from year to year. In return, the zebra are protected from the great predators—mainly the big cats like the lions, as well as crocodiles—by the sheer numbers of wildebeest,' he enlightened us.

We hung around a long time marvelling at this extraordinary scene, and felt privileged to have experienced it.

'Yes, it's all about timing, and you have timed it very well,' Robert said. 'You want to catch the movement of the animals like we are seeing now, and you have avoided the rainy season when the tracks are impassable. But you have also to avoid the tourists who come in great numbers in the later dry summer months.'

'Of course,' Brian quipped, 'the annual migration of tourists.'

'Yes, and I've met some of their predators and scavengers,' Leonie added. 'From what I've seen of northern Tanzania, it appears to be richer and more full of pickpockets in comparison to Kenya.'

'Maybe there's a connection between the two?' I suggested.

Brian's eyesight was quite bad.

'Look, quick, what's that animal moving beyond the trees?' he yelped on one occasion later that day.

It turned out to be a distant jeep. So, we did not have the Serengeti to ourselves after all. We trained our binoculars on some rich Americans in their over-the-top safari costumes; they were wielding cameras with huge telescopic lenses and taking endless photos of a very ordinary acacia tree.

'I spot a smaller specimen of this tourist animal,' Brian remarked. 'But it has got an even longer lens. It's the Japanese variety.'

At times, we travelled for ages without spotting anything interesting, especially in the heat of the day. Occasionally we played host to swarms of flies.

'God made the fly, he just didn't tell us why,' Robert announced, in his wisdom.

We spent some time observing a male gazelle continually trying to mount a female who kept hopping away. Thereafter, he tried it on with all the other females who also kept skipping away from his amorous approaches. At this point Leonie started humming the jaunty tune at the end of *The Benny Hill Show*. We all joined in, getting faster and faster until we were convulsed with laughter.

At our campsite in the evening, I watched in a state of near paralysis as a gargantuan bull elephant sauntered past our tent in search of water. It was only a matter of feet away. Before I drifted off to sleep, I heard lions roaring quite close by, their pronouncements echoing regally over the star-covered savannah. Bríd was petrified on hearing something scratching at the tent, and gave me a dig to wake me up.

CHAPTER 21 SAFARI IN THE SERENGETI

'Probably a rodent of some sort,' I suggested.

She did not find that very reassuring, for some reason.

Sometime in the middle of the night, I had to step out to relieve myself. Now it was my turn to be paranoid. I was imagining a hungry lioness jumping on me from behind in the pitch darkness. And now it was Bríd's turn to mock me. On my way back in, I stamped and galloped around the tent a few times in an attempt to frighten her.

'I knew it was you all along,' she claimed, calm as you like.

As we neared the Ngorongoro Crater next day, we passed numerous Maasai boys wearing their distinctive red blankets and begging by the rocky track. Their dark faces were painted white.

'This is part of the preparations for their circumcision ceremony to become a Maasai warrior,' explained Robert. 'Another part of the preparations is that each one of them has to catch and kill a wild animal. Yet another common custom is the removal of one front tooth. This is to enable a sharp whistle for controlling their cattle.'

Brian speculated about which to choose if you really had to: being circumcised or having a front tooth removed. Both would be without benefit of anaesthetic!

A Maasai in the city can easily be identified by his great height, his slender frame, his distended earlobes and, sometimes by his missing front tooth. Being semi-nomadic, his is the only tribe freely allowed to cross the Kenyan-Tanzanian border. Maasai territory straddles the border. Nowadays, the tribe is sidelined in the politics of both countries. They are constantly under government pressure to move out of the country's many game parks.

The Maasai have already been removed from the Serengeti.

NO HURRY IN AFRICA

They still have grazing rights around the Ngorongoro Crater, but the blanket-clad herdsmen that we saw rounding up cattle right beside four huge elephants on the very rim of the Crater, may be forced to evacuate in the near future. It seems unfair to me. It was Lord Delamere, over a century ago, who was among the first people to recognise that the nomadic pastoral lifestyle of the Maasai can exist quite harmoniously with the African wildlife.

Our campsite, high on the crater rim, was freezing cold at night. As I made my way from the tent to the toilet, I could identify buffalo and zebra cantering nearby in the moonlight. Early the following morning, descending into the basin through the thick shroud of mist that had formed around the crater rim, was like entering a lost world.

'I think we are in *Jurassic Park*,' Bríd commented.

Ngorongoro Crater is truly one of the wonders of the natural world. A mere twenty kilometres wide, it has perhaps the greatest concentration of wildlife on earth. As we drove down and out under the cloud, an entire ecosystem trapped in a bowl stretched out before us. Biodiversity takes on a new meaning here.

Rich in vegetation, the Crater attracts most of the big beasts of the plains as well as a great variety of herbivores such as wildebeest; there are even flamingos in the soda lake at the bottom of the crater. A freshwater lake guarantees an amazing variety of bird life. Exotic birds compete in colour with a profusion of plants and flowers of every hue. Unlike the wild, endless, open, and largely featureless landscape of the Serengeti, you have a sense here of concentration, distillation, essence—the ultimate zoo. The creatures here are encaged by the crater, but naturally so, and that makes all the difference. I was so glad we had kept

Ngorongoro Crater to the end of our safari. It made for a perfect climax to our trip. *Safari njema sana!*

Returning to Arusha and the noise and bedlam of humdrum urban life was anti-climactic, a shock to the system. Back in the hotel, many visitors to the major game parks were griping about their safari experiences: their jeep broke down; there were no lions to be seen; there were too many jeeps around one lion; there were too many Americans; their guide was not fluent in English; their meals were of poor quality; they did not get on with their companions in their jeep; their jeep kept getting stuck in the mud because of recent rain—and so on and so on. As Brian, Leonie, Bríd, and I got together for a meal that night, Brian spoke for all of us.

'Maybe we just got lucky, but I'd say we have just had the perfect safari.'

Over drinks, I told them some stories of horror safaris, some of them probably the savannah equivalent of urban myths. The *Daily Nation* in Nairobi was full of these stories. One of the best known concerns a group of Japanese tourists in the Masai Mara game park, the northern extension of the Serengeti in Kenya.

'Apparently,' I continued, 'several Japanese stepped out of their jeeps to take pictures of themselves in front of a pride of lions. Days later, they had not returned. The park rangers eventually called out a helicopter to help search for them. Anyway, there was no sign of the Japanese, but their jeep was found with a camera on the bonnet set to automatic mode. When the photos were viewed, the last ones showed the pride of lions sneaking up behind the group, getting closer and closer and closer . . . '

'I hope you make it back into Kenya alright,' Leonie wished

me luck at the end of the night, as we parted company.

They were heading for Rwanda the following day. Bríd and I were still unsure exactly where we were going, and chose to sleep on it.

My first thought when I woke up the next morning was figuring out how to make it back into Kenya. There are only four border crossings between Kenya and Tanzania. One is Namanga, which was obviously no-go. The one near Lake Victoria would take many days to reach because there is hardly any public transport, or indeed roads, from Arusha. One is near Mombasa, but it is always busy, with long delays. So we settled on Taveta, a no-horse border post east of Mount Kilimanjaro.

Our first attempt to reach Taveta failed, when the police outside Arusha impounded our bus for having people hanging off the sides. We had to walk back to town and get another one. That is how we found ourselves travelling through the savannah aboard the 'Snowbuster'! Sitting beside us on the Snowbuster was one of those African geniuses that I came across now and again. When Bríd mentioned that we were from Ireland, he launched into a critique, long and loud, of seemingly nearly every novel and short story that James Joyce had composed. He claimed to have never been to school. Having encountered his like before, I was inclined to believe him.

When we eventually reached the border post at Taveta, I nervously spun a yarn for the benefit of the solitary bored immigration official.

'I have to escort my wife to Nairobi Airport, sir, and I will be travelling on to Ethiopia once I leave her there,' I assured him.

He stamped me in for another three-month stay . . . with the correct date. I checked!

'Told you it would be all right,' I said to Bríd, not entirely convincingly, when we were out of earshot.

Just like that, the Border Foxes were back in Kenya. I would say that there were probably only half a dozen people who passed through that border post the entire day. A few days later, I read in the *Daily Nation* that fifty-four people died when a bus crashed over a precipice into a river between Arusha and Moshi, just one day after we rode the Snowbuster on the very same route on our way to Taveta. Such are the vagaries of life—and death—in Africa.

CHAPTER 22
A BIZARRE TALE OF ARMENIAN ROYALTY

TRAVELLING ALONG THE BUMPY dirt road from Taveta to the town of Voi in early June, our slow bus encountered so many elephants at one point that even the Africans hollered to the driver to stop so they could look. There must have been forty or more in the herd. In Africa, you can never predict what will slow your progress. We were late in reaching Voi—not that anyone seemed bothered. Over 100km east of Taveta and about six hours from Nairobi, Voi is a busy but unremarkable town. Except, surprisingly, there are street bins, and people actually seemed to be using them—uniquely for Kenya, in my experience.

Bríd and I got off the bus in Voi and ordered *ugali* and black beans at a café. There was a tree trunk growing through the café roof, but at least it was convenient to the railway station. Voi is another East African town, like Nairobi itself, which has grown around the station. When we went to book tickets for our onward journey to Nairobi, we found the station itself to be a living museum of the early twentieth century. The stationmaster, dressed in a white bushjacket, was stopping the trains by holding up a red hurricane lamp; he was changing the tracks manually by yanking big levers, and ringing hand bells prior to shouting announcements on the platform while his assistant was using the wind-up phone in his office. The entire station interior was made of dark unstable wood panelling. There were notices on the walls that had been there since before Independence; a few words had been updated in pencil. Barefoot children were rolling an old bicycle wheel along the platform while we sat waiting for our train to arrive.

Fr. Liam told me one time about an Irish missionary from Kitui (the same one who hoisted the boy in the air for calling him British) who went to collect an important parcel in Voi railway station in 2003. He began to protest loudly when he discovered his parcel had been lost. Unimpressed by the priest's belligerent attitude the stationmaster told him,

'You are late.'

On hearing this, the missionary raised his voice again,

'What do you mean I am late! It should have arrived here last week.'

'You are forty years too late!' came the loaded reply from the stationmaster, implying that since Independence, he deserved more respect.

Upon boarding the train late that night for the 350km journey northwest to Nairobi, we discovered that someone was occupying our pre-booked compartment. After several minutes banging on the door, out stepped two men in uniform, a yawning soldier and a hefty policeman who was rubbing his eyes. Each of them was wielding a Kalashnikov. I was momentarily silenced. But they both apologised to us, and vacated the carriage. The train went clickety-clickety all night long.

I poked my head out the window at dawn to relish the breeze on my face, waved to the Maasai who were waving back, and pointed out the zebras, giraffes, and ostriches to Bríd as we approached Nairobi. The thrill of spotting game animals never ended for me. The train was soon trundling through the slums into the awakening city. The makeshift shacks of the slums are built literally just inches from the track. The Kibera slum market stalls are also strung along both sides of the railway track; because of the pressures of population, every square inch of land is at a premium. There are no fences between the hovels and the railway line.

Bríd and I had allowed ourselves a day to spend together in Nairobi. I wanted her to get a feel for the place and some of its colourful characters before she returned to Ireland. The touts on Nairobi's streets were familiar with me by now. In some instances, we were on first name terms, but not yet with that 'Sudanese refugee' conman. When I identified myself as Italian this time, he was about to complete his doctorate in theology at the Gregorian University in Rome, but first he needed a lot of shillings to reach Tanzania. Once again, he appeared not to remember me.

When not fending off touts and hawkers, we spent a lot of time wandering around and dodging the maniacal Nairobi traffic. We observed a man with the words:

Corruption Is Evil
Parking Attendant

inscribed on the back of his coat. Since the departure of President Moi, the anti-corruption message is everywhere, but sadly is more honoured in the breach than the observance. As we sat on a wall enjoying an ice-cream, we saw the righteous parking attendant being slipped a bribe by a driver who was allowed to park where clearly he should not have been.

NO HURRY IN AFRICA

For our last night together in Nairobi, we enjoyed a meal in the all-you-can-eat 'Carnivore' restaurant; on the menu were crocodile, camel, and ostrich. For conservation reasons, the government had banned them serving the meat of other game animals in 2004. It is somewhat incongruous that such a place exists only 100km from Kitui District where the people had been suffering food shortages for the previous five years. At the same time, the 'Carnivore' is vital for entertaining tourists and financial investors who pour money into the local and national economy.

Bríd and I very nearly did not have enough cash to pay for the meal, just about scraping it together with a mixture of three currencies. Bríd flew out early the next morning after a long goodbye. It had been a fabulous few weeks. I had been able to introduce her to a world far removed from her own experience—in Zanzibar, on safari, and on our extensive travels through two countries. Our time together had further cemented our relationship. It had also made me think seriously, for the first time, about returning home to Ireland.

Bríd's departure was not without complications. There were lengthy delays because of heightened security. The previous evening, the now infamous 'Artur brothers' had briefly seized control of Nairobi Airport. I did not seem to be able to avoid these ruritanian conmen. Every time I had tried to renew my visa or cross a border, these two youthful characters were high profile in the media and seemed, indirectly, to cause me bother at critical moments. Their quite incredible story is also worth telling because it may shed some light into the murkier corners of Kenyan politics.

The brothers had entered Kenya around the same time as I did

CHAPTER 22 A BIZARRE TALE OF ARMENIAN ROYALTY

in September 2005, claiming to be members of the Armenian royal family. The Armenian people, incidentally, have not had a royal family since 1375. Anyway, their claim to be serious business investors meant they found ready acceptance, and they were very publicly paraded around Nairobi for weeks.

The Arturs first came to national prominence during the constitutional referendum campaign. Somewhat melodramatically, the then opposition Orange leader, Raila Odinga (now the Prime Minister), claimed they were mercenaries hired by the government to assassinate him. Shortly after that, they were chased down Nairobi's Kenyatta Avenue in the city centre by a 'spontaneous' lynch mob one afternoon.

Having escaped the mob, they then staged a major press conference at Nairobi Airport. At it, they took the media by surprise by producing a photo of themselves with Raila's main rival for the leadership of the Orange movement, the Akamba politician Kalonzo Musyoka (who is now the Vice-President—incidentally, his science teacher throughout secondary school was my friend, Fr. Liam). They went on to claim that both Raila and Kalonzo owed them over a million dollars—all this in a press room that is normally reserved solely for the use of the President. Clearly, things were not as they seemed.

In the months that followed, the Arturs went on to reinvent themselves as celebrities. They appeared frequently on TV shows, opening shopping centres and sporting events, and being guests of honour at fancy award ceremonies among Nairobi's elite. One of the Artur brothers was also supposedly having a romance with a woman who was rumoured to be President Kibaki's illegitimate daughter. The other brother boasted he was spending over one million shillings (€11,000) a day on his girlfriend. On live TV, they taunted a cabinet minister and the country's police commissioner, hinting strongly that they would unleash their ferocious alsatian dogs and crocodiles on them if either ever dared call to their plush mansion to investigate them. Was the confrontation staged? The plot was certainly thickening by the day. Someone will surely write the book.

It was obvious someone was protecting the brothers. The wheels came off, however, the evening before Bríd left. They stormed Nairobi Airport with high-calibre weapons to free some comrades, who had been arrested for using fake documents and importing a private arsenal. This incident forced the US embassy to demand action against them for a serious breach of international airport security. The Americans were jittery ever since Al-Qaeda killed over two hundred people with a bomb at their Nairobi embassy in 1998, and one of the 9/11 twin towers plane hijackers had come from Akambaland.

Incredibly, the Arturs even made it back to their suburban mansion, unimpeded, after the airport incident. That night, however, instead of being arrested to stand trial for a catalogue of extremely serious crimes, they were quietly and quickly deported to Dubai.

When their mansion was searched, it was found to contain weapons belonging to President Kibaki's personal security staff. Clear evidence was also uncovered that they were the masked men who had raided the offices of Kenya's main independent TV station and newspaper at the beginning of 2006. At the time, the raid had sparked mass protests against the government's crackdown on press freedom. The Arturs were also found to possess a registered government vehicle, had used forged documents identifying one of them as the deputy police commissioner of Kenya, and freely used fake security passes to sensitive places such as the airport. It goes on and on and on.

And it gets worse. It later transpired that they were not officially deported at all, but were free to return whenever they liked. An official had even given them a return plane ticket! Their exiting documents had been stamped with wrong names and dates. In fact, throughout the year they had operated under at least four different aliases. It is uncertain whether they are really Armenian; there has been some suggestion that they may be Russian, Czech, Ukrainian, or even Indian. They had certainly been using forged Kenyan passports for a year. It is not even clear if they were really brothers either.

The two Artur brothers appear to have been clever criminals who left huge debts behind them everywhere their high-flying lifestyles took them in Kenya. They simply duped everyone around them in a country with more than its fair share of chancers. Nobody is sure why they chose Kenya in the first place. Whatever the reason, one upshot of their high profile was that this *mzungu* was being asked at border posts and by people on the street, 'Are you one of the Arturs?' The Arturs do not know the trouble they caused me!

The big question remains: who was protecting them? Those in the frame included the police commissioner, some opposition leaders, the security minister, the immigration minister, and even President Kibaki himself. Some, all, or none of the above? Or were the Artur brothers just a pair of extremely audacious confidence tricksters? President Kibaki, while being weak on tackling corruption, had appeared to be relatively clean himself through-out his long career. His government was thought to be moving the country generally in the right direction.

However, the circumstances of his re-election at the end of 2007 were hotly disputed. The worst street violence in decades erupted over this, and resulted in hideous tribal massacres that left over 1,500 people dead and around 600,000 people displaced. My friend Sr. Cecelia, whom I stayed with in Turkana, fled along with her mother with only the clothes they were wearing when they were burned out of their home near Londiani in the Rift Valley. The Kiltegan missionaries with whom I stayed in Londiani, were attempting to feed and care for at least 3,000 people who sought refuge in their compound. In the process, they were endangering their own lives. At the time of writing, it is unclear how this sorry chapter in Kenya's history will conclude. A fragile all-party government has been formed, but the longer-term fall-out may last decades.

After Bríd left in the middle of June, I arranged to meet in Nairobi a Dublin student whom I had met in Tanzania. He had suggested the possibility of both of us travelling for the following six weeks in Ethiopia. To explore that ancient land was certainly tempting. But the other option I was considering was to return to the missionaries of Kitui to volunteer with the street-children. In the end, my Dublin friend went back to Tanzania to chase after a woman he had left behind. It was not the first time that I had struck up a friendship with a love-lorn Westerner, only for him to prioritise his love life.

My decision was effectively made for me. I would be return-ing to living with candles, fetching water from wells, and eating *ugali* everyday in dusty Kitui until my return to Ireland. The often-delinquent street-children would be a tough assignment. But after all my travels, I relished another challenge.

CHAPTER 23
THE STREET-CHILDREN OF KITUI

BEFORE I RETURNED FROM NAIROBI to Kitui in the middle of June, I spent the weekend in and around Mukuru slum, at the invitation of a missionary I had met on a previous visit.

I had not been in Mukuru since April, in the immediate aftermath of the devastating fire that had left about a tenth of the slum's 300,000 inhabitants homeless. By now most, but not all, of the hovels had been rebuilt from the charred wood and buckled corrugated sheeting which survived the flames. I spotted one elderly man ankle-deep in an open sewer picking out scraps of wood with his bare hands, probably trying to source material to re-build his shack. It was in this unlikely setting that I watched the World Cup, in a small makeshift tin hut described locally as 'the cinema.' Regardless of who was playing, every kick and tackle was watched with noisy excitement and intense interest. For ninety minutes, these people were transported far beyond their miserable surroundings.

Outside there were inescapable foul smells emanating from the rubbish heaps and sewers, blending with the not unpleasant whiff of smoke wafting from the numerous outdoor charcoal fires. The people seem inured to these odours, the inescapable miasma that envelops everything. Theirs is an enclosed world, relatively self-contained; many do not step outside the slum for weeks at a time. The whole of Mukuru is smaller than a square mile, but it is teeming with tiny shops and businesses and is, in its own way, a community throbbing with life.

Rent in Mukuru equates to about two euro a week for a room for a family of four or five or more, and note how it is *one* room for a family. In comparison, a home with two or three small rooms (again they are rooms, not bedrooms) in Kwa Vonza village in Akambaland can be rented for less than a euro per week. Neither home has running water nor electricity or anything Europeans would consider essential.

From what I observed, and from what the missionaries and Africans confirmed for me, the social dynamics of Mukuru are quite different from a longer established slum like Kibera. One cannot, as one might first imagine, consider all slum communities to be the same. As Kibera is much longer established, for instance, there exist extended family networks that are not present in a newer slum like Mukuru. In Kibera, people are also more likely to help themselves, and be more resilient in the face of common tribulations like disease. The people of Mukuru are a bit more dependent on help from outside. It would be farcical to speak of infrastucture, but Kibera is much better organised and, indeed, cleaner than Mukuru.

Mukuru is home to vast numbers of people from all over Kenya who have been displaced in recent years by famine and drought, and who have come to Nairobi in search of jobs and a new life. I spotted cows and goats wandering the alleys in the middle of the slum, animals that the pastoralists had brought with them. Territorial disputes are common in Mukuru, and sometimes turn murderous. This is partly because of the density of population, and partly owing to cultural and tribal differences in what is a more disparate and less settled community. In both Kibera and Mukuru, however, it is all too often a case of dog eat dog.

And yet, the sense of menace I had experienced on earlier visits was now lessening as my familiarity with the place and the people increased. Most people living in the slums have great dignity. They are particular about their hygiene and appearance despite the lack of facilities. The women dress in vividly coloured clothes, the children smile shyly at strangers, and the men are rarely less than welcoming. Not once during any of my visits to the Nairobi slums did anyone ever beg off me. This was in marked contrast to so many other places I had been to in East Africa, especially in Tanzania. It is ironic but true that you are more likely to be pestered by beggars in those places where people are relatively better off because of the income generated by tourism.

My thoughts on beggars and begging were inspired by a man I encountered in the bus station where I went looking for a return bus to Kitui. He was scrounging money off people waiting in the queues, claiming he came from Kakuma UN Refugee Camp. The Akamba people beside me, with little enough money for themselves, were emptying their pockets for him. This simply confirmed my feeling that the very poor and the destitute were more likely to get assistance from the merely poor than they were from the richer elements of society. It also confirmed my sense of the Akamba as a very generous people. I was glad to be back among them.

On our way back to Kitui, somewhere past Machakos away up in the mountains, an elderly Akamba man somehow managed to pull the door straight off its hinges when he was alighting from the bus. So much for vehicle maintenance, I thought. The conductor immediately shouted that we were stopping to 'take a short call or a long call'—and he was not referring to phone calls!

So, as some women on the bus took the opportunity to relieve themselves in the middle of the road, I aimed for a bush by the roadside. Seconds later a police car appeared from around a bend. They targeted only me. They may have been looking for a bribe from the only *mzungu* on the bus, without ever putting it into words. A second police car followed a couple of minutes later. They stopped to chat to their colleagues. I recognised one of the cops from Kitui; indeed, I had become quite friendly with him, so the charge of indecent exposure was dropped before it had even been properly pressed.

Once the door of the bus had been re-attached, the man seated next to me began to tell me about how people become victims in the most random of accidents. In Kenya, stories of these accidents were always told in an entertaining manner by people who enjoyed having an audience; I often found myself laughing— until the punchline arrived.

'An oil tanker crashed off this road a while back, near my own village,' he began. 'People headed for the scene and began siphoning off the oil into jerry-cans. After some time, one man decided he had collected enough oil and went for a rest under a tree. He lit his cigarette and dropped the match. The match lit a bit of oil that had spilled on his trousers. He danced around, trying to put the fire out, but the fire spread to one of his jerry-cans.'

I was amused, picturing a *Laurel and Hardy* situation, or maybe the hapless *Mr. Bean*.

'The jerry-can exploded, and it spread to the oil tanker. Eleven people who were still siphoning oil were killed. One of them was my cousin.'

Most accidents in Kenya are the result of human error, negligence, or ignorance—just like everywhere else. But the one area where Kenyans seem to be out-sprinting the rest of the world is death on the roads. I met Mwangangi in Kitui village the day I returned. We greeted each other warmly and, after exchanging stories for a while, he told me matter-of-factly that he needed to go to the market to buy a new shirt.

'Oh, is it for a special occasion?' I enquired.

'My older sister died in a bus accident coming from Mombasa. I have to be at the funeral in an hour,' he replied resignedly.

I felt devastated for him; he was a good friend but I really did not know what to say to him. Painful memories of Mutinda's death came flooding back to me. Mwangangi's sister had been on a Kitui-bound bus that crashed near Kwa Vonza when the driver fell asleep. Rumour was that the driver had been awake all night, chewing *miraa*. Sixteen people were killed. Most people passed off this accident with little more than a shrug of resignation. Carnage on the roads of Kenya is an unending horror story.

What pleased me though on my return to Kitui was that the horrors of drought and famine had eased, at least for the time being. There was still sporadic rain into the middle of June; it would normally have stopped at the end of April, but there was nothing normal about this season.

I passed my second day back in Kitui in the shade of a red-flowering bougainvillea tree at the mission house. I was reading the poetry of Patrick Kavanagh and enjoying the nearby angelic voices of children singing in unison in the inimitable African style. Out of the corner of my eye, I saw the local school principal approach; he was relatively new to the school and did not know me. He was looking for Fr. Frank.

'At last they have sent us a young priest,' was his parting shot to me. 'Those Irish are always sending us old priests!'

By coincidence, and as proof of the second part of the teacher's statement, an elderly Kiltegan missionary had recently returned to Kitui to fill in for a priest who had gone back to Ireland for a break. Fr. Eamon, a jolly character with a moustache, had served in Kitui during the 1960s. He was one of a group of us who went together into the village to cheer on Ghana against Brazil in the World Cup. We shared the Africans' disappointment at the result. There was further excitement on our way back. Fr. Eamon nearly crashed our small pick-up into the car of an African priest who lived beside me.

The Irish threw a party to mourn England's exit from the World Cup. As we were driving back in the dark that night along the dirt road, Sr. MM frightened me when she revealed,

'Last night about twenty young men attempted to hijack my car. I put the foot down and raced straight through them. They would definitely have robbed me if they had managed to stop the car . . . and perhaps worse . . .'

Whilst I was thinking about the courage of people like Sr. MM, we came upon a police checkpoint further along the main road. The presence of armed police was indicated only by a paraffin hurricane lamp planted in the middle of the road. We came close to driving over it—which could have been a fatal mistake.

CHAPTER 23 THE STREET-CHILDREN OF KITUI

When we arrived back safely at Sr. MM's home, she ran up the hall shouting,

'Come quickly, Brendan, there's a big monitor lizard in one of the bedrooms!'

It turned out to be a relatively small and perfectly harmless yellow lizard. He was reluctant to leave, though; we had a job finally brushing him out of the house.

'You amaze me,' I joked, 'you're not afraid of twenty African bandits, just scared of a wee lizard.'

'Could have been worse, I suppose,' she replied. 'It could have been a spider!'

In fairness, her home had witnessed its fair share of insect and animal attacks over the years. Scorpions were a perennial problem; they can deliver excruciating stings. There were large black moths that can be very unpleasant indeed if provoked, as Fr. Paul mentioned quite casually one day. Many of the feral cats have rabies, and some pass it on to unlucky humans. A rabid dog viciously attacked one of the boarding students at Sr. MM's school while I was staying at her home. The student would probably contract rabies from the bites. This meant an emergency trip to Kitui village searching the place for a vaccine, and would also require lengthy follow-up treatment later on. Fortunately, the student made a good recovery. Students and children are particularly vulnerable because they are less alert to potential dangers.

The most vulnerable children of all, of course, are the street-children. My last six weeks in Africa during June and July were spent volunteering with these orphaned and abandoned children in Kitui village. They are housed in a purpose-built building known as the 'Saint John Eudes Rehabilitation Centre.' It is run by several African nuns of the Sisters of Our Lady of Charity, and is yet another project of the Diocese of Kitui. Ironically, the Centre is situated in the Muslim quarter of the village. That end of Kitui is dusty, dirty and over-crowded; it is said to be populated by descendants of the nineteenth-century Swahili slave traders.

The Centre's principal aim is to return the street-children to mainstream society through care, compassion and education. I was very impressed by the good work going on at the Centre, and wished to lend what assistance I could. Fr. Paul arranged for me to talk with Sr. Florence, the formidable, but very caring, young Akamba nun who was in charge. She and I agreed a teaching role for me at the Centre until I would be returning to Ireland.

These children, most of them aged from seven to fourteen, had already lived more than I had in some ways. Most were the victims of indifferent, destitute, violent or exploitative adults. Sr. Florence introduced me to some of those who were hanging around the hallway after our meeting.

'Brendan, this is Nduku.'

A shy girl politely shook my hand, then moved on.

'She arrived here having fled her own Akamba circumcision ceremony,' Sr. Florence explained. 'That would have marked her initiation into womanhood in her community. We have to be very sensitive where tribal customs are concerned.'

I was told about other girls as young as eight years old who had been working as prostitutes, some employed for that purpose by local bus drivers. The Centre offered them the possibility of a better future.

I got a vibe from the nuns that they would rather not go into detail about the backgrounds of some of the children who ended up in their care. And indeed, I was happy just to get to know the children for the individuals they were at that very moment. Some were bursting with vitality, while others were timid and withdrawn. Whenever a row broke out amongst the children, which happened frequently enough, I would be given more background information to provide me with some understanding of where the children were coming from. Sr. Concepta, another young Akamba nun working there, was particularly helpful in this respect.

'See these boys, Brendan, their parents died in an accident and they have been very slow to adapt to life without them. They can be difficult,' she warned me.

On another occasion, she explained 'These twins have been physically and sexually abused. Many street-children like them have been forced into sexual intercourse as young as nine or ten years old. Many take to drugs at an equally early age.'

Indeed, some children were nearly always as high as kites on glue that they bought off the shoemakers in the village. Glue sniffing was a very common problem with street-children in the bigger villages and towns throughout Kenya and, inevitably, in the Nairobi slums. They turned to glue in an attempt to escape briefly the harsher aspects of their lives.

The Centre was a modest building that accommodated over thirty resident children. They slept in bunks in two dormitories, one for boys and the other for girls. Each morning I was welcomed off my bicycle by a sprightly mob of youngsters who crowded around me and cheered. I was reminded a bit of the people at the orphanage in Lasse Hallstrom's film *The Cider House Rules;* there was an almost tangible sense of impoverished togetherness among the children. Most of the time.

On one hot afternoon, they all went swimming in their pelts in a natural pool in the nearby river. This upset the Rodney and Del Boy of Kitui, who happened to be fishing from the rocks with bows and arrows, a makeshift net, and a crudely fashioned rod cut from a tree. The exuberant splashing and screaming of the children must have put to flight every fish within a wide area. Twenty minutes later, a huge rumpus erupted among the twenty-five or so children. They had taken sides over a piece of bread supposedly belonging to Fundi, a deaf mute boy who had only entered the Centre that very day. Sr. Florence, Sr. Concepta and I had to try frantically to separate the brawling children. Fundi could throw some punch. My glasses were broken in the commotion—again.

Most mornings found me sitting at my classroom table teaching a bit of English and basic mathematics. During my final year in DCU, I had conducted tutorials in a few subjects with some undergraduate classes. This was a different proposition altogether, and it was not just the age difference. Probably the biggest challenge was linguistic; most of the children only understood Kikamba, their tribal language. So, as I was teaching them English, they were teaching me Kikamba, and we had great fun. One young lad named Mutua had a natural flair for teaching. I could not help thinking that he had the makings of a great teacher one day, if only he gets the opportunity. The street-childrens' English, when I arrived, consisted mainly of telling me, 'I am not a glue,' and, 'Your name is a-British, you come from America.' I decided I would add geography to the curriculum.

The Akamba tribal language, in my view, must be one of the

hardest languages on earth to learn. For example, there seems to be about a dozen ways to say 'hello' depending on such variants as the time of day, the age of the person whom one is addressing, and the degree of respect he or she merits. Each greeting comes with a different reply. Every word seems to have four vowels for every one consonant. Despite these complexities, Fr. Frank is regarded by many as the foremost authority on Kikamba anywhere in the world—even more than any Akamba person. He has lived in Kitui since 1961.

I had picked up some Kikamba by listening to people in Nyumbani and Kitui over the months. I never saw it written down, even though there are books in the language. Perhaps because of the amount of vowels, it is a wonderfully musical language. 'What is your name?' for example, sounds something like 'waazz-ee-attaa?' Kitui people used to laugh whenever I used Kikamba. This was quite off-putting at first, until I was assured they were laughing, not at my clumsy attempts to communicate, but at the sheer novelty of hearing a *mzungu* speak their tribal tongue. They must think of Fr. Frank as a native speaker by now. Compared to Kikamba, I found that Swahili was fairly easy to speak.

One morning, about two weeks after I started in the Centre, I arrived full of enthusiasm for the day ahead, just as I did every morning. Immediately I sensed a rather tense atmosphere; everybody seemed unusually sombre. I could hear raised voices somewhere in the building. Eventually Sr. Concepta arrived and gave me the story in a hushed voice,

'Four of our street-boys left the Centre last night and raped a grown woman in the village.'

She pointed three of them out to me. One still had not returned. The shock at hearing this was momentarily overwhelming. I was full of conflicting emotions, mainly sympathy with the victim, as well as disgust at the perpetrators. But this was tempered by an awareness of the abusive backgrounds of the boys in question. I could not help contrasting in my mind how different my own innocent childhood had been. The children who raped the lady were around eleven and twelve years old. Two of them I had been getting on especially well with, and another of them was the hotheaded deaf boy, Fundi. I had developed a good rapport with him too.

This incident happened a month before the end of my time with the street-children. When I moved on, the boys were still at the Centre, much subdued; I was told the situation was still being assessed. There was, apparently, confusion over the circumstances of the assault. There was reluctance on the part of the nuns to go into any detail. They did not reveal the extent of police involvement, if any. There was a sense that the community had their own ways of dealing with these situations. There was a sense, too, that the business of the Centre was rehabilitation, not punishment.

The rape incident did not detract from the huge enjoyment of working with street-children. I spent some afternoons learning to play traditional African rhythms on a goat-skin drum. The children used to spontaneously and joyously dance and sing to the drumbeat in the timeless Akamba ways. It was almost as if they were hypnotised and possessed by the rhythms; they were simply incapable of keeping still on hearing a beating drum— even when played by a beginner like me.

CHAPTER 23 THE STREET-CHILDREN OF KITUI

On other occasions, they loved to dance to a different, modern style of Akamba music that you could hear playing loudly from tapes in Kitui village every day. This music is known as *benga*, and is characterised by lively crisp high electric guitar chords and heavy bass rhythm interludes. Ordinary people never sing it or play it themselves, but they love to listen and dance to its infectious rhythms.

On some afternoons, I hoisted Mutua or Fundi or some of the other children onto the bar of my old bicycle and cycled down to the river to wash clothes. It was marvellous to see how these destitute children were all bonding together—though not always. One hot afternoon, they were all playing football with a ball made from plastic bags tied tightly with string. (The Dutch girls, Ilsa and Yvonne, had left them a proper leather football, but they often preferred the plastic bags because they were easier on their barefeet). Suddenly, World War III broke out among them. The usual suspects got stuck in, including the four who had raped the woman. Within seconds, though, Mutua and even the girls had joined in.

What had caused the free-for-all? I had no idea.

Eventually I got one word out of Mutua: 'witchcraft.'

When I heard this, I let them at it; I was seriously outnumbered and had my glasses to protect!

'It often happens here,' Sr. Concepta explained afterwards. 'One team is accused of placing a spell on one of the goalposts during the game. They take their witchcraft very seriously.'

'Now that you mention it,' I recalled, 'the score was eight or nine to nil, and the ball did always seem to roll up short for the losing team, or hit the post.'

NO HURRY IN AFRICA

'Maybe you have been here too long, Brendan,' she smiled.

There was another occasion, shortly before I left Kitui, when the children were having a party and everyone was happily dancing and singing. Suddenly, Mutua accused a cheeky boy called Mumo of performing witchcraft on him. Mumo produced a sharp knife in the fight that inevitably ensued. It was only with difficulty that I managed to break it up and prise the knife from his grip. They were both sky-high on glue. With many of the street-children, it was often a matter of two steps forward, two steps back.

A couple of days later, Mumo and a small moody boy called Kilonzo came to my rescue when they stoned a light-green snake they spotted slithering towards me, as I stretched out in the shade of a tree. Kilonzo had been in a foul mood all morning up to then. To thank him for his alertness, I placed my khaki hat over his head and let him wear it. He was a sight. He could hardly see out from under it as it covered his eyes. It cheered him up no end, and he went round impersonating the *mzungu* for the rest of the day.

That week I heard Kilonzo and Mumo plotting to rob a lemon orchard. I just hoped they would not make a career out of thieving or banditry, as so many street-children do. In the English lesson that morning, I asked my pupils to finish the sentence 'When I grow up, I want to be . . . ' Nduku, the shy little girl who had escaped circumcision, replied,

'A car.'

She had not understood. Some of the others laughed, and her big eyes grew tearful.

It was Kilonzo who asked the day after, 'Is your hair real?' while plucking at my arm.

On another occasion he enquired, 'Is your father's skin white?'

'Yes,' I said, 'but my mother's skin is pink.'

He looked really perplexed until I told him I was just teasing. It was around this time that I picked up a cold. The nights are relatively chilly in Kitui during June and July. When I phoned home, my mother was very concerned—as usual.

'It could be malaria you have, Brendan. You should get the plane home.'

My cold lingered for a few days, forcing me to stay at home in the evenings. I whiled away another sunset by reading Thomas Pakenham's fascinating book on colonialism, *The Scramble for Africa*. From my perch on the verandah, I could hear nearby children singing as the light faded and the stealthy female mosquitoes moved in for a nightcap of blood. Driven indoors, I retired early to bed, but was soon awakened by the sound of gunshots not very far away.

Although used to such nocturnal gunfire in Africa during my year there, it always made me fearful; and it made sound sleep impossible. I just lay there, restless, in the menacing darkness. I was imagining the gunman and his violent mission. I dozed a little. In my semi-conscious state, the gunman got mixed up with the early rifle-toting colonists—images from Pakenham's book. Then, in the stillness, another familiar sound: the high-pitched and highly irritating buzzing of a solitary mosquito. It was hovering inches from my ear, trying to infiltrate the mosquito net hanging over my bed. Big fears and small irritations meant I awoke next morning from a night without restful slumber.

After a couple of days, I felt perfectly well again and had very mixed feelings about returning home. I had really enjoyed my time volunteering with the street-children, trying to get the best out of each one of them. I had loved working with children the summer I spent at an activity camp in America, but working with Kitui's abandoned, abused and orphaned children was so much more challenging, and more rewarding because of that. Some of them still had monstrous behavioural problems by the time I left, and other broken children were continuing to arrive on a regular basis. But I had become a father figure to many of them. I could see a difference in them myself. I had a feeling that many—I hope all of them—benefited at least a little from my time with them.

I also came away with the greatest admiration for the nuns who were dedicating their entire lives to giving these children a chance in the world. The sisters were doing truly trojan work in caring for and offering love to children who were not just un-loved but, as often as not, abandoned and abused. In educating them, the nuns were also offering them that most precious of gifts: hope.

What was most encouraging was that the children were en-thusiastic about education (as indeed they seemed to be every-where I travelled in East Africa). They were also learning essential life skills beyond the limited curriculum. Despite the sudden, occasionally violent flare-ups, there was a spirit of camaraderie among them. Most were bonding with each other and learning to trust; to trust each other and to trust the sisters. Prior to their arrival at the Centre, their entire life experience had taught them not to trust adults. It took some of them several weeks to come round, but all of them learned to smile again. That, I thought, was the real measure of the nuns' success.

At my going away party at the Centre in late July, the children and I were dancing for ages to the hypnotic beat of the African drums. As I was leaving, Nduku, Mumo, and Kilonzo came up and shook my hand. In their broken English they murmured shyly,

'*Bwana* Kyalo (my Akamba name), thank you . . . tell your father thank you . . . we love you . . . don't tell your people at home we take glue.'

Then Mutua tugged my shirt. I turned around to him.

'Are you cycling back to Ireland?' he whispered in Swahili.

Maybe I was not such a good geography teacher after all.

CHAPTER 24
REFLECTING AT THE END OF TIME

ONE WEEKEND IN THE FIRST HALF of July, I cycled towards Sr. MM's home having bought a small henhouse from a young skinny lad I happened to meet walking down the dirt track. It was an impulse buy, but it would make a good present. The henhouse was skilfully made from branches and woven ferns. I tied it on to the back of the bicycle, and was pedalling very awkwardly as a result. I did not get too far, however; the combined weight of the henhouse and me was too much for the ancient bicycle. I ended up throwing the bike and the henhouse on the back of a cart pulled by two oxen and two donkeys, as I grabbed a lift up to Sr. MM's house.

I found Sr. MM in the dining room with Nzinzi, an elderly silver-haired barefoot man whose gummy smile revealed that he was about twenty-eight teeth short of a full set. The Ursuline Sisters have been looking after him since their arrival in 1957, long before Sr. MM came to Kitui. Like many elderly Kenyans, he does not even know the year he was born. He was a product of the last decades of colonialism, a link with a largely forgotten past. While Sr. MM was still busy with Nzinzi, I took a wicker chair outside under a purple-flowering jacaranda tree on the lawn, and began reading *A Grain of Wheat* by the Kenyan nationalist writer, Ngugi wa Thiong'o.

NO HURRY IN AFRICA

This historical novel tells a vivid story of *Mau Mau* resistance to British rule in the period before Kenyan independence in 1963. This would have been the world of Nzinzi's youth, I reminded myself; he would have been around the age I was at this point. He would probably not think of it as 'history,' though. In the novel, a departing colonial laments at one point, that if he ever returned to Kenya in the future, he would never again see that way of life he had known. It set me thinking—about time, history, memory, things moving on.

I knew if I happened to return in ten years, and certainly in twenty years, a new chapter of Kenya's history will have been written. The country I had visited in 2005 and 2006 will have changed for me in at least one significant respect: I will feel less at home! From the Kitui desert to the Nairobi slums and on to distant Turkana, I had availed of an extensive network of Irish missionaries. They had welcomed, housed and fed me and provided me with contacts on my travels. These were the nuns and priests, now mostly elderly, who had played such a large part in the development of Kenya, post-Independence—and not just in the religious field. As I have witnessed myself, their contribution to the health and educational infrastructure of the young country has been immense.

Now in their sixties and seventies, they and their way of life will soon disappear. As the Kitui headmaster pointed out, the old priests are never replaced by younger men. The Africans themselves will have taken over—which is as it should be and, indeed, was always the plan from decades ago. It is just a pity that the herculean efforts of the Irish missionaries have not received more recognition at home. They surely merit more than the footnote that they will be lucky to get in the histories of their native Ireland. In the modern world of celebrity, these for me are the anonymous heroes and heroines.

In Africa, you are not allowed to be solemn for long. That weekend in July, Sr. MM was throwing a party. There were three Irish missionaries from different parts of Kenya staying with her. They were women of considerable experience and long service, and very good company. That evening, we all sat down to another one of Sr. MM's meals that I looked forward to so much. The table was perfectly laid out, as if it were for a black-tie function. The food, as always, was much more basic than in Ireland, but, as on every occasion, she surpassed herself with the delicious sauces she conjured up from local ingredients. There was even a small drop of alcohol that she had hunted down in Nairobi; she had been saving it for visitors.

All present were curious to hear what I had made of my time in Kitui District, now that I would be leaving soon. I had to think about it. I told them that I had been somewhat overwhelmed at first by my experiences of Kitui, but that I had quickly been won over by the warmth, decency and joviality of the Akamba people. It was a place full of character and of characters; even the crazies, and there were plenty of them, were mostly entertaining.

As they knew themselves, I kept coming back to Kitui. I had had a vague notion at one point of moving on to the Middle East, and beyond. But of course, I never really left for long. Kitui always exercised its gravitational pull—I had caught the 'African bug.' Everything happens for a reason, as the Africans often say. I had enjoyed my months in Nyumbani, but working with the street-children in Kitui village was probably my most rewarding experience in Africa.

NO HURRY IN AFRICA

Over dinner, I recounted stories about recent encounters and events, a kaleidoscope of memories I would take home with me: getting a take-away 'dip fried chicken' wrapped in the café owner's bank statement; regretfully declining when being asked by a waiter if I wanted margarine with my beer; laughing at the dance moves to the *macarena* being performed to an Akamba hymn at Mass; seeing a father and his four small children all perched on one moving bicycle, two of them gripping hens in their hands; encountering young men flying downhill with a hand-pulled cart stacked to the clouds, all looking at *me* incredulously; feeling like a zoo animal as some Akambas queued up to stare at me reading on the verandah as I listened blissfully to nearby children singing their African songs; watching men running after and jumping onto the moving 'Lucky Escape' bus (whose slogan was brightly emblazoned 'Network Search'—whatever that meant); attempting to repel cats jumping on top of my dinner in a café; being amazed at people selling everything and anything, from hillocks of second-hand tights, to piles of old plastic bottles from higgledy-piggledy stalls by the roadside; enjoying banter with the women stitching garments on the foot-powered sewing machines along the footpaths; frequenting such establishments as 'The Misplaced Saloon,' 'The Precious Iceland Hotel' and the 'Mogadishu Complex Shop'; dodging the wide metre-deep pot holes in the footpaths along Kitui main street in the darkness; meeting a black Brendan and several black Brendas . . .

I would remember too the sinister side of life in Kitui. I would long recall the unsettling sound of gunfire in the night. In late June, locals burned to death some of the bandits (the 'hole-in-the-wall gang' we had nicknamed them) who had been terrifying the district for months with raids and hijackings—the very same gang, indeed, who had attempted to stop Sr. MM that night in her car. The police simply informed their families they had been lynched. There would be no question of the mob ever being charged with murder. There was the pitiful sight, too, of convicts in black and white stripes being marched off in chains to prisons where conditions are reputedly horrendous.

I recalled the time I saw an excitable mob rushing towards women brawling on the street. The raucous crowd let them fight it out for a while, and then took sides and joined in the fight themselves. But my abiding memories of Akamba women are favourable ones. Like women everywhere in Kenya, they work hard and are not always shown the respect and gratitude they deserve. I was always greatly impressed everywhere I travelled by the resourcefulness and resilience of African women, and I would remember them too.

A very common sight around Kitui was of children and women carrying heavy bundles of sticks on their backs, held by a rope tied around their foreheads. This is the Akamba method, as distinct from other tribes who carry bundles on top of their heads. An odd time, I would see someone with a second-hand Western style bag, but with the straps around their foreheads instead of over their shoulders or in their hands. If a woman has a baby on her back, though, she will carry a bundle on her head. I often watched women laden with fruit ambling to market in this way, with the mother also holding an umbrella to shelter the baby from the sun.

At the outdoor fruit market in Kitui, I used to ask for twenty shillings (twenty cent) worth of oranges from Mumbua, a wizened old lady who spoke only Kikamba. She would first throw five into the cardboard box on the back of my bicycle, then ten, then fifteen, then hand me twenty succulent fresh oranges—all for twenty shillings. I always threw a few extra shillings to her, though she often tried to refuse it. Twenty shillings for twenty oranges was the going price for locals, so she was being exceedingly generous to the *mzungu*. It wouldn't happen in Nairobi, I thought. With men, I might have been offered ten or fifteen for twenty shillings.

I will always remember the primary colours, the healthy smells and the organised chaos of these markets. What pleased me most of all now was to see that fruit was plentiful in Kitui again, following the rainy season that began in March. Prices had dropped substantially from what they had been during the drought. In Kenya, prices of basic commodities such as grain and vegetables vary wildly from district to district and from month to month, largely depending on the timing of the rains, or lack thereof.

At the outdoor markets, if I handed over a one hundred shilling note (about one euro), I was nearly always asked, 'Have you something smaller?' No one seemed to have a float big enough to give me change. Sometimes the ladies eventually reached into their bras in order to locate their coins, chatting to me all the while in Swahili, and end the transaction with a friendly smile.

The small number of fruit sellers who could speak English were quite fond of quoting Akamba proverbs in their conversations with me.

'Freedan, a stranger's excrement smells nicer than your neighbour's,' one once advised me.

They tended not to use the word 'excrement,' though. There

were other vulgar proverbs of that ilk that did not make a lot of sense to me. Many could not manage to pronounce my name correctly. I quickly gave up telling them it was not 'Freedan,' or 'Bradan.'

I loved the comical banter with the street hawkers selling their wares. I was partial to just sitting down in the shade and watching them—and life—pass by. At such times, I was a disciple of the 'no hurry' philosophy that I so admired in the Kenyans. The hawkers used to stroll up to me and offer some trinket for a ridiculous price; I would offer them a lot less than what they asked for, and then the fun would start. I soon got to know most of them, and they me. Once they made their sale, most usually started a conversation on any random topic of interest to them.

I had been told many times that I was famous throughout Kitui District for my Akamba nicknames, one of which translated as 'tired white man who can ride a bicycle with the horn.' I had gained notoriety in July when flying down a dusty street of Kitui village; my front wheel fell off the boneshaker and sent me flying over the handlebars. A crate of eggs tied on at the back landed right on top of me. It was my own *Mr. Bean* moment, enjoyed by all who witnessed it.

There were more formal entertainments to remember too. The '*Fleadh Ceoil*' of Akambaland took place in Kitui in mid-July. It was a truly memorable affair. All the performers were flamboyantly decorated; some in hay skirts and wearing feathers on their heads, others had painted bodies and sported bells on the arms and legs. A number of them used long straight sticks as part of their routine. There was much spontaneous dancing, singing and drumming in the rural way, and a really lively atmosphere. Old men sauntering by on the track would suddenly erupt into limb-flailing dances on hearing the drums and music. The whole week was electrifying, captivating, and wonderfully African. As was so often the case, I was the only white person present, and felt lucky to be there.

The competitions were of an extremely high standard, especially the traditional Akamba, Meru, Embu, and Maasai tribal dances. These are the dances normally performed throughout the year at weddings, harvests festivals, circumcision ceremonies and so on. The Akamba style of dancing is said to closely resemble that of the Tutsi tribe of Rwanda. It is quite distinct from the 'jump-up-and-down' dancing of the Maasai tribe, for example.

There were long rambling speeches at the end of each competition. Two themes seemed to be common to these orations: how very important the speaker thought himself; and how 'fervent drumming is needed to call God down upon us,' or words to that effect. I really wish I had taped a few of them.

One of the speakers at the 'fleadh' kept telling me, 'The King of Germany is here.'

If he was, I did not meet him. I did not have the heart to tell him that the *Kaiser* was no longer with us for nearly a hundred years. However, I did manage to get within a few yards of President Kibaki and the entire cabinet at a different event a few days later. I even got to shake hands with the then main opposition leader, Raila Odinga. He looked very distinctive in his black and red polka-dot suit and oversized cowboy hat.

The occasion was the funeral in Kitui of the husband of the Minister for Health, Charity Ngilu, who was the local MP. She was leader of one of the government coalition parties. In his sermon on the Grim Reaper, the Archbishop of Nairobi referred respectfully throughout to 'Mr. Death.' After his sermon, the funeral effectively became another huge political rally, with the bigwigs addressing the wildly cheering multitudes gathered in the middle of the field where the funeral service was taking place. I chuckled when one of the government ministers stood up to address the crowd in English and began,

'A speech should be like a woman's dress—long enough to cover the subject, but short enough to retain your interest.'

The old jokes are best, I was thinking, but maybe not so appropriate at a funeral.

Even during the funeral, light aircraft kept landing and taking off beside it at Kitui's tiny airstrip, which was really just a flat field. As the planes taxied, hundreds of people kept delightedly racing along after them. It was a comically chaotic scene, like something out of Ken Annakin's film, *Those Magnificent Men In Their Flying Machines*. It was such a novelty for them to see the planes. They were enjoying the funeral hugely. Deafening roars of excitement erupted when the President's fancy helicopter took off at the end. One Akamba among the crowd turned around to me.

'I work in the Office of the President, you know,' he boasted.

'Oh, what do you do there?' I enquired, impressed.

'I sweep floors,' came his reply.

One weekend in late July, I cycled back out to Nyumbani for the last time. I had a live kid goat inside a box tied on to the back of my boneshaker as a gift for my friends. Along the way, I met two men on bicycles each carrying a wooden chair over his head. Further along the rutted dirt track, I passed a donkey and cart, and as I did so, the kid and I were nearly run down by an old Volkswagen beetle beeping me out of the way and smothering me in a cloud of red dust. How the memories of so many other bicycle rides came back to me.

I got a great reception in Nyumbani, quickly surrounded by familiar smiling faces. Another new manager had been appointed since my previous visit. He was a friendly well-groomed man called Francis, an Akamba from Machakos. When Nancy told him of my computer skills, he roped me into giving him a bit of advanced training.

'I am a bit frustrated, Brendan,' Nancy later quietly complained to me. 'I am now very good at the computer but I have not been given any extra responsibility.'

Perhaps the reason was that nothing much was happening. I was sorry to see the whole place was pretty much at a standstill. The AIDS orphans and their carers were now not expected to arrive until the end of the year (they did so in 2007).

Nancy insisted I visit her home one last time, and I was pleased to be invited. I managed to hitch a lift on an ox-cart carrying hay, in the direction of the mud-huts where she lived. There was the usual warm welcome from Nancy, her extended family and her neighbours. I had to tell her of all my adventures since last we met. Once again, her five children ran away from me at first, still scared of the *mzungu*. Nancy laughed out loud, rolled her eyes and escorted them over to me. I was sorry to say goodbye to this remarkable woman, her family and friends. I had to promise that I would return some day and visit them again.

When I left Kitui for the very last time in late July, Sr. MM took me to Nairobi Airport. She insisted on driving me there, despite the fact that she was recovering from yet another dose of malaria at the time. As we drove along, the pure randomness, diversity, and unpredictability of living in Kenya hit me yet again.

In the few hours that it took to reach Nairobi, we met Fr. Frank in his small jeep, passed a wayside hyena, drove past the 'Sea Breeze Motel' (500km inland) and the 'Saint Josephine's' shop (she never existed), overtook buses called 'Secret Admirer' and 'King Judah I,' then got a speeding fine from a policeman who was hinting at a bribe, became stuck behind a barefoot man pulling an overloaded rickety hand-cart named 'Moscow Express,' declined to buy a six-foot high hat-stand being sold through our car window from the centre of the road (the man chased after us with the hat-stand when we sped off again), and encountered a crazy old woman dancing around in circles at the next junction. The day ended with audible gunshots from the slums nearby as we retired to bed that night in Fr. Jimmy's home in Nairobi. Where could you find the like of it? These were vivid memories to be filed away for future times.

My parting from Sr. MM was an emotional one. She had been like an aunt to me for the best part of a year. I would always appreciate the welcome she had given me, and her support and advice and encouragement throughout, as well as her parties and the craic we had shared. We promised to meet again next time she returned to Ireland. Then my flight was called.

I was finally leaving 'home' in Kitui to return home. The end of time, African time, was approaching on the 'dark' side of the world; the 'real' world was beckoning again, and I had to bid farewell to this misunderstood and compelling continent. Geographer George Kimble once mused, 'The darkest thing about

Africa has always been our ignorance of it.' At least now, I was a little less ignorant than before.

In one sense, I had lost time in Africa; my parents had both retired while I was away, my youngest brother left home, and a treasured relative died just days before I flew back. I dreamed about bonfires being lit on the hills of Donegal to welcome me back to the shores of Lough Swilly on my return home. I was just longing to see everyone again.

One month before I left for Africa in 2005, I had spent three days on a penitential pilgrimage on Lough Derg in County Donegal, praying that I would come back safely from Africa. Now I was grateful that I had returned unscathed. But for all my mother's sleepless nights when I was away, it was within weeks of returning to Ireland that I fell off a ladder, suffered a bout of food poisoning, and got lost descending the wrong side of an Inishowen mountain after the mist came down. It did not happen on Kilimanjaro or Mount Kenya!

Once in a philosophical moment, that wise old medicine man Mutinda said to me,

'Life is part of a greater story, Brendan. We are all part of a bigger picture—we are just too close to it to see it right.'

If I had to sum up my year in Africa, I would say that it opened new perspectives. Africans were fond of saying that everything happens for a reason, and I had come to an understanding of what that means. It is meant to be, they would say, whatever happens—so what's the rush? No hurry in Africa. In Africa, there is daytime and night-time—people seem largely indifferent to tracking the smaller fractions of the day or night. Life is for living in the present. People happily wait for ages, laughing away the whole time; the bus will leave when it is full, and get there when it arrives. And whatever happens, it is all meant to be.

'*Whites have watches. Blacks have time,*' as the proverb goes.

They do not know how blessed they are in some ways.

EPILOGUE

ON THE FLIGHT BACK TO IRELAND, and many a time since, I found myself thinking over my year in Africa and on how volunteers can best help that continent. From my experience as management accountant at Nyumbani, and later working with the street-children, I could see that there is more to volunteering in Africa than simply a matter of flying out to 'do some good' for a few weeks and flying home again. Nor is donating money to poor families *willy-nilly* much help, though I always found it troubling when a barefoot child would stare at me with hungry eyes, hoping I would give. 'Doing good' in these ways can be counterproductive. It breeds a dependency culture, and can be generally wasteful of resources that could be more beneficial if properly and more precisely targeted.

My first piece of advice to anyone thinking of volunteering in Africa is: be prepared to embrace their culture and their very different ways. Leave your preconceived Western notions, attitudes and expectations at the airport. One has no monopoly on understanding what is acceptable behaviour. Polygamy may not be to your taste, but it is still a fact of life. A man might work away from home for two years at a stretch without returning to his family, but this may be out of sheer economic necessity, not indifference or neglect. It may seem to you that many Africans treat their animals rather cruelly, but this may be down to survival or the stage of agricultural development at which they find themselves. You do not have to approve of any of these things, but as a volunteer, you should usually accept that it happens.

You will be surprised that some very intelligent and well-educated men have three wives, paint their fingernails, or wear polka-dot suits. It is different, but you get used to it. There are valid reasons for most of the differences, serious or trivial. For example, Bríd gave out to me in Kwa Vonza for throwing the remains of a piece of fruit onto the ground. It is called littering in Europe; in Kenya, it is called feeding the goats.

Secondly: many people arrive with only a vague desire 'to help.' This may be fine for short-term emergency work. But for your efforts to be of long-term value to the people, you should have a skill—preferably one you can pass on. Otherwise, you might simply be taking a manual job from an unemployed African who would be delighted to be paid less than two euro a day to do the same work. A skill, on the other hand, is more durable and can be left behind. For that reason, I saw it as being more important for me to train locals like Nancy in basic management accounting and a variety of computer skills. I saw how Nancy and the others grew in self-worth by acquiring skills that they in turn can pass on. It is all about empowerment, to use that overused word.

Thirdly: any voluntary work should be for three months' duration at the very least to make any significant difference, and ideally much longer than that. Also, some of the organisations that ask you to raise €4,000 so that you can volunteer with them for six weeks as a radio presenter in an exotic sounding country may not be using all that money to help local people in the developing nation—instead, they will more likely plough money into keeping their organisation running, and thus gaining a greater share of 'the volunteer market.'

Fourthly: do your homework. There is the well-known story that the fuel for your flight to Madagascar probably would do more harm to the environment than your four weeks trying to save the endangered Madagascan tortoise will benefit it. So it is important to choose carefully, if you have good intentions and a desire to do voluntary work. Read up and ask questions, and do not immediately fall for the story of a charming sales rep who tells you all the ways you will be helping, and automatically assume your money is going directly to a good cause. If you do find an organisation with worthwhile projects, you can make a valuable difference, and if you donate your money to the right places, it can be of huge benefit.

Finally: any cash donations to individual Africans should usually be given to pay for such things as education or to help start a small income generating enterprise. It comes back to empowerment and breaking free of the cycles of poverty and ignorance (in the sense of lack of schooling). Africans make a go of it if given half the chance. Many are naturally enterprising. It could be as simple as buying a bicycle for someone: this could enable him to find work further afield; he could hire it out; he could even charge a few shillings for giving someone a lift—simple ideas which obviously would not apply in Europe. It is about helping people to help themselves. I sometimes speculated that the people in some of the larger administrative towns of Kenya could benefit

hugely from a facility like our own Credit Union.

I have noticed that, in Ireland, many people often contribute to trusted missionaries on the ground, rather than to some of the well-known charities or aid agencies operating in Africa. This is despite the fact the charities are audited and the individual missionaries usually are not. Many people appear wary of the amount spent by some of the best-known charities on general administration, and things such as taking the plane across Kenya instead of a car, being chauffeured around, or staying in four-star hotels. Many people are aware of the frugal lifestyles of the missionaries I met on my travels and know that they prioritise the people they serve.

In fairness to the charities, they often need to spend money on these things in order to attract quality professionals to work for them. But I still have reservations about some of them. I recall being at lunch once with the 'country director' for Kenya of one well-known charity. The bill came to only a few hundred shillings. I insisted on paying for my own lunch, but she was happy to put everyone's lunch on expenses.

Many of the larger charities are doing excellent work; their efforts are precisely targeted. They work tirelessly to improve health and education, to establish water infrastructure, and they feed many hungry people in emergencies. Less well-known charities like Childaid (whose work I got to know from my climb of Kilimanjaro) were also doing invaluable focused work, funding schools and clinics. None of Childaid's staff was salaried. At the same time, a few Africans I spoke to view some Western agencies with suspicion, accusing them of profiteering, political interference, and arrogantly tramping on the wishes of local people. Some

even speak of neo-colonialism. As with everything in this world, some charities do it right, others do not manage it so well.

Lifting the debt burden on African countries is important, but perhaps more so is helping to build up their infrastructure. Even in the more developed urban centres of East Africa, I encountered rutted dirt tracks, power failures, and taps with no water. Proper roads, ports, water and power installations are urgently needed if Africa is to move beyond a failing subsistence agricultural economy. The Kenyan government can balance its own day-to-day spending from its own resources without recourse to foreign aid or borrowing; the difficulty is that it has little or nothing left over for long-term infrastructural projects.

It is certainly not a case of throwing money irresponsibly at sub-Saharan Africa. Corruption is still a big problem unfortunately, being endemic throughout every single level of society— as I saw myself all too often. At the same time, corruption should not be an excuse to withhold properly monitored funding to the continent. Corruption is a fact of life in Africa that will not disappear by simply cutting off the money. To the Kenyan government's credit, probably for the first time ever on the African continent, ministers resigned from the cabinet over corruption allegations during my time in the country. Sadly, this progress seems to have been reversed in more recent times.

The Irish missionaries draw from a deep well of experience and wisdom where helping Africa is concerned. They often cooperate with and get assistance from the well-known charities on specific health, educational, infrastructural, and employment projects. They have been in the field longer than most of the charities, though, and they often work in much more remote ar-

eas that the charities do not reach. There tends to be a much more personal dimension to the assistance rendered by each missionary as well.

A typical missionary might have fed a baby girl after her father died, then paid for the education of the same girl in the school where he or she taught her. Some time later, they might have donated money to her so that she could start a simple business, and a while after that, drop everything in the middle of a very busy day in order to drive her to the nearest hospital to give birth. Sadly, and all too frequently nowadays, the missionary might have to arrange for someone to nurse her, and then bury her if she dies from AIDS a few years later. The missionary would then take on the responsibility of clothing and looking after her now orphaned child, and the whole cycle would start again for the next generation. It is this personal cradle-to-grave involvement, tending to their spiritual needs along the way, which makes the role of the missionary unique.

It is not always easy to get it right, and I certainly did not at times. There was a desperately poor single mother called Mumbe, whom I knew well in Nyumbani. She literally had not a bed to sleep in at night. I gave her money to buy schoolbooks for her three children. I heard a few weeks afterwards that she was walking around with a mobile phone.

'Are we saints or fools?' Sr. MM queried, when I told her this.

The missionaries themselves admit to being taken advantage of from time to time, even after living in the country for decades. It is not an easy life, it can be lonely at times, and people they know well can burden them with the expectation of solving their

problems, whether financial or otherwise. Yet most of the missionaries told me that it is extremely fulfilling work, if thankless at times. (Incidentally, Sr. MM, Fr. Paul and Sr. Mary Dunne amongst others, have since returned from Kenya.)

For my own part, during my months of volunteering, I nearly always felt I was exactly where I wanted to be. I was greatly enriched by my work in Nyumbani and at the Centre for street-children. I believe I made a small difference to the lives of some people.

USEFUL WEBSITES AND READING MATERIAL

Some websites that prospective volunteers might find useful:

Comhlámh: www.volunteering-options.org

Combined Agencies: www.HowYouCanHelp.ie

Irish Aid: www.irishaid.gov.ie/centre

Volunteer Centre Ireland: www.volunteer.ie

VSO: www.vso.ie

Some books that visitors to Africa might find of interest:

Chinua Achebe: *Things Fall Apart*

Felice Benuzzi: *No Picnic on Mount Kenya*

Karen Blixen: *Out of Africa* and *Shadows on the Grass*

Joseph Conrad: *Heart of Darkness*

James Fox: *White Mischief*

Elspeth Huxley: *The Flame Trees of Thika*

Ryszard Kapuscinski: *The Shadow of the Sun*

Martin Meredith: *The State of Africa*

Thomas Pakenham: *The Scramble for Africa*

John Henry Patterson: *The Man-Eaters of Tsavo*

Ngugi wa Thiong'o: *A Grain of Wheat* and *The River Between*

Lonely Planet: *Kenya* and *Africa on a Shoestring*